Lisa Wright spent her childhood in large and draughty English vicarages and rectories in the Black Country, the Essex Marshes, a Dagenham housing estate and East Ham near to the Woolwich docks. There was very little money to run these huge old places, and wartime rations and coupons made life even more difficult, but her parents, J.O. and Margot worked marvels with practically nothing, and they were all happy, exciting and characterful homes. The one thing they all had in plenty, especially East Ham, was space.

Lisa trained as a Drama teacher at the Central School of Speech and Drama, at that time housed on the third floor of the Royal Albert Hall. In 1953 she set off to America to teach in Connecticut for nearly three years.

She married Martin in 1957 and they had five children.

She was a drama teacher for 35 years mostly in large inner city comprehensives, where she wrote and directed large scale shows with elastic casts.

She started on her second career in middle age as one of the first women priests in the Church of England, still continuing to write shows, though now for parishes and diocesan activities.

Now she has embarked on a third career, as writer and performer of one woman shows.

Lisa lives in South London v

D1351880

for dear Anne + Robin.
with love from
Lisa Wright.
19.8.2010

Spilling the Beans
Letters from East Ham Vicarage
1953 -1956

by
Lisa Wright

Spilling the Beans
Letters from East Ham Vicarage
1953 -1956

Published by
Fisher King Publishing
The Studio
Arthington Lane
Pool-in-Wharfedale
LS21 1JZ
England

ISBN 978-1-906377-15-1

Edited by
Mary-Ellen Wyard

Printed in Great Britain by the MPG Books Group,
Bodmin and King's Lynn

CONTENTS

Chapter   *Page*

BY AIR MAIL
PAR AVION

2/6
POSTAGE

LONDON. W.C
3.45PM
12 APR
1954

BRITISH INDUSTRIES FAIR
54

Miss Lisa Nicholls.
St Margarets School
Waterbury
Connecticut. U.S.A.

The First Letter

Tuesday September 14th 1953 My Darling Lisa, Oh! What a lovely day for you to set off on your travels. It is heavenly here and simply baking on this seat on the sun patch. Rupert is barking himself sick, he thinks there are Robbers on the Roof. I have been following you all day in my imagination and we are so glad it is such a lovely sparkly day. The sea must be beautiful. After the train went out to Southampton, Daddy insisted on a taxi to the Lyons Corner House in Charing Cross, and there we had a nice HOT cup of tea, not like that filthy dish slops we got in the station, and then we got the Underground home. We got in about 10.20a.m. and I made some more coffee, and then Daddy went off to the Rural Dean's Conference at Barking.

It was Mrs Pooler's day off, but she had not gone out. She had had a very hot bath, and made herself feel sick and faint, but she managed to revive enough to come down when she found I had made the coffee. Gran appeared on the stairs, in her yellow nightie and her Bandeau round her head like a bandage, and her old gray coat, and was very disappointed to see that I wasn't crying, and didn't look as if I was about to start! She wanted to know if you had cried, and was equally disappointed when I said, No, what had you to cry about? But I was really grateful to her, for I was feeling more than a little like having swallowed a doorknob that would neither shift nor melt – and she completely dissolved it.

1

Introduction

Margot Dodman and John Osborne Nicholls were born in the same seafront road in Whitstable Kent in the early years of the 20th century. His forebears sailed their oyster fishing boats from Whitstable to Billingsgate and her forebears had been builders and architects in Canterbury for a couple of centuries. He went to Christ's Hospital School and then on to Lincoln College, Oxford. Her mother was a music teacher, her father a photographer and an excellent amateur cellist. Margot danced and sang her way through her school years in Norwich, acted with the Norwich Maddermarket Theatre with Nugent Monk and trained as a professional singer. John, always known as J.O., first proposed to her when she was 13 and he was 17, and they finally married in 1925. J.O. trained at Wells Theological College and was ordained in 1928; and so began the long round of tough parishes, first in the Black Country where Lisa, their only child, was born, and the Potteries, then, during the war years, first down on the Essex Marshes in Pitsea, and then in Dagenham near the Ford works.

In 1948 they moved, with J.O.'s mother, to East Ham, a huge thriving parish in the East End of London, near the Woolwich Docks. Although the war had taken its toll of the buildings it was a place of full employment, clerks and shop assistants going up to the City and the West End, dockers to the Docks, and many to small workshops and factories. The people were thrifty, kindly, rough diamonds and cheerful. Margot and J.O. were very happy there.

Margot loved the cold rambling, handsome William IV house with its twenty-three rooms and made it elegant and beautiful – on no money. Every room was distempered white; floor coverings were coconut matting and a few Persian rugs. She made every curtain, every bedcover, sofa cover, matching cushions, professionally piped and finished, and meticulously fitted. She coped with the housework, and a friend who lived with them, Annie Pooler, widowed in the last days of the war, coped with most of the cooking.

£25 a week was a good stipend in those days, but the house was a daunting place to furnish, decorate and keep clean, and keeping five people fed and clothed and warm meant constant planning and saving, not without blood, sweat and tears. Only a person with her vivacity and spirit could have survived the pressure.

Margot was an able administrator, organising large occasions as well as every day parish meetings and groups. She was a friend and confidante for all sorts and conditions of folk, from the market traders to Mayors, and at ease with all, from Bishops to the smallest choirboy. She would suffer fools as gladly as she could, but she was a realist, and no one could pull the wool over her eyes. She always saw through insincerity. She was elegant, and devout, and fun and magnetic. She had a huge influence on those around her. She neither led from the front nor the back, but from the midst.

Lisa finished her training as Drama Teacher at the Central School of Speech and Drama in 1953 and set off to Connecticut for her first teaching job. And remained there very

4

happily for two and a half years. They all wrote to each other weekly. It never occurred to them to telephone each other and they only cabled once – after a hurricane. J.O. wrote short notes about church doings in his crabbed academic script, Lisa wrote breathless, ingenuous puppyish scribbles; and Margot wrote these loving racy diaries in her expansive unique handwriting.

"About 6p.m. I went over to church and helped with the floor polishing. We did all the Lady Chapel as far as the first pillar".

Final touches for the Rededication of St Bartholomew's

From 1948 to 1953 J.O. had overseen the revival of the parish of Saint Mary and Saint Bartholomew and the rebuilding of Saint Bartholomew's church. This had been the most enormous task. When he and Margot arrived in East Ham only the huge red brick walls remained standing, the charred timbers and the rubble still lay inside, ragwort and fireweed and brambles ramped over the burnt pews, birds nested in the alcoves and stained glass ribbons swung from the windows. The faithful few had continued to worship in the vestry since the night in 1941 when the cluster of incendiary bombs fell. Mercifully, the tiny Norman jewel of Saint Mary Magdalene, down on the edge of the parish, had been spared. It nestled in its twenty-acre graveyard, and Rollie, the curate, looked after its day-to-day affairs.

The first task was to clear the rubble and to turn the interior into a neat space with benches and tubs of shrub and flowers, and to open the doors for those wanting a quiet place to sit during the day. No one recalls it ever being trashed or misused.

The next stage was to fundraise and rebuild the South aisle. While this was in progress the growing congregation moved into the Church Hall a few streets away. The choir re-formed, boys and men only. Mrs Gilson the parish worker arrived, and ran a Women's Group and the Youth Club. The Sunday School grew and grew. Father Witcutt arrived, as the second curate, with initial unwelcome publicity; he had converted to Anglicanism from being a Roman Catholic priest in the Midlands. Newspaper hounds arrived at Sunday services. Was there a woman in the background? But no, there wasn't – the change was purely for theological reasons – so the newspapers soon lost interest.

After the rebuilding of the South aisle, a brief respite, and then work started again for the other two aisles. And once the roof was on and the floor laid and the plastering done, Margot was of enormous help with the decorating and furnishing, choosing colour schemes, carpets, altar frontals, hangings, stools candlesticks. She made countless visits to ecclesiastical furnishers, comparing prices and quality of fabrics. But she was no mere consultant. A true artist, she was interested in every detail behind the scenes, scrubbing, sweeping, sewing and all the practical details.

The day grew closer, about a month after Lisa had set off for America.

September 21ˢᵗ 1953 About 6p.m. I went over to church to help Mrs Bush do the floor polishing. Daddy has appealed for help for Church Cleaning every night from now to the Rehallowing, but only Mrs B. and I were there tonight. She came over and had a cup of coffee afterwards and Rupert FLEW at her so I had to beat him. We did all the Lady Chapel as far as the first pillar. Doesn't sound much – but it's a good stretch when you come to do it and my back and knees ache.

Monday September 28th 1953   I took lots of church measurements and then Johnnie Griffiths and I went up to the Warham Guild for Church Furnishings to look for a little flower stool for the side of the altar. Then we went to Mowbrays and bought some Christmas cards – ! – then looked at pulpit crucifixes and prices, and finally bought one. Then had beer and sandwiches at the Blue Poste in Newman Street where Cuth and Doris used to go. Then we went to the Civil Service Stores in the Strand and looked at Oriental rugs. All the ones I liked were around the £75 - £95 mark – one beauty – the first I picked out was £400! Champagne tastes and beer money, me! In the end I found two gay little twin Anatolian ones, lovely colours, orangey, sea greeny, mustard yellow and white ones with a good flare of rust in the middle, but even both together they may not be wide enough for the top altar step, but the man said I could have the two together for £37 – and it is tempting. I got them to send a beautiful one as well, cost £69, same sort of colours, but a lot more green. By this time Johnnie was bored stiff.

Tuesday A nasty day. Dull, windy weather – cold – gusty – and everything frustrated. I'd begin on a job and get taken off it every time until I could scream. I began to wash cushion covers in the sitting room to look smart for all the bigwigs at the weekend – then Daddy wanted all the quarterly returns for the marriage registers to be sent to the registrar done AT ONCE – so I left the covers – went back to the washing and he wanted the strings for the pulpit cushion put on AT ONCE. He didn't get it done AT ONCE, but I had to do it

NEXT, which made me late to get the bread and Rupert's rabbit – and by the time I had done that it was time to get tea for Mrs Jefferys who was polishing furniture like mad, and so I got some for the workmen as well, and when they had finished the second pot Daddy came in and wanted some, and so it went on.

Jessie the sacristan had thrown a temper in the morning and he had thrown one back. A pretty exhibition between the two of them. I should think Harold the churchwarden, whose head they were hurled over, must have been much edified while counting the Free Will Offerings. I was measuring the altar step and looked for escape like a frightened rabbit, but found no bolthole. Jessie is mad because she has had no say in choosing the altar frontal and said in a very Poophy voice, "Too many colours that do not tone -!"

Friday Luckily there were lots there to polish the church on Wednesday and Thursday, so I didn't feel I had to .I concentrated on making the house look shiny and smart.

In bed just on midnight My feet ache, my arms ache, my back aches, my head aches and my eyes ache, and I'm Tired. Been on the go since 6.30a.m. Did flowers all over the place in the house here, yellow and bronze chrysanthemums and large long Michaelmas daisies and turning leaves. They really look lovely. In the church they are putting lovely gold bronzy chrysanthemums and reddy bronze beech leaves which blend in with the hangings beautifully and great jars of them all over the church. A large consignment of stuff is coming up from the Parks Department tomorrow, so we shall be decorated up.

I tidied round like mad this morning and dashed into the Bargain Shop for some yellow and gray check for the bathroom curtains but it had all gone so I came home with two yards of 42" blue and silver shot organza (a remnant) for 6/-. Then I went over to church and stayed there doing flowers until 10.30p.m. It really does look LOVELY and Daddy ought to feel very proud. It is a wonderful achievement. The little Lady Altar has stolen the powder though. It looks so dainty and feminine and young, tucked away down beside the resplendent greens, reds and golds of the High Altar. It is like a small shiny blue icicle. I wish its rusty red and silver cross and candlesticks were ready, but they won't be here until the end of the month. Jessie was working herself up into a temper because she had not chosen the frontal herself. She wanted to make a crepe de chine one if you please! However I swept up all the flower mess out of both vestries so that cheered her up a bit. She can't stand having to do a menial task!

Must go to sleep. Am too tired to hold the pen.

Saturday night October 3ʳᵈ 1953 Darling, thank you for the letter which arrived by first post – bang on the day. It set Daddy up for the day. Everything has gone right all day. No one could ask for more.

To begin with it was a lovely sunny day, not too hot, just right for my black wool dress and ceremonial hat! I think I looked very nice.

The church looked lovely, really LOVELY! The men came up from the parks and they decorated with wonderful ferns and queer leaves in pots, red striped ones and yellow and red striped ones and pale green striped ones and they banked them round bald spots quite beautifully.

In the afternoon there must have been a thousand people in church. Folk were standing in rows at the back, and mostly church people and they all joined in the prayers and the hymns.

Canon Styler, the Chaplain of Brasenose College, our patrons, arrived from Liverpool about 2.30, in good form. Old Canon Hodson and Mrs Hodson were brought by car by their son in law, Commander Robinson. Canon Hodson had been the vicar when the church was bombed. Mrs Hodson said how glad she was that the Canon had been able to see the church and get it over before preaching tomorrow, as when he went inside and saw it all restored he broke down, poor old dear, and just sat down in the choir stalls and wept. He cheered up soon, but it was an emotional day for him. He is very tottery now. They are coming to tea tomorrow, and are dying to hear all about you! They were bowled over when they heard where you were.

Daddy will tell you the details of the proceedings, I expect. In the end we put the twin Anatolian rugs on the altar step. The £69 one did not blend in with the hangings, so it now reposes on the top landing until they collect it next Thursday. It looks fabulous here, but alas, we can't keep it! Rupert thoroughly approves and spends all his odd leisure moments sitting on it in state.

The Bishop of Chelmsford came and the Bishop of

Barking, and Mayors and Mayoresses and Corporations, and the M.P and lots of our friends. Ilma and Johnny Fox came and she looked so pretty in a soft suit of Jaqumar tweed, black and white dogtooth check with a grey and white fox fur collar, very "model" and a little beret type grey peachbloom hat.

There were four East Ham Vicarage wives there, and I must say, we were a jolly good looking lot considering all things; Mrs Ware, 1895, Mrs Porter, somewhere in the 1920s, Mrs Hodson, 1940s, and me. Mrs Ware at over 80 is still very attractive and so is Mrs Hodson, and Mrs Porter was very trim in a very good gray suit and white shirt with diamond brooch and small pillbox hat and blonde silver hair and very well made up face.

I can't say how many there were at the tea. But they milled around in St. John's Hall, both upstairs and downstairs, both halls full and everybody seemed to be meeting everybody and all were happy and welcoming. Charlie Allchurch and Ralph Gilson on the door of the halls handed people in and hailed them and began the show with bonhomie! Charlie even had a crack at Ilma and she responded with pleasure!

We stayed there until 5.45 p.m. and then Styler and I felt we had had enough of smiling and small talk and backchat, so we slipped off home and had a drink of Dubonnet and a quiet little talk until Daddy came in half an hour later. We had supper in the dining room, roast lamb, sprouts, roast and boiled potatoes, stewed pears and baked custard and cheese and biscuits, and the men had beer. Then we had cups of tea afterwards and Poo and I washed up and we all went to bed

13

fairly early – and thank goodness it was the night to put the clocks back so we got an extra hour in bed.

Sunday night   Oh! Lisa, how sleepy I am, but I shall have no time to write in the morning as I have to go to Chelmsford for the Mothers Union Diocesan Council by the 7.35 bus.

I got up at 6.15 and tidied round. Styler is afraid of the bathroom geyser, so I had to run his bath, stupid great baby! I went to 8a.m. service, a lovely lot there, and we communicated at the High Altar. Styler celebrated and Daddy and Witcutt assisted and ALL the servers came and made their communion, a corporate one, so the chancel was full of servers. It was a real treat to see them all. Then we had breakfast in the dining room: bacon and eggs and tomatoes and the usual toast and marmalade etc. Then Styler went to prepare a sermon because the Bishop had stolen his yesterday! I cleared breakfast and laid lunch and laid the fire in the sitting room and laid the tea trolley and we had lunch in the dining room early as Styler left at 1.30p.m. for a train for Waterloo as he was preaching in the evening at Wellington School! He certainly gets around.

As soon as he had gone Pooler and I got the rooms tidied and prepared and we did the washing up and then I changed and then the Hodsons arrived with their daughter, Mrs Robinson. She was very attractive too, pretty gray hair, about my age, smart and friendly, wearing a bluey gray velour coat over a steel gray grosgrain frock and a black hat. She looked over the house again and was most interested. Mrs Hodson said she was so disappointed not to see you. I thought I would privately ask you to send them a Christmas card. I will send you their address. Pooler gave them a smashing tea – she has turned up trumps this weekend, it has been non-stop cooking for her, and every meal has been grand. Then about eight of their relations shewed up! I bunged them all together in the sitting room and we drifted out and got ready for church quite leisurely for once! It was a bit of cheek really on their part – but the Hodsons are such dears that I forgave them.

The old boy preached the sermon. He is very tottery but still very game and it was a good sermon. After church they came in for a glass of sherry and then they went home and I could have cried with relief! So we went and had cups of tea in the kitchen, almost in silence. It was so nice not to have to be social!

Rupert has been quite perfect all weekend. He has been charming and welcoming and has sat quietly on a chair at the side of the dining room by the window at mealtimes and on a cushion in the sitting room at teatime today, and has been a dear good boy and a credit to his Mother. I expect we shall pay for it later!

"This has been the most awful week. It has been colder than I ever hope to have it again. I have done nothing but carry coal and coke and stoke fires and saw wood…"

Running the Vicarage

Like army wives, clergy wives are constantly ready to be on the move. The houses they live in do not belong to them and they have no choice in their size or location.

Since the Second World War, vicarages and rectories have undergone a sea change. The vast, often very beautiful, dilapidated mansions have been sold off for profit by the Dioceses, and purpose built houses have been provided for the clergy. A clergy house now must have at least four bedrooms to allow for priests with large families and for visitors, a large sitting room that can be used for small parish meetings and social gatherings, a kitchen suitable for the same, and a study situated close to the front door. They have central heating and fridges and washing machines, and most have a decent sized garden with a large patch of grass suitable for summer fetes and parish gatherings. The clergy wife is expected to give hospitality to all and sundry and to be ready for whoever may call.

Such niceties were not the case when Margot became a parson's wife. As a curate, J.O. rented two rooms in a house in Wednesbury, Staffordshire, then was sent to a small house in Tunstall as priest in charge. In 1933 they moved back to Wednesbury to a vicarage built thirty-five years before when the parish was created. Lisa, their only child, was born there.

In 1939 they moved to Pitsea on the Essex marshes, a strange shantytown of flimsy bungalows and wooden huts with no electricity or inside sanitation that grew up after the First

World War. Now it has been completely subsumed in the great Basildon housing estate. The huge rectory had begun life as a beautiful eighteenth century white clapboard Essex farmhouse with dairies and outhouses and storerooms that had then been greatly extended in the nineteenth century, with high drawing rooms and nine bedrooms, and long rambling corridors leading to blocked up walls, and great cellars which flooded every winter so that Margot had to wear Wellington boots to fetch up the coal. During the war it was impossible to provide black out curtain material for every room so many could not be used. Lisa and her friends loved the house, solemnly going round knocking the walls to try to find secret passages, and running wild in the old stables and woods and the overgrown orchard. Margot knew it was haunted, but loved it all the same.

In 1943 the family moved again, this time to Becontree, the great interwar housing estate built to take the slum clearance of Stepney and Poplar. There the vicarage was a redbrick box. One bedroom had to be turned into a furniture repository to store all the furniture that had been spread sparsely around the Pitsea Rectory. That furniture came in very useful in 1948 when the family moved to East Ham Vicarage with its twenty-three rooms.

Margot turned these houses into charming homes. In every move, dining room ornaments and pictures always moved on to the next dining room, sitting room ornaments to the next sitting room. They felt comfortable and reassured at once. She made every curtain for every room in every house all her life. (And the curtains for many of her friends too.)

Monday October 19th 1953 Now that the Rededication of St. Bart's is over, I have turned my attention back to the Vicarage. Everything needs smartening up. Every time I go upstairs the chest of drawers on the landing sends me reproachful signals. So I went over to Sharpless, the ironmongers, this evening and got some paraffin and some linseed oil and began to clean the chest up. It was too dark to do much to it, but the top has come up beautifully and I'll have another go tomorrow.

Tuesday I had another go at the chest of drawers and got a fantastic amount of dirt off the sides. It begins to look a glorious nutty brown colour. Heaven knows when, or if, it has ever been cleaned or polished before. Certainly not while it lived in Whitstable, I bet. A good hundred years of neglect, and it's such a pretty shape!

I also rang up Jamie Mileson, wearing his hat as Diocesan Surveyor, to ask if we could have another boiler in the kitchen. This one has been on its last legs for years, and I dread another winter of its puffing and blowing and coughing and sulking. He was out, but I left a message, and also a note about dry rot in the cellar.

This was the note about the dry rot Lisa found years later.

Notification of Dry Rot sent to the Diocesan Surveyor

There are queer things from the ceiling in our cellar,

19

They aren't the usual dry rot sort of lark.
They are white and soft and shiny
Like the foam upon the briny
And they feel all wet and sloppy in the dark.
I don't expect this means much to an expert,
But the sight of them has filled me with dismay.
It puts horror in my soul
When I go to fetch the coal,
And it isn't any joke,
When I go and get the coke
And I wish the beastly things would go away.

Saturday night Had breakfast and then did the flowers and got some of the beech leaves that have been soaking in glycerine water in the attic all summer and washed them and they have gone the most beautiful goldie brown. I put them with the rust and red and gold chrysanthemums and they looked wonderful. Then I took the cutting shears to Sharpless for sharpening and then I began to wash towels, a big pile, and boiled them. It was a lovely morning while they were boiling but then it went all overcast. However there was a good breeze so I risked it and hung them out in the garden. Then I went and had a bath, and of course went to sleep in it and when I woke up it was pelting with rain and Pooler never bothered to go out and bring them in. I brought them in wetter than they went out and shall have to rinse them all through again tomorrow. She is a snivelling, lethargic, streaky Cat -!

Sunday The sun was shining beautifully early on so I hung out all the towels again and went to early church. The church looked lovely in the sunlight. When I came out the streets were running with water. I bought the papers and went home and said to Pooler, "Did you get the towels in?" She said, "No. Why? It hasn't been raining, has it?" So they will all have to be rinsed for the third time and it has rankled all day.

Then I concocted a table lamp for the attic out of that old sugar bowl of Granny Camburns because we need a squat one on that little corner table in the attic. I had to cut up the lid of an elastoplast tin to make the top fit and had to cut it with a tin opener which was very hazardous. But it works! Clever Mother!

Friday Jamie Mileson says we must hang onto the old boiler until we have heard from the Dilapidations Board. I was all for putting one in and then asking them afterwards but he didn't think that was tactful. So it looks like we shall have to put up with the creaking old grate puffing smoke in all the wrong places some more. Mr Parrish came in the afternoon to shift the coal in the cellar so we could get at the coke! I decided it would be foolish to try to do it myself, so he came. 10/- and a bottle of Worthington. Well worth it for him AND me.

January 29th 1954 Bitter, bitter cold. Freezing hard and a frightful cutting wind. Gran went out as far as the Co-op and came straight back and said it ought not to be allowed. I thoroughly agreed.

We had the radiator on in the hall all day and all night and I decided I must knit another jersey for Rupert as if this goes on he will need two on at once. So I have found two ounces of dark green wool which you must have had over from something and began that after they had all gone up to bed. It was pleasant to sit in peace. I was too tired to haul myself up to bed anyway. When I DID go it almost hurt to breathe in that attic. But we had the electric fire on and Rupert had his little hot water bottle and I had two and we were very cosy once we were in.

Sunday February 7th 1954 It's Sunday and I am only just making a start to this letter and to tell you the truth this has been the most awful week and for most of it I wished I were dead. It has been colder than I ever hope to have it again. And I have done nothing but carry coal and stoke fires and saw wood. And I have had the most awful cold on the chest. I felt so lousy I had to go to bed on Monday with whiskey and hot milk.

Wednesday It was not quite so cold and the frozen geyser in the bathroom came back to life in the morning. My cold was still vile but I battled on. I did have a little weep on the lavatory seat, but was afraid the tears might icicle. The Gilsons were frozen up everywhere! They had done nothing to stop it. No candles, no oil stoves or heat at crucial points. So although we kept most things going, as soon as it got over to their side they let it freeze up again. I could slit their silly throats! Pooler had just got the tea ready when down came the water, AVALANCHES of it, all down the Gilson's stairs and landing and out the side door, and through the ceiling by the cellar door. We had to get mackintoshes and umbrellas to get from the kitchen to the dining room! I rang up Mr Stokes the builder, and he sent Mr Hale, and he, clad in my mackintosh cape and sou'wester, knocked up the pipe in the roof and then turned off the water – and told us to let the kitchen boiler out! I thought Pooler was going straight to the station for a ticket to Walsall to her sister! She has taken the whole cold spell as if it was a personal grievance and no one could feel it as badly as she could! Considering I took her up breakfast in bed for five days last week when she was bad, and I have been JUST as bad, and she has not even brought me up a cup of tea – not ONCE! – I gave her a piece of my tongue, and she cried! She said she was so strung up with the cold that if I wasn't careful, she would have the screaming hysterics. And I said, if she did, I should have the greatest pleasure in pouring the remaining bucket of cold drinking water over her. And I meant it, so she shut up and became a little less self-pitying. But Wednesday evening was miserable. We spent the rest of the evening buying buckets and cadging water off the neighbours.

But on Thursday morning golden little Mr Hale arrived at 8 a.m. prompt, and worked hard until 11a.m. and mended the pipe and left us with injunctions to be careful as there was plenty of ice left to thaw. Thursday night we relaxed a bit until about 8 p.m. when the temperature went down with a bump and when I went to bed I couldn't see out of the window for the frost on the inside in spite of having the electric fire on for an hour. And the disinfectant in the po had frozen solid!

November 30ᵗʰ 1953 I darted around in the morning and did the chores. Pooler's day off. Lou rang and said she was coming over shopping and would I have lunch with her at Wo Pang's? I was planning to do the washing as Daddy had a meeting in Bishopsgate, but I thought why should I? I'll take the washing over to that new Bendix place they've got over the road and have a bash. So I waited till Lou came and we sallied forth.

Lisa, it was a wow! They have got about twenty machines over there and you can take nine pounds of washing for 2/6. No soap powder needed either – they provide that. You put the whole lot in the machine and shut the door – it's your machine for the time being, no one else's washing goes in except yours – and then you turn it on and they all swish round, and after a bit a red light comes on, and you pour the soap powder in the top and it goes on soaping and after a bit rinsing, and then the red light comes on again, and you pour more soap powder in the top and this time it gets really lathery and gaily sloshes round. And meanwhile the wireless is on, and the old girls sit and gossip, and Lou and I leant on the machine and smiled at the folk watching from the pavement and invited some in, and they came, and we demonstrated, and after a while Lou began to do it with actions, so I thought we had better beat it, and we went up the High Street and posted your letter, and when we got back it was going round so fast you couldn't see it! And as it slowed down it made a clucking noise and Lou said, "MY GOD, it's going to have a new laid egg and all!" Then it stopped and we opened the door and scooped it all out into a little basket on wheels and wheeled it down to the end of the shop and put it into an Extractor. The washing was not at all wet, it was just as if I had put it through the mangle. And we put a penny in the slot in the extractor and off it went again and you saw MORE water coming out of a pipe in the side. And it was quite dry enough to iron after half an hour in the garden.

It's MARVELLOUS! And it's all DONE in NINETY MINUTES!

April 4th 1953 It would have been a lovely sunny day only they had decided to have an eclipse on it, so it all went dark at midday until 3.30p.m. Mr Parrish came to mow the grass and said he could have done with a fog lamp. He has just become a grandfather and is very excited about it. His daughter is forty, and has been trying for about ten years, and had a bad time with blood pressure, and then the baby was born early, and then she collapsed with worry when she got home that she wouldn't be able to manage the home and the baby. So her sister Mag, who lives with Parrish, was sent for. Parrish said, "To see the two of 'em with this 'ere baby was enough to make a cat larf. May was scared to touch it, and Mag's got a 'and as big as a 'am. She was afraid of breakin' its bones!" I said, "For Gawd's sake, 'andle it, it won't explode!"

Tuesday The workman has come from Crabbes to distemper Pooler's bedroom and to put the wall right where the snow came in. We asked Mr. Stokes for an estimate for doing the wall and distempering walls and whitewashing the ceiling and he sent an estimate for £21.00! We asked Crabbe for an estimate and he asked for £8.00! So Crabbes got the job! Stokes seems to be going sky high with their prices. Harold Tomlinson had his little tiddy kitchen painted by them – it's not as big as our downstairs lavatory, and got a bill for £22.00. Whether Pooler comes back or not the room had to be done.

August 17th 1953 We have a REFRIGERATOR. Yes, really. The men brought it yesterday afternoon. I rang up Mr. O'Donnell at the Gas Office and told him it had come. Then I cooked the lunch and we ate it and I washed up. Mr O'Donnell rang back to say that they couldn't fix the fridge till Friday week. I said, O.K., only, that being so, they must send a couple of men to move it as I couldn't get to the cupboard. He sighed and said if they had to do that they might as well fix it! In the end he said they would come at 5.30p.m. and do it at once! I then had to clear about three hundred weight of muck out of the old fireplace in the back kitchen where the thing was to stand, and had just finished this when the men arrived.

I dispensed tea and dripping cake to everyone. The fridge looks as if it had always been there. They got it going, but said they couldn't fill in the back of the fireplace with asbestos until next week. I said, fine by me. After they had gone I got everyone's supper and washed up and wrote out four wedding registers and starched some tablecloths. But Daddy and I wouldn't go to bed until we had seen the ice really freeze in the little pans.

June 20th 1953   A perfect summer's day. Mr Parrish came to mow the grass and at coffee time he regaled us with an account of a Sunday afternoon drive with his daughter and the new baby.

"Cor!" he said. "Talk about a bleedin'outin'. First me and the boy gets in the front. Then May and the baby and my other girl gets in the back AND 'er 'usband. AND a mass of clobber for the baby. RIGHT! We gets orf at larst and the baby 'ollers from the word go. Gets into Eppin' Forest and the 'ole place is ringin' with its 'ollerin' and it ain't no bigger than a rabbit! A little pree-matured baby it is, feel you want to pick it up by the back of its neck like a cat! Well! I says, fer Gawd's sake feed it! So art comes its bottle and an 'ole lot of paraphernalia – charts and diagrams and measures and Gawd knows what and they put four ounces, I think it is, into a bottle and the kid wolfs the lot in no time. NOW! I fink, we'll 'ave a bit of peace but oh! NO. NAH it's got the wind. If you fink it cried loud before, you was mistaken. It was nothing to this lot – Well, it shifts that lot and then it goes to sleep. I guarantee it wasn't asleep for more than eleven minutes – JEST about eleven minutes, and then it opens its eyes, goes puce in the face and fills its nappies up, and then yells again becorse it ain't comfortable." May says, "It ain't no use, we'll 'ave t go 'ome." "Whaffor?" I says. "We ain't bin 'ere 'arf an hour yet!" "Ain't got no more nappies, Dad," says May. "Wipe its arse along a bit of grass," I tells 'er. "Goo on. Run it along this 'ere verge. But no! Off we 'as to go 'ome. NOW! There's an old cat down at the club with four kittens – 'ad 'em in an upturned bucket on a bomb site. Four of the fattest balls of fluff you ever did see. No fuss – no palaver – purfick management. And they calls this civilisation!"

Friday after lunch I went and bought two towel rails for the bathroom and screwed them to the wall. Then I took the old wooden one and decided Mrs A. must have one in her room. So I bought some paint and varnish remover and had a heavenly session stripping all the paint and varnish off it, and washed it and dried it, and it was real oak under all that, so I linseed oiled it and it looks very nice indeed!

Then I cleared out the kitchen table drawer and reorganised THAT! Then I cleared the back kitchen mantelpiece and washed and reorganised THAT! Augean Stables!! After supper I began on the middle dresser drawer and reorganised THAT! By this time the dust bins – emptied in the afternoon – were nearly full and six days still to go. Then I had a grand washing up session, listening to a programme with Noel Coward and Joyce Grenfell the whiles, and made a thorough job of cleaning the sink and wiping the washing up bowl out, and I left it on the draining board and went to make a telephone call and when I got back little Tiggy was asleep in the washing up bowl. By this time I was tired enough to go to sleep in the washing up bowl myself!

Monday in Holy Week 1955 I got up early. Lots of visitors to cope with this week, and I had planned to have a good spring clean with Mrs Jeff. My heart sank as Mrs Jeff's Marjorie scuttled past my window about 8.30 a.m. "Mum can't come. The stuff as she's bringin' up is something awful! The doctor's given her somethink as is doin' it to 'er. But you should jest SEE it!" – ! – "Yes! Well! Thank you, Marjorie. Give my love to your mother and tell her I hope she will soon be better again. (I certainly do!) and tell her that we can manage until she is fit again." (Like hell we can!) Spent all morning turning out the dining room, study and hall. Went to have a bath and found Gran had run off all the hot water, so gave her a good dressing down for luck.

Tuesday April 26th 1954 I spent most of the afternoon sitting on the step in the sun patch drinking tea and cleaning the brass with Mrs Jeffreys. I am afraid she is getting past the work here and I shall have to find another cleaner and keep her on for a few light things from time to time. I think it would break her heart to leave altogether. She is such a dear and she keeps me sane with her quiet commonsense and it is such a damn nuisance.

Wednesday May 10th. A woman called to see if she would do. She said she had heard that I wanted a cleaner. She seems a decent sort. Her name is Mrs Nicholls! She said, "Call me Daisy, Madam. The whitest flower in the field, you will remember it by that!" So "Daisy" is starting tomorrow and I hope she will be as brisk and helpful as she appears on the surface. Her brother is the valet to Heifetz the violinist, so they must have something about them as a family.

May 15th 1955.   This time next month you'll be home for the summer. Glory be! You won't get much from me this week as Johnnie G. is here and he and I are distempering the attics in your honour. He has got a lovely new little lambskin roller thing and he won't let me have a decent go at it as he says I'll get too tired! But he doesn't mind me washing down the walls and ceilings which is a damn sight more hard work! Rupert is very interested and has got distemper on his tail and his ears so he is satisfied.

"Daisy" has done her three half days and makes us die with her noisy repartee but she sure can polish! I shall have to keep her apart from Mrs Jeff though, for Mrs Jeff would think she was too familiar by half! To give her her due she treats me with great respect, but she calls Poo "Toots" – which goes down better than you might think, to do Poo justice. Mr. Parrish was here one afternoon while she was here, and he has had a bad cold. I said to him while we were all having cups of tea in the kitchen, "You don't seem to be able to shift that cold, Parrish!" Whereupon Daisy chips in, "What 'e wants is a good dose of gin and harpic. Shift anything – shift pianners given time!" To which Parrish replied, "CORRR!" She works quite differently from Mrs Jeff. Mrs Jeff gets in a lot more but doesn't go hell for leather at it. This one polishes everything she can see in a room, which means she doesn't get in the mop-dusting, but you can see your face in the furniture, and her brass cleaning is as good as mine. Which is high praise!

November 8th 1955 A terribly hot – November – day and damp, damp, damp! The walls literally ran with water. The banister rail was too wet to hold, gray bloom all over the furniture and the walls -! Awful!

Saturday January 10th 1955 Cold, gray and cheerless with a raw damp that rots your bones. We had a super load of coal in this week, lots and lots of it, so I have been surreptitiously been putting a little fire in the sitting room for the last three days as it really was as cold as the tomb in there and began to smell like death, it was so dampish cold. So after three days it began to feel much kinder and to be warm enough for me to be able to slip in there on the quiet to be on my own, only Rupert nearly gave the game away by whimpering be let in too! Anyway, I got up late this morning and having two fires to see to kept me heaving coal for quite a while. Then I did the chores and went to do the church flowers and got daffs and white tulips and bunches of a little white whiskery flower that looks like big snowdrops on a white stem. I just filled the bowl with them and they looked lovely, I am SO TIRED of chrysanthemums!

February 6th 1955 Colder than ever, but no, it was colder than ever yesterday, so today it is colder than colder than ever. We all huddle round the fire. Rupert wears two jerseys to play outdoors and Tig is all bushed out and fluffy. I put on three cardigans and a jersey and my tweed coat and thick scarf and go to the Tailoring Class. I do an infinitesimal amount of sewing and come home again and huddle by the fire! Rupert has a hot water bottle in his basket each night and my quick knit cardigan AND his white blanket over the top of his basket. He has got his life sorted out well. Wish I had.

April 28th 1956 I am thinking very seriously of getting Daddy to set motions afoot for the disposal of this house, and building a smaller one on the lawn. I know you will shriek your disapproval and I expect I shall hate it too, but I really don't think any other Vicar will live here when we are gone. Twenty-three rooms is not SENSIBLE. It is a fearful drain on the income, over seven pounds a week goes out in wages alone. I get frightened now when I think of having to manage on my own. Whereas six years ago I managed it fairly well I just could not do it now. The carpets are wearing out and the renewal of such vast areas of floor – even if only coconut matting – is well nigh prohibitive. Keep this under your hat. Before anything can be done we must have the approval of our patrons, Brasenose College, the Church Commissioners, the Bishop of Chelmsford, the Parochial Church Council AND J. O. Nicholls. Anyhow, I am going to have a bash!

"Here are some of the hats I sold at the Bazaar!"

Parish Life and Parishioners

Margot always played a large part in the life of any parish she was in, and made good friends, and was a confidante to many, particularly the women of the Mothers Union, most of whom had hard lives, holding their families together on too little money, too little leisure and too little attention. She enjoyed the pleasures and shared the sorrows and they all had a good deal of fun together along the way.

20th September 1953 I did the most enormous wash all day. I went on till about 5.30 and my head and my back ached, and I had just settled down with a cup of tea and the newspaper when Daddy came in and said, "Had you forgotten you were going to the Thespians Society tonight to help make them all up for their show?" Of course I had completely forgotten, so I scuttled round and found there were twenty-two to make up in about forty minutes. However Alec King (Siddie Taverner's buddy) turned up and helped valiantly. It was a Revue called Beaux and Belles. We got them all made up by 7.50, simply marvellous, and then I went to watch for bit and sat next to Netta. It was NOT the best they have ever done! Olive sang fearfully sharp all the while. Derek and the red-headed girl did some terrible double number turns, forgot every other line and swayed to and fro as if they were in a draught. Jean kept changing her dresses and looked more like a pearly queen every time she appeared. Her ensembles were wonderful. One was a dove gray effort with silver bells on it. Another was a black silk jacket and skirt with lots of brassy buttons and one of those little fish slice hats with white sequins, and she proceeded to sing, "We'll walk down the AvenOO," showing with relish that she had nothing in her pockets. I said to Netta," Well! Twice up and down the AvenOO ought to solve that problem!"

I sat there for an unconscionable time waiting for the interval until Netta informed me that it was a Non Stop Show and that There Weren't No Intervals. So I crept out during one of the interminable blackouts between each scene. If that's a Non Stop Show it's a new one on me as I thought it never WOULD stop, and for all I know it may be going on yet.

Tuesday October 27th Pooler lit the boiler fire today for the first time this season, not bad, end of October. Then the bell rang and the nice policeman Smith who has the boy David in the choir and the smart pretty wife who was so talkative stood there looking lost and asked for Daddy. I said I was sorry he was not in but he would be back in half an hour, or would he risk it and come in and wait, or would I do? He simply said, "My wife has committed suicide." I nearly dropped. It appears she has been under a nerve specialist for some months and has had fits of depression, but seemed no worse than usual and he had gone to work as usual at 6.30 this morning and came home at 2.30p.m. to find her with her head in the gas oven. David, thank God, is staying with some cousins in North London as it is half term. I got him some coffee and talked to him for about 20 minutes till Daddy came. Gosh, it knocked the stuffing out of me.

Saturday night November 7th   I went down to visit old Mrs Kerr and she sent you her love. Rollie brought her Communion and I knelt by the side of the bed and she was so pleased. She is such a pet, so merry and uncomplaining and in such dreadful pain at times. Her nice smiley little husband is so good to her too, so uncomplaining, they are an object lesson to the likes of me.

Sunday night I went to St. Bart's for evening service and sat next to the nice policeman Smith who was all alone. The funeral of his wife is tomorrow. David was in the choir and he said he was sending him back to school tomorrow and was going to try to manage and to get along as normally as possible. It is dreadful for the poor man, but the boy seemed quite perky and cheerful.

Friday I had to have Jessie to tea on Friday as she is helping with the catering for the Deanery Mother's Union Festival. It's a case of "Mother, is it worth it?" and if only she had got up and gone when she had stopped being helpful she would have been much MORE helpful. Instead she gave me a bellyful of her love life! HONESTLY! She said he – (H) – was 41 when he declared himself. He's got to be late sixties now, doesn't seem to have much sense of urgency! She said she knew in church his thoughts were all for her. (I didn't think this said much for his churchmanship, but suppressed it.) She said those sisters of his hated her and that the main reason was that though she – Jessie – was not as good-looking as she used to be – she knew – she had managed to retain her looks and her figure, and they were just plain jealous of the fact. I am NOT making it up. She actually said all that and a whole lot more. It was not my lucky day.

Monday March 29th 1954 Father Witcutt came as usual for the office hour to arrange baptisms and weddings in the front hall, just as Daddy was darting into the church for a service at 7.45. I pottered back and forth from the kitchen to the dining room doing your petticoat. Pooler was draped over the wing chair with her head in her hands most of the evening. I noticed a school satchel in the hall by the Indian box, but thought J.O. must have put it there, as indeed he had, but had thought it belonged to a choirboy. Witcutt was extra busy in the front hall most of the time but just before he went home he gave me a letter to read from his publishers. I took it into the study after he had gone and made a phone call and put it on the study table. Then I went to help with the supper sandwiches and Daddy came back from church and went into the study – and then came out with a girl about 13 who had been crying and hustled her out of the front door! Some time later he came back and said, "How long had that girl been in there!" I said, "Didn't you bring her in?" He said, "No! I found her hiding up by the bookcase. She said she had run away from home and had got in by the garden door and hidden behind the curtains in the study!" Don't ask me why she picked on us! She must have been there the best part of an hour. She didn't take anything. J.O. took her to the police and they said yes, she had been missing from home since the morning. So now we have to keep double watch on locking all the doors, now that we know how easily folk can enter and hide up without our knowledge.

Thursday I was having a root around in the Bargain Shop today and came across the most exotic gunmetal and bronze silky organza frock which looked worth at least eight guineas. I asked the man and he said, "You can have for 35/- if YOU want it. YOU know what it's worth and will appreciate it. It's more than this lot will!" It fits perfectly. Very sombre and rich. I will make a stiff black petticoat to go underneath it. I didn't wear it at the Parish Social though! I wore my black and white check cocktail suit with the red lining and looked VERY nice. And I am glad to say I caused a stir. Netta and Bessie both wore identical taffeta spot dresses except for colour. Netta's was cyclamen- pink - shot- purple and Bessie's was bright yellow- shot- orange – both bloody. By the way, the Obelisk – or was it Odalisque you called her? – is engaged. She was so animated that her eyes moved! I congratulated the happy pair and she clutched him tighter as if I was going to snatch him from her, and he just grinned and breathed with his mouth open.

Sunday night When I got home from evening service I opened the front door and the most terrible smell hit me – burning – acrid – foul – disgusting – I dashed in the kitchen – nothing there – Rupert all right but looking pained. So I went up the stairs and there it was, smoke all belching through

Gilson's connecting door on the landing. So I fled back to church and threw Rupert at the organist who had a clean shirt on and didn't look too pleased, and rushed to Ralph Gilson who was at the back of the church with Mrs Bush. I said, "Something is on fire in your house, Ralph," and he said, "Oh! God! FISH!" and began to run like hell. A whole great bowl of cat's fish they had forgotten and it had burnt the lot to cinder – at least one and a half pounds of heads and tails!! The STENCH! People passing held their noses. Gilson's room downstairs was BLACK with smoke. However, no harm done to the property and Daddy didn't get home till 8.30p.m. so the smoke had gone by then, but the smell will be here for weeks!

Sunday night August 17th I helped Daddy clerk the baptisms and then went down to St Mary's for Evensong. Charlie Allchurch sat next to me in church. When I told him to go and sit with his wife he said, "No! You come so seldom, I want to sit next to you!" And then he said, "Do you know what?" and I said, "No! What?" and he said, "Next to keeping one smashing woman, I'd like to keep TWO smashing women." I thought he hardly looked the type to keep a fancy piece in a flat in Knightsbridge.

Florrie Allchurch told me to tell you she was saving a tin of salmon for you when you come home!

Saturday In the morning I had a talk to old Miss Brewer who helps to clean the church. She was telling me what a Christian man her father was. She said, "He suffered terrible at the last. For the last two years of his life he couldn't speak a word – nor stir hand and foot – and Mrs Nicholls, we never got a murmur out of him!" Not surprising, I felt!

I was talking to one of the choirboys. He said he was born in Staffordshire. I said, "Where?" He said, "In my Auntie's front room!"

Sunday night Mrs Bush's Renee is getting married on January 1st. Such a to do. Mrs Bush will dissolve in a whirl at any moment. I went to church tonight and sat next to Hilda Spivey who is very friendly with Mrs Bush. Hilda said in a loud stage whisper, "Isn't it a shame, poor Mrs Bush can't get no one to lend 'er a pianner." I said, "Oh, dear, hasn't she got one?" "No!" said Hilda, "And the woman next door 'as got one and she's not being obligin' neither." I began to feel sorry for the woman next door, so I said, firmly, "Well! Hilda, I can't blame her! I wouldn't lend my piano to anybody." To which she replied, surprisingly, "Not likely! It only wants one person to knock a 'arf of bitter inside of it and it's 'ad it." All this during the Exhortation.

As we were going out of church Mrs Cloake said to me, "Wait for me. I want to see you but I just want to give this to Mrs Gilson." So I waited, and Mrs Gilson was about ten yards away. Mrs Cloake went up to her and in a voice you could have heard as far away as the Denmark Arms, she said, "Pooh! Good Lord, gel, you want to take a walk round the block and fumigate yerself – stinkin' fish and lamp oil – I nearly passed out." It is quite true, her coats simply reek of it, but Mrs C.

never wraps her remarks up. Pooler laughed herself sick when I told her!

Mrs Beaumont is getting married next Thursday. Probably the very moment you are reading this she will have lured a third husband into her web. She is eighty-one and the fiancé is sixty-eight! She told old Mrs Brown over the road that it was not a case of platonic friendship at all – it was pure love! Mrs Brown said to me, very seriously, "It's all very well, Mum, but I reckon she's got a pluck turning into bed with a fellow at 'ER age." If you ask me, I think it's the fellow who's got the pluck!

Wednesday In the evening I went to the first Evensong of the Ascension at St Bart's and then went round to the Church Hall to get ready for the East Ham Boys Grammar School Breakfast. Muriel and Charlie Middlebrook, Jessie and me. We laid the tables, and then Muriel and I heard a dreadful "set-to" between Jessie and the caretaker, Pettifer. We listened in and nearly killed ourselves. It appears there is a very old piano and harmonium in the hall, and Jessie had sent for a rag and bone man to shift them both. On Tuesday Mrs Gilson was giving a film slide show to the Women's Fellowship, and the rag man came, and poked his head round the door and said, "Where's the pianner?" Mrs G., who was mad at being disturbed, said she didn't know what he was talking about. "Is THAT it?" he said, pointing to the one they had just played the hymns on. Mrs G. said, "No! We are using this one." Off he went and came back and said, "What's this 'ere pianner with it's face to the wall?" and Mrs G. in a paddy, said, "I don't know if it's the one or not, but it's not THIS one!" Off the man goes and carts off the piano with its face to the wall in the front hall. When Jessie came to the Hall to get the Grammar School breakfast ready, she said to Pettifer, "What has happened to the Male Voice Choir Piano?" and Pettifer says, "I don't know, but a man came on Tuesday and carted off a piano and a harmonium, and said you had arst him to." Whereupon Jessie blew up and Muriel and I held each other and rocked with glee!

Anyway they went round to the ragman and he said he had sold it straight off the cart to a man who he didn't know who he was nor nothink! So the Male Voice Choir will have to practise singing unaccompanied for a bit! I got home about 10.15p.m. and recounted the fracas to Daddy and Pooler.

Thursday To Mass at 7.45a.m. Forty-six boys at the Communion Service. Very good indeed. We gave them a grand breakfast. Boiled eggs, rolls and butter and marmalade, coffee and tea. Roy Waters, once the most diminutive boy in the choir, now a Sixth Form Giant, made a very nice speech of thanks at the end, no trace of nervousness and very neatly put. How you do all grow up!

Tuesday I went down to St Mary's to the Women's Fellowship where the committee was giving a sketch. It was TERRIBLE. It couldn't have been worse. I laughed every now and again, but I had no idea at what. It was supposed to be funny, I believe. It was quite deadly, and Golly! It was cold down there.

Thursday I went down to St Mary's for the M.U. and expected there would be very few there as it was a cold and cheerless day. We had twenty there and I gave them a talk on preparing for old age – and how to do it gracefully -!! I must say they were all very quiet and most appreciative!

The fog was awful in the evening but I went straight from the M.U. to the Choirboys' party. They had some lovely slapstick Laurel and Hardy films which left me helpless. In one a whole governess cart and donkey came tumbling down the stairs, and every time Laurel wanted a light for his cigarette he snapped his thumb and a light came out of the top of it, and then the fat one tried and couldn't do it, and the one time he DID manage it burnt him – and then the choirboys and I all yelled and stamped and whooped with glee.

Sunday evening Young Hunter was too late to go into the choir, so he came and sat by me at the back. The Second Lesson was the beginning of John's Gospel, "In the beginning was the Word etc." and he nudged me and said, "Excuse me, but they've made all that a bit involved, don't you think?" I grinned and winked and let it go at that, and then afterwards felt how inadequate I had been and how I ought to have told him to come round afterwards and I would help him out with it – or let Daddy do it!

January 1ˢᵗ 1955 My sweet Lisa, Happy New Year and all that bilge. I am tired of all these compliments of the season. I've caught Gran's cold as I knew I should and I feel Lousy.

My hands are ingrained with dirt, my nails are broken, I've put on about half a stone in weight with Christmas booze, my hair is filthy, my nose is chapped, and by the time you read this I shall have a cold sore on my lip. It hasn't begun yet – but it will. Still, I feel a bit better for the grizzle and thank you for listening! I daren't let off steam to Daddy; he takes it as a personal reproach! Also, I haven't had a letter from you since Christmas and you are a pig, so there!

Today was Elsie B's wedding. Goody Goody. Now you know as well as I do that Elsie is very delicate! She can be relied on to faint five times out of seven at early Holy Communion. But did she bat an eyelid at her wedding? Not she. She came full early. She stood at the back of the church in the baptistry on her father's arm while Daddy told the guests what to do and what not to do and she never even trembled. She swept up the aisle with the utmost sangfroid in white rayon brocade and coronet of orange blossom and a bouquet of red roses and stephanotis. After the ceremony they walked round to the Vicarage garden and stood there for a full ten minutes – no coats – in a biting wind with little costive pellets of snow chasing round while Dennis Large took Photographs. Did she faint? Not she. Did she turn blue and shiver? Not she. She just stood there clasping the arm of her new husband and she smiled and she smiled. She was MARRIED!

Now it's Monday at 3p.m. and your lovely letter came at breakfast, so you are not a pig, but a nice plump creature.

"Gran has shortened her skirt for Spring, NOT
a success!"

Battling with Gran

Old Gran had been born Annie Camburn in the 1870s in Whitstable Kent. An exceedingly pretty little girl, she had been one of a family of nine, only three of whom reached adulthood. She was the only remaining girl of the family and was consequently much petted and cosseted. Her family were staunch Congregational Chapel goers, and I have a photo of her parents, Granny and Grandpa Camburn on their sixtieth wedding anniversary in 1921, both with strong kind faces.

Pretty Annie married strikingly handsome Edward John Nicholls in 1900 and proceeded to make his life a misery with her spoilt ways and social pretensions and tantrums. He was an easy-going sweet tempered man who gave in to her for the sake of a quiet life. He and his partner ran a thriving ship's chandlers and ironmongery store in Whitstable. His ancestors were fishermen, his father one of the founder members of the Whitstable Oyster Fisheries. He had grown up around boats and his great love was racing small yachts. For many years he was the Commodore of the Whitstable Yacht Club and this suited Annie very well. She pressured him to retire at fifty, to give more time for her social activities, and he was prosperous enough to do this. She preferred to be the Commodore's wife rather than the wife of a ship's chandler. But he had enjoyed his life in the store, which had kept him in touch with all the sailors and life around the working boats in Whitstable Harbour. Now he hadn't enough to do, and positively enjoyed the war years as an air raid warden. He was well known and

47

respected in the little town, riding his sit-up-and-beg bicycle unbelievably slowly – why didn't he overbalance? – and courteously raising his straw boater to every lady he met along the High Street.

Their two sons, John Osborne and Philip Edward were born in 1901 and 1907. J.O. got a scholarship to Christ's Hospital and then to Lincoln College, Oxford, before training for ordination at Wells Theological College. Philip went to school in Canterbury and then worked in a bank until the war when he joined the Navy. He married when the war was over and then had various jobs abroad in Finland and the far East.

By the late 1940s Edward John was in poor health and they had to move to East Ham where he died in 1948. Old Gran, crippled with rheumatism and arthritis, tried to carry on in Whitstable, but had to come and live with Margot and J.O. in the early 1950s. It was a trial for all of them, but Margot bore the brunt of it. Old Gran was entirely self-centred and had no inner resources. She neither read, nor sewed, nor knitted, nor had any friends, nor made any contribution to the household. The one great thing in her favour was that she never complained of her aches and pains which must have been legion.

Thursday September 16th Gran said she didn't have a good night last night because of the Warning, and when we said what warning, she said she had heard a Flood Warning. And so she got up, she said, and cut her corns and toenails with a new pair of scissors that she had bought in Woolworths. Just why one needs must cut one's corns and toe nails to deal with a Flood Warning I would not know! Must go to sleep now and perhaps it will be clearer in the morning!

Sunday night 11.50p.m. This morning I thought Gran had gone to church so I went up to make her bed about 11.30a.m. and found her still there and in a rearing temper over her green hat. She said someone had been in and Mucked it Up Completely. She had "trimmed it most Nicely – really well – most carefully! And NOW look at it!" And my golly, you couldn't take your eyes off it! She had evidently done it in the twilight with a very large needle and some black thread – a green felt hat and some lighter green ribbon, but to make a really good job of it she had turned it inside out first, and it was one of those cheap hats that wouldn't turn inside out, and having done it she couldn't get it back into any shape at all. It was all I could do not to have hysterics and when I took it down to Pooler she let out real hoots of laughter. I spent a good twenty minutes trying to bash it back into something like a hat and put the ribbon on and she was pacified, but she has been muttering about spiritualism all day, and "One Woman's Right Up". Very touch and go.

September 22nd Pooler picked another great saucepan full of grapes and made some more of that wonderful grape jelly. I then cut out the scarlet lining for Gran's coat. She came in from church and was most irritating and I could have willingly throttled her. She said she had been looking at the

Lady Altar and it reminded her of the daughters of Gann the butcher at Whitstable, God alone knows why! She then gave us a complete history of the Gann family, who they married and why, and why not, and then she screamed with laughter and her teeth fell all over the place and her hat went over her ear, and Pooler said, "I don't know what all that's in aid of, do you?" However, she stomped off "Out for a Bit" and I got the animals their food and then went all tired and just COULDN'T go to church.

Monday Pooler and Daddy both went off up to London for the day, she shopping and he to get Sunday School prizes. Gran and I had lunch on our own, and I made a semolina and made it pale pink with a few drops of almond essence and called it Japanese Custard, and Gran was enchanted and said it was so good of me to go to all that trouble! It's wonderful how two drops of cochineal and four drops of almond essence can transform the atmosphere!!

Monday November 9th 1953 Lord Mayor's Show Day and DON'T YOU FORGET IT!

Dear Lisa Lou, Gran has been incensed that none of us has been up to the Lord Mayor's Show. It's been a TERRIBLE day – rain – mist – fog – dark – London MURK. Every bush you see outside the window has little globules of water hanging tremulously on the twigs and leaves. When, exasperated with all this idiocy, I testily said, "If you want to know all about it, why didn't you go yourself, Gran?" she replied blandly, "I don't want to catch a cold!" Johnnie Griffiths is staying with us, and he has got a most lovely fire going in the dining room and I have sat by it as much as I could and knitted the socks Gladys Riley has ordered for the Bazaar, and made myself a paisley scarf from the back of Uncle Lewis's old dressing gown and fringed the ends. It goes beautifully with my navy twin set and a blue straight skirt. My cold is very much better now, thank God, and the cough much looser.

Gran has been very naughty all day. She would sing "Turn again Whittington" all through lunch. I couldn't stand it and took my Oxo into the dining room. Then after tea she sulked because she wanted Johnnie to play draughts with her and he didn't want to. I gave her a pile of magazines to look at and she pushed them all on to the floor. So I picked them up one by one and slapped each one very firmly on the stool by her side, and after that we had no more trouble. She thought I wasn't feeling well enough to withstand her, but she was never more wrong in her life! Now I am going to bed and must pray for patience and charity – the old faggot!

Tuesday night   My first day back properly on the rat run. Pooler went off for a holiday at her sister's and when I got up I found dear Johnnie had already got up all the coal and coke and had washed the hearth before he went to bed!

Gran has been in a devilish mood all day and I am not strong enough to cope with her. She started a racket about her gloves so I told her I didn't know where they were and then she banged with her stick until I nearly screamed and kept telling me to wrap up and go to Oxford Street. I told her the sooner she practised what she preached the better. But just as it was getting really dark and getting cold she set off – only up the High Street. I cooked bacon and eggs and sausages and tomatoes for supper for all of us and she said she only wanted bread and cheese. Every time I slosh her one, either verbally or by frustrating her I think, that's another one I have paid her back for how she treated poor Grandpa. But she got it back on me for she sat down after supper and talked about the Lord Mayor's Banquet from 8p.m. until 9.45p.m.

Saturday night I dashed around shops all morning and the electrician was here again all morning and he makes as much mess as he can for a hobby. The Lord was on my side as Daddy had to go to some Dedication Service somewhere and they provided lunch, and Gran waltzed up to Aldgate! She has caught my cold! "There is a lovely fire. Why go out?" I said. "I must," says she, "I am a great believer in OXYGEN!" and off she went. I was very grateful to Oxygen – but I bet she will pay for it tomorrow – or I shall!

November 14th After tea Gran comes into the dining room with that lovely bit of fine wool I had made up into a shaped cravat for her to wear under her blue coat. She then proceeds to take out of her bag a skein of bright red floss silk and a darning needle the size of a poker and said she was going to embroider a few flowers on it to brighten it up. So I exploded. I told her I had taken time and money to make her something that was in good taste and suitable for her and that if it wasn't to her liking I would have it back and send it to Aunt Jo Prentice for a Christmas present, but I was not going to sit there and watch her ruin it before my eyes! So then she said it was a dowdy old thing and she wasn't going to wear it as it was! So then I really let go and told her just what I thought of her scarlet lined coat and told her to go out and buy some scarlet sequins and sew them on with scarlet thread to brighten THAT up. She then said she had had no consideration from me ever since she came here and that I was utterly selfish, so I gave her a bellyful in reply to that, and altogether I should have been ashamed of myself! But we both had a thoroughly good shouting match! RIGHT!!! Anyway I ended up by saying I only hoped when I got to my eightieth year I should have the good luck to be as uncomfortable as she was and in the care of someone as selfish! She has been as good as gold today. Most obliging.

Thursday night I started to cut out your blue silk frock and have cut out half the bodice. It's a queer pattern and looks like a combination suit for an octopus when laid on the table. Gran can't make head nor tail of it and looks at me as if I am just buggering about to befogg her – and to tell the truth it was some time before it made any sense to ME! But now it is all light and joy and peace and I can get on with it in the morning.

Friday night in bed It has been a non-stop day starting at 6a.m. The day before the Bazaar. The stalls are duly up and decorated and all are pleased except Jessie the caretaker who is flouncing round like a maniac. And I've thrown away Gran's hat and she is looking for it everywhere. The Spirits again! It's that awful thing she turned inside out and I had a presentiment she was going to wear the damn thing tomorrow so I've liquidated it! I heard her say, "I shall simply have to buy another tomorrow if I can't find it." I wish she would go and live with Jessie. It would do them both good. And me too.

Saturday Gran has been to Anne Rose and bought a green velvet hat and a green chiffon scarf. Not bad at all. Well done the Spirits.

Sunday night Got up early and fell into church at 8 a.m. Gran's cold is shocking. Sniff, sniff. Sniff – sniffle – snuffle – sniff. Pooler and I decided we could stand it no longer and retired to the kitchen, she with her knitting and me to do some ironing.

Tuesday night Gran has sniffled all day, juicy revolting sniffles. We shouted at her to "blow your nose Gran" – but she merely replied, "Oh, that's all right. I've got all that seen to!" She has not been out but won't stay in bed and does not look at all well. She is a terror to try and deal with.

Thursday It's now thick fog, most peculiar weather. Gran's cold is awful, but she WOULD go out shopping yesterday and then went to one of Daddy's interminable carol services for schools, so came home half dead. She really looks ill tonight and I shall have the doctor tomorrow if she is no better. Pooler and I are quite worried and are both being nice to her, so you can see it must be serious!

Friday night and dead-beat I swept the church all afternoon and it was awful after all those people Carol Servicing in it. But we got it done. Mary came for supper, and she read your letters while Poo and I washed up and then we had a nice cosy meandering talk by the fire. Mary thought Gran looked very rough, as indeed she does – but what can you do with her – she won't stay in bed – or even in the house, and this morning when I went to call her for dinner, I found her happily chucking wet disinfectant all over her bed on account she said she had run out of talcum! I told Pooler if we needed a wreath I should put "Bon Voyage" on my card -! "In Loving Memory" would be too much!

Saturday Fell asleep at that point. I phoned Doctor Ollie Thomas and he came, and we went upstairs to see Gran and found her with the window wide from the bottom and the curtains blowing out straight from the rod at the top into the room with a howling gale. Dr. Ollie said, "Brrrh! You ought to have that shut for a start." She said, "I will if you are cold but I'M not." He told her she ought not to go out. She said she MUST. So, That's That! However, I am covered all right and when we got downstairs he said she was very poorly but it was no one's fault but her own, so that's likewise that. Pooler and I both went out shopping this afternoon and when we got back she was washing in the coal bucket in the sink and was wet through all over her diaphragm and up to her elbow. I made her take off her blue check coat and it was so wet I wrung the water out of the sleeves, but she was quite annoyed I made her take it off.

Wednesday night. January 5th Whew! I am so sleepy that I won't be able to write much. Bishop Henry came to stay the night and wants to come back for Maundy Thursday; he is preaching somewhere in Ilford. He said, "I don't want to keep cadging, Margot, but I HATE sleeping away from home and it's homely here and I know where things are and have got used to it!" So this morning I got up at 6a.m. and did the chores and the fire. We had breakfast at 8.30 and Henry was gone by 9.30 and then – I went to the M.U. Corporate Communion at 10a.m and then made coffee and went to the hairdresser and wrote M.U. notices under the drier, and got macaroni cheese for lunch and apricots and custard, and washed up and tidied the Bishop's room and did some ironing. And then I went into the dining room to have a little sit, and I made the fire up and the front bar fell off and the whole lot fell out onto the hearth and it was too hot to tackle and I was in a bad temper and it took a good half hour to clear it all up.

I had just about got it all back when Gran came in and said, what a dreadful fire, and had I been asleep and let it out? BEEN ASLEEP! I ask you! I nearly burst into flames with internal combustion! But I suppressed it and got her some tea and got the animals their food and then Daddy came in and said, "What about a little something to eat?" So I cut pilchard and tomato sandwiches and made lashings of coffee – and I put the dining room clock and the kitchen clock on an hour and ten minutes and took the whole tray in by the dining room fire and said breezily, "Supper!" And Gran looked startled and said, "But I've only just had my tea! What does that clock say?" And I said triumphantly, "It says a quarter to eight" and she said, "Does it indeed?" Anyway, I got her to bed by quarter past eight – correct time – and Daddy went off on the spree and Pooler had gone to her sister in – laws for the evening.

So it was heaven! I just had the reading lamp on and I put the lights out in the hall to discourage visitors, and I got a very large glass of sherry and a large piece of cake and I just WALLOWED in the solitude.

Monday morning I don't care if they don't get their dinners until 3p.m. I am going to write to you. Pooler has been sick with a stomach upset, so I have had it all to do. Saturday, it was bitterly cold and Gran had got a devil in her. She would not wear her new coat in the morning and her other coat is a thin little rag of a thing. However off she went to the Sunday School Prize Giving. And when she came back I realised why she hadn't worn it in the morning. She had turned the bottom up with grey wool – ! It looked awful. Still, I held my tongue and when I went upstairs with the hot water bottles I neatly unpicked it and left it and said nothing.

On Sunday I went to 8a.m. church and when I came back I saw at once that Poo's number was up. She looked rather green about the gills and had a frantic headache. She went back to bed and so I slammed into the tasks – coal, coke, lay fires, wash up, make beds, get coffee, make Rice Krispie cakes, cook vegetables, rabbit, pork, stuffing, pudding, lay table, wash up, coals, coke, Pooler's trays, and to crown it all, Gran decided not to go to church.

About 1.30p.m. I found she had sewed up the hem of the coat again, this time with pink cotton. I neatly unpicked THAT! She then came down in the back kitchen trembling with rage and said her coat had been tampered with! I asked her in what way and she didn't want to tell me she had shortened it, so she just said, "Tampered with! Tampered with!" "Oh!" said I, "I expect it is one of those unpleasant Spirits. You have evidently done something to the coat it doesn't like. I should leave it alone for a bit. They get a bit violent at times, I believe," and she banged off into the dining room, knocking over Rupert's bowl en route. With this uncharitable story I will now close and get the dinner. Mrs Jeffries came and is cleaning round in her usual valiant fashion. I'll go and see if Poo is strong enough for a little Bovril and Toast! I am a cat – but I'd like two hot water bottles and to be in bed today. I don't feel ill, but I'd like to BE there. I love you dearly. Ever and always your loving Mother.

Tuesday June 8th Yesterday was a long day. I rose at

5.30a.m. to get everybody up and fed, and cut the sandwiches and pack the bag with fruit etc. and everybody out by 8.25a.m., ready for the annual Whit Monday Charabanc outing, two coach loads! This year we all went to Rye and Battle Abbey, very nice, too. Johnny and Gran and I went in one coach and Daddy in the other, which was sporting of him, as he does LOATHE these outings. He smiles valiantly, but I tell him it's no good if he smiles AND grits his teeth, it gives an ambiguous impression.

It was a gray chilly day, but it didn't rain till we were on the way home and everyone had a good time. Rye is so pretty and Battle Abbey is beautiful.

On the way home we all had a good knees-up in the coach and sang the usual frankly unsuitable songs for a church outing. Jessie pressed her lips together, but the rest of us roared them out.

Halfway home, when everyone decanted into a pub, Gran said she didn't want to get out, but we were to "Get Jack!" So we sent Daddy back to her and got off the bus. It appears she said to him, "Jack! Fetch me something!" He replied, "Gladly, Mother, what would you like? Tea? Coffee? Biscuits?" To which she replied, "I don't want anything to eat or drink! Just use your intelligence!" He came into the pub and told us. Johnny G. said, "Well, that narrows it down a bit!" In the end he got her a couple of packets of crisps and she threw them up on the rack in a rage. And we are still left guessing what we are expected to have fetched.

Friday During the morning Gran's teeth fell over the

banisters and broke! Whether she threw them over or whether she was having a good spy to see who Daddy was taking into the study we shall never know, but the top set broke in two. Oh! Dear! Oh! Dear! NOW what? She must have them seen to at once, Jack, AT ONCE! Mr Revell kindly fitted her in straight away and she went up there after lunch, but she insisted on wearing the bottom set without the top and the result was like a dying warthog. Ralphie Gilson said she had better have an X-certificate.

Saturday I am now about to make a most solemn pronouncement, Lisa, which I wish you to store upon your memory. If I die before Gran and she is still living here with Daddy – if you come home to look after her, I shall HAUNT you until you go away again. And not a nice gentle haunt – a nasty vicious haunt. She is an evil old woman and you owe her no allegiance. If I am not here he will have to get her into a home as no one else would stomach her, and it would be better for him in the bargain. If Daddy dies first, I turn her out the day after the funeral. So now you know. We might as well get that straight from now on.

December 20th 1955 Sunday. I went to early church. Gran did not go to church but had a bath instead. Outer cleanliness as opposed to inner cleanliness. I have to help her now, and Rupert comes as well, and tries to look over the side of the bath and Gran screams with girlish laughter. All very macabre.

Then we had a cup of coffee in the dining room.

Darling Miss Broderick has sent me a reproduction of the head of Botticelli's Venus and I have put it on the mantelpiece. Presently Gran said, "Who is that. Margot?" I said, "Venus." "Who?" she says. "VENUS!" I bellow. "Oh! I don't think I have met her have I?" "NO!" I shout. I give up.

After Evensong Gran said why did the wireless keep fluctuating so? The wireless wasn't even on at the time. She heard bands in the night. Brass bands? At 4a.m.? Surely not the Heavenly choirs? Alas, not my luck!

Ladies at the Mayor's reception.

Civic Duties

East Ham was solidly Labour, a one hundred per cent Socialist Council, proud of its respectable working class roots and determined to provide first class education and opportunities for all. The Library was excellent, there was an extensive programme of Evening Classes, Maths and Sciences, Languages, Woodwork and Sewing, Law and Philosophy, Book Keeping and Accountancy There were several Choirs of more than competent standard. East Ham was among the first Councils to provide innovative and exciting old people's accommodation, and somehow managed firstly to attract outstanding contributors to Education schemes, Youth Employment schemes, and secondly to give them their heads. The East Ham grammar schools sent far more than the average pupils to Oxford and Cambridge, and the Secondary Schools tapped into first-rate apprenticeship schemes. Alas, where are they now?

Like all true Socialists, East Ham people set great store on people earning their own way. They wanted to do things RIGHT and they wanted to feel the equal of every one else. East Ham Councillors were determined that their Town Hall activities must be able to rank with any other Town Hall in the country. So Council Receptions and Dinners were conducted frequently with dignity and formality.

J.O. as Mayor's Chaplain, was required to attend many of these functions and Margot was often invited.

Sunday   8am Church, and then home to do the fire and the beds and dusted and did the flowers. Gales of wind and lashings of rain! I began this letter to you and then made myself a nice waist petticoat out of that old black taffeta "choir" skirt of yours and finished it by dinnertime. Roast Lamb – mint sauce – roast pots – greens and prunes and rice pudding. There goes my diet.

Then I got myself ready to go to St. Mary's as the Mayor and Councillors were attending Evensong and there was to be the usual bun fight in the Hall afterwards. So I put on my cleaned elephant gray Marks and Spencers wool frock and my black coat and my black pill box hat and the reflection in the glass looked about as bloody as the weather -! I felt like Gran, "Must have something to brighten it up!" So I had a brainwave and twined your green and crystal beads round my cornelians and put on my diamond earrings and the result looked very tasty, and most expensive. I then wrapped myself up in my red mac and braved the weather, could not hold an umbrella up in the gale!

The Church was full. I sat with Siddie Taverner. The Deputy Mayor read the First Lesson, very halting and jerky, but O.K, and then came the piece de resistance. The Mayor read the Second Lesson. Oh, Calamity, Calamity! He stutters a bit anyway, and it was those frightful verses, earth-earthy corruptible and incorruptible and corruption and incorruption and Poor Mayor got so flummoxed he grasped his jabot of lace and it came off in his hand! I thought Siddie Taverner would choke! Anyway, he tucked the jabot away in the folds of his robe, and stuttered to a close and then left the lectern – when to my astonishment he turned his back on the altar and made a DEEP bow to the West Door and sat down. This completely finished Siddie, who wiped his eyes for minutes afterwards. Why he did it and what he thought he was doing I cannot fathom. I went into the hall afterwards and was very social all round and got a lift home in the Mayor's car which was much nicer than standing outside Burgoynes for a bus!

Wednesday May 14th Lovely hot day, but stormy looking. Had a salad lunch and then went to the Mayoress' Farewell Social in the Town Hall; it was chronic. I never saw so many fat, sweaty women in my life. I wore Doris' yellow and gray silk frock and my "Henry Wilson" hat and felt quite elegant. We listened to interminable speeches and back slappings from the Mayoress to all who had helped her during the past year. She was presented with a wristwatch. She presented her secretary with a cheque. She presented the Deputy Mayoress with a brooch. She presented Shepherd with a cake stand and Mrs Ames with a butter dish and someone else with a tea cosy. She then gave the Mayor a present and her daughter a present and about fifteen other people little gifts, and the Mayor gave HER a present and then they began handing out bouquets to each other and finally we got home. All WE got was a cup of tea! Meanwhile it got more and more airless and the heat was stifling and the old girls clapped and wiped their faces and fanned themselves and sat with their legs wide apart and their hands on their knees! ALL the elite!

I came home and spent the evening doing my costume jacket on the sun patch ready for the tailoring class on the morrow.

Thursday January15th A bit of snow and foggy. I did the flowers as the Bishop of Chelmsford was coming in the evening before the East Ham Male Voice Choir and The Ladies Choirs rendering of "A Messiah with a difference" -! I changed into my black twin set and thick skirt and pearls and told Daddy if he wanted me to wear a cocktail frock I would not go at all!

I got the trolley ready and tidied up, and Pooler got coffee and ham sandwiches and pressed beef sandwiches and coffee cake for the Bishop who tucked in. By this time it was snowing good and hard and I began to think of how long it would take to air the big bed if he had to stop the night! However we set off for the Town Hall and got ourselves in the Mayor's Parlour with the Mayor and Mayoress and Deputy Mayor and Mayoress and the Mayoress' son, who is a rising young dentist and VERY full of his own importance. We tried hard to keep the ball rolling and finally all trooped up to the gallery to listen to and look at this dramatised version of The Messiah! This was a very regrettable incident. I send you the programme and most of the comments are on that!

The choir was very passable and pleasant to listen to, as always. Quite frankly, the Tableaux were a horrid mistake and I am quite sure that everyone in the audience thought that John the Baptist was the Messiah. I didn't know who he was until Daddy told me, but still couldn't see why he had to fall off a painted tea chest and apparently suffer agonies with the colic on the ground – but then I didn't have a very good allegorical education! I did wonder if he had eaten too many locusts.

Tuesday March 14th   I got up early and did the chores and went to the Mothers Union Service at 10 a.m. Then I went as stand in for Daddy to the official Opening of an art exhibition in the Town Hall. Art from the Borough Schools from five years old up to Adult work from the Technical School. It was certainly a very good show. I was struck by some of the extraordinarily good work by the six and seven year olds. Good form and good colour and most imaginative. Some of the adult work was good too. I shall keep the catalogue. I stayed there about two hours as the Opening took up a lot of time and I came in for a lot of handshaking.

Thursday April 29th   We had to go to a Civic Dinner in the Town Hall in honour of the 50th Anniversary of the beginning of Higher Education in the Borough of East Ham. I attacked my fingernails, late afternoon. The left hand was passable but the right hand nails all lengths and mostly split! Then I had a bath and changed into the gray lace frock I had just finished and we sallied forth.

Well!! It was a SMASHING do and I really did feel good in my lace dinner dress. I didn't feel it was home made and I felt very smug. We went to the reception first and then we had a short drink before the dinner. I had a gin and tonic as I was thirsty and I could finish all the tonic. We sat at the top table which was placed lengthwise along the left side of the large hall as you face the stage which made a very long table and got lots in, and the other tables went crosswise. We had a VERY good dinner. Turtle soup, Scotch salmon and salad, roast chicken and peas and French beans, iced pudding and strawberries, petits fours, cheese and biscuits, coffee – white wine with the dinner and a liqueur with the coffee. All off the rates – Daddy trembles! I sat next to the Town Clerk who was quite nice but a bit heavy going, and we listened to the speeches. They weren't bad at all but all a bit long. It was scheduled to finish at 10p.m. but was not over till 11.30pm. and some folk got a bit restive. One man said he had ordered a taxi for 10pm. And I did think this was a bit hard. But it was a good dinner all the same and I WOULD NOT HAVE SWAPPED MY DRESS FOR ANYBODY'S! So there!

Saturday May 1st 1955 I shopped and did the church flowers, white iris, and deep bluey red tulips, and parrot pink and white ones, and forsythia green leaves all trailing, very nice, I thought! Daddy said put some red in the vases as it was Ss Philip and James' day. I sewed all afternoon and in the evening went to East Ham Central Hall and listened to a concert of the Barking District London Co-op Choir with Mrs Cloake in it, still conducted by Edward Taylor, your old piano teacher. It was really VERY good. I went alone as Daddy went to St Thomas Becontree, for the induction of their new vicar. I sat next to the Mayor and Mayoress for the first half, and then they vamoosed and I sat next to Mrs Elson and a friend and enjoyed it. Then home and cups of tea with Pooler and Daddy and then I took little Rupert up to bed.

June 3rd, Tuesday It has been a decent day. Mrs Jeff came in the afternoon and we washed a rug, ostensibly for your attic sitting room, but since washing it I've decided I don't like it there, so it's nice and clean for wherever I do decide to put it. Then I did some mending and had a bath and got dolled up to go with Daddy to the new Mayor making.

I have to say I am glad the Methodist minister is to be the Mayor's Chaplain this year. The new Mayor is a proper herb of a chap! The sort that would whistle through his teeth to get the Mayoress' attention! He informed me that his wife went all black before she died, and "she was a decent looking woman". His Mayoress is his sister-in- law and I shouldn't wonder if he doesn't marry her before the year is out! He hoses down the cars at the South East Essex Electricity Company. Proper democratic, we are! Anyway, it was all very amusing and I got my fun out of it.

Saturday September18th I had a fly-a- round, scrubbed both bathrooms, did the flowers, got the bedroom ready for Mary Eaves and tidied up and got myself ready to go to the Barking Road Recreation Ground to a service of Dedication for a new wrought iron gate in memory of Bert Monk. Daddy was not asked to take any part in it so thought it better to stay away.

I went because I was fond of Bert Monk; he was one of the best churchmen I have ever come across. WELL! You never saw such a shambles. I walked in through the gate and there in front of me, about 70 yards away, was a large dark bell tent, one of those thick army ones, camouflaged ones, as black as pitch inside. I stood as near the gates as possible so as to get a good view. Pollard the Methodist Central Hall man was to dedicate them as he is Mayor's Chaplain this year. It was a nice sunny afternoon with a good stiff breeze. The Mayor arrived and after a bit everybody was motioned towards the tent, and all the Councillors and their wives moved inside and I stayed out with Mrs Middlebrook, Mrs Cloake, Mrs Lockyer, Mrs Broadbent and others. Presently – from inside the tent – which must have been like the Black Hole of Calcutta by this time – the East Ham Male Voice Choir struck up and they sang All in an April Evening. It being a September afternoon I felt it a little inappropriate -! They rendered a few more muffled numbers and we sang a hymn and then a councillor thanked everybody for their "Benefactions". Then the Reverend Pollard dedicated the gates, still inside the tent! None of them in there could even SEE the gates! Then we had The Glory of the Lord from the Messiah sung by about ten men and the pathetic crowd shambled out of the tent, hot and sweaty and blinking in the light of day -!

Thursday November 10th I thought when I woke up I was in for a cold, but it seemed to go away during the tailoring class. Came home and helped with the lunch as Poo wanted to do shopping in Ilford, and spent the rest of the afternoon getting ready for the Medical Health Dinner and Dance at the Abercorn Rooms. Daddy and I were guests of Dr. and Mrs Stanley Thomas. I wore the gray lace dinner dress as I didn't think I would get asked to dance seeing Daddy is a dead loss at it, but I got off with the Medical Officer of Health for East Ham and danced quite a lot and the skirt was too tight for enjoyment! Also danced with Reg Slater and Dr Bell. The latter was well away and kept calling me Margery! T'was a very good dinner and I put on pounds.

The next morning the cold comes back with a vengeance. I suppose I should be grateful to the Good Lord for deferring it so that I could go to the Dinner! My nose is bunged up, my ears are bunged up, the top part of my head has been boiled and my eyes are going to fall out. I shall be better by the time you get this. .

Sunday February 6th 1956 After dinner I changed into my gray flannel suit and white nylon blouse and began to wonder what hat I would wear to St. Mary's in honour of the Mayor and Corporation. I finally decide on a white straw beret thing that I bought at a jumble sale. I turned it inside out and bashed it about and finally wore it back to front AND inside out and it looked A.1. Even Pooler said so.

The usual scrim of Councillors and their wives, and Town Clerk and Mayor and Mayoress, and Deputies. Tea and cakes in the hall after Evensong. Smile, smile. Shake hands. Talk, talk, talk. Smile, smile, and finally they all went home and kind Rollie brought us both home. I took off my glad rags and donned my dressing gown and had more cups of tea.

Wednesday 23rd May Mrs Jeff came in the morning and Mr Parrish too. We all had coffee in the garden, a most beautiful day. Mrs Jeff returned in the evening to be with Gran and I went with Daddy to the Mayor making at the Town Hall again. Mrs Dyer was there dripping with furs with an old-fashioned crochet straw hair tidy with tassels on her head. It was £2.2.0 from Dickens and Jones. I saw them there next day. I don't know how she does it, a widow with six children and no pension on a Lady Welfare Worker's pay. And a new beige suit too! Very dressy! Heigh-ho! A hot Cha-cha and a home made cheap flannel suit for me and May Tomlinson's last summer's straw hat inside out -!!

The mayoral party were pretty pathetic but THEY were as pleased as Punch with themselves. PUNCH is right. This old Judy came home and made tea and went to bed.

June 4th 1956 Daddy and I set forth to the Mayoral Reception about 7p.m. We both looked extremely smart. I wore Doris's red lace and tulle evening dress – new in 1938 – but I had spent three evenings taking the sleeves out and re-draping the top and turning it ballerina length, and that meant re-hemming both skirts, yards and yards and yards. It looks very up to the minute now.

Inside the Mayor's parlour was the usual set of the Mayor and Mayoress' relations. The Deputy Mayoress must have been at least 60 inch hip. She had on a dress of bedspread material and some nice long gloves. She had the most graceful lovely daughter, a dream of a girl and such fun. Incredible. The Mayoress wore black with black gloves with gold butterflies and a face set in a wooden grim fixed glare. Like a malevolent Dutch doll. They had no idea what to do when the visiting Mayors and Mayoresses came in and so did nothing but stare and hope for the best. In the end Daddy and I took control and greeted the Mayors for them.

After a bit they went down to the hall to begin the official reception and we were left to shepherd the other mayors down at the appropriate time. Doctor and Mrs Barker both asked after you. Mrs Edwards was wearing a frock too young for her and Mrs Dyer a frock too striking for the company. Mrs Barker's was charming, heavy, navy moss crepe, smothered with lemon and olive green hearts.

We had a good meal and a cabaret, and the Rabbi, who looked as if he had been lunching on a diet of vinegar and lemons with rough cider, did NOT approve of it. Me – I thought they were two very funny men and so did most of the others.

"So it was heaven…I just had the reading light on and I got a large glass of Dubonnet, and a large piece of cake and I just wallowed in the solitude!"

Margot's Friends and Free time

During the First World War Archie Dodman had been conscripted into the Air Force – at that time a very small section of the Armed Forces; not as a pilot, but to use his photographic skills flying in the reconnaissance planes taking photos of the French and German countrysides, factories, and enemy lines.

In this job he made contact with many photographers, and after the war, through his connections with a Dutch photographer, the family moved from Whitstable to Norwich, where he worked in a studio in Castle Meadow and the family lived over the shop.

Margot went to school at the Norwich Girls High School and made several life long friendships there. She excelled at English, Music and Drama, taking the lead in the school production of Iphigenia in Aulis. She also joined the Maddermarket Theatre, then in its infancy, and formed and run by the remarkable Nugent Monck. There she met, in her late teens, a very young married woman called Doris, the daughter of Sir George and Lady Holmes, who owned large shoe factories in Norwich. Doris and she became fast friends. Doris was Lisa's godmother and was loyal and generous far beyond the line of duty. It was Doris who bought Lisa's first bike, paid for the first professional hair styling, bought the first evening dress, took her out to theatres, showed her how to eat lobster – all facets of her education that the Vicarage salary could not afford. Doris understood Margot's need for fashion and

artistic stimulation, and even during the war years, helped to
provide the splashes of colour and excitement Margot craved.

September 23rd 1953 Doris rang up today. She wants
me to meet her for lunch on Friday. She says her mother, old
Lady Holmes, is being very difficult and they have discovered
she is blind in one eye and can't see very well out of the other,
so no wonder they kept saying her flat was dirty! Doris says
she and Cuth have bought a house in Lyminge – a big house –
a modern house – somewhere round the back of the village,
and it's called Iron Gates, as it has some very beautiful
wrought iron gates. It is built in the middle of an old garden.
But why they want to move from that magical cottage in
Rhodes Minnis I shall never understand.

Friday Crumbs! What a day! And oh! My feet! Got up
too late and rushed round the chores and then met Doris at
11.30 outside Charing Cross Station. She looked extremely
smart as usual in a black suit and broderie anglaise blouse, a
black beret and an Aquascutum proofed soft wool coat in small
grey and white checks. I wore my new winter costume that I
made for the first time, with your discarded red blouse and the
white and black handwoven scarf and it looked good. Doris
was very taken with it and thought I was very clever. We went
to the Civil Service Stores to buy some floor felt to go under
the rugs in church and I introduced her to the nice sales girl
there. Doris bought a large rug costing £55 for the new house!
So that did the girl a bit of good, and me too, as I shall get the

top brick off the chimney there in future! We then walked to Bond Street and had a very indifferent omelette in some fancy place of hers where it was stuffy and overcrowded with scent laden women who made me think of a luncheon party in one of Ruth Draper's monologues. She asked all about you and I told her all I could and she told me how awful all her relations were and all the family tiffs, and we enjoyed ourselves.

September 30th Cousin Queenie has been staying. It has been very unexciting for her, I fear, but I think she is just happy to have some one to talk to. On Saturday it poured with rain all morning but in the afternoon we went to Woolwich over the ferry! And we both enjoyed it! And the fates were kind for we sat on top of the bus in the front and when we got to the road bridge it went up and a ship from Canada came in. Queenie was thrilled to the marrow! We looked at every shop in the High Street and went round the market and had a cup of tea and came back over the ferry. The river looked absolutely lovely. There were great dark stormy clouds and a wild pink patch of sky reflected from the sun which had set, and the river looked like Lalique glass, all opaque and creamy and gray, with translucent streaks of bluey gray and queer jade green and pink from the road lights that had gone up suddenly – and misty smoky outlines of the buildings on the other shore. By the time we got over it was dark, and the water looked black and oily and the smell from the gas works was vile. But fate was on our side again because as the bus got to the bridge it went up again, and we saw the liner Esperance Bay go out on her way to Australia – we saw the passengers in evening dress and fur coats, watching over the rails, and the chefs cooking the dinner and the lights in the portholes and it all looked so gay and adventurous, and made me think of my darling crossing the Atlantic on the Caronia.

November 2nd All Souls Day Went to church and prayed for all my dear dead ones. Doris rang. She said that Cuth wanted her to leave Rhodes Minnis because he did not like her being alone there in the winter as it was isolated and liable to be cut off in snow and bad weather. And when she said she could not leave because it would upset Mrs Regamey – who has been a loving and faithful daily help since they moved there in 1935 – he said that much as he loved Mrs Regamey he could not allow her to decide where he lived! And Doris saw the point of this. Mrs R. will not continue with them regularly, she is getting very old now. Doris says she will have her down every fortnight to clean the silver or something. She is too old for the scrubbing and the hard work. But I said I would help with the move when it happens. Curiosity really.

November 16th I've had a day off today because I have put the sewing machine needle through the first finger of my right hand – SO helpful! Right through the top and it throbs. Pooler has bandaged it up. I sat in the sun this morning. A perfect spring like day, crazy weather. The breeze is warm and the sun shines and the birds sing and we have two primulas out and the japonica, and the catkins! In mid-November. This afternoon I had to go to deliver Mary's cocktail frock, so I went up to St Bart's Hospital and handed it in at the Nurses home and then went on to Oxford Street and bought a hat at Jays! A little black peachbloom pillbox. Daddy said, "Another peculiar hat!" But it's very ordinary really. Then I went to Libertys and bought you a mohair scarf for Christmas, and don't you bally well lose it or leave it on the subway or I'll haunt you.

Monday December 7th I put your letter in the box on my way up to my check up with Dr. Levin in Park Lane. He said all was satisfactory but that I had been going hell for leather by the look of it, and so he has given me some vitamin pills and some thyroid increase. He was very suave and debonair and I felt quite elegant out in the street – and very shot- at as I entered the superb waiting room. It's been redecorated – pale tangerine leather chairs and grey walls and an extremely pretty faded buff and rust and khaki green oriental carpet. And it all looks so expensive and I felt a little out of place in my homely tweed suit and my black stockingette blouse. But I expect we pay the bill quicker than most!

December 28th 1953 Johnnie Griffiths is staying, and after tea we went to the Gaumont in East Ham and saw Odile Versois and Stanley Holloway in A Day to Remember. It was a lovely picture of how the Englishman enjoys himself, the local pub darts club annual outing to Boulogne. Odile Versois is the loveliest thing I have seen on the screen. I could have looked at her forever, wearing merely a pleated skirt and a shirt blouse and a shapeless cardigan – so it wasn't the CLOTHES! There was a girl behind us who got so excited. She kept saying, "THAT'S tore it!" "She'll never make it!" "Ere comes a bloody lorry!" "THAT'S tore it!" I enjoyed her as much as the film, and she simply MADE the second one, which was a frightful American thing, all Red Indians and a full-blown Floozy in immaculate crinoline under gunfire!

December 29th Pooler and I went off up to London this morning and left Daddy just up and Johnny and old Gran still in bed! We stood in the Aquascutum sale for half an hour and I got a smashing tweed coat which will last me for the next twenty years. It's a black and beige heavy herringbone tweed with a black satin lining, raglan sleeves and slit pockets and a little collar and I got it for £9, reduced from £15. It took every penny I had, all my Xmas money AND the last £5 from cousin Noel, but it's worth it. I shan't wear it until next winter, but Aquascutum only have one sale a year. Pooler got a proofed West of England cloth coat in beige and donkey brown, reduced to £7 from £14. My coat goes perfectly with Rupert!

February 3rd We are recovering from our burst pipes saga. Johnnie G. came to stay for the week just after it, thank God, and has spent most of his time here in bed. Can't quite make out what his ailment has been, but he thinks it was a bout of kidneys – wind – and exhaustion coupled with a bad cold, incipient pleurisy and a touch of sciatica! He was back on his feet yesterday and tonight we had a drink at the Earl of Essex in Manor Park and then went to East Ham Palace to see Ian Hunter and Joyce Heron and Sophie Stewart in Dark Secret. It was great fun, very well acted and produced. Hardly anybody in the theatre at all, which was deadly as it is a vast place, as you know. We sat in the stalls and I enjoyed it. They have a new manager there and are getting new plays and quite good actors, so shall go and have a bash when I can. They have Noel Coward's Relative Values on next week so shall definitely go to that. I would much rather that than the pictures and it probably won't last long if the audiences don't get better!

February 22nd On Tuesday night I packed my suitcase ready for going to Doris and Cuth early in the morning. As soon as Rupert saw the suitcase it was all up! Down went his tail and he just humped himself up in a dejected little heap in the big chair and looked reproachful and resigned! Poor little dog.

On Wednesday, I was up at 6a.m, got up the coals and did the fire, made the beds and was out of the house by 8a.m.and met Doris and Cuth at Charing Cross by 9.15a.m. We picked up the car at Ashford and went to the cottage at Rhodes Minnis where we found the removal van already installed and the men packing and moving out things and Mrs Regamey also packing and looking as miserable as hell, poor old dear. She was pleased to see me – but said she couldn't think why

Madam was leaving when she had spent so much money on the cottage and got it so nice! I must say I felt much the same way!

After a cup of coffee Doris took me to see the new house. It is very big compared with the cottage. You can throw the whole ground floor open into one space if you want to give a whale of a party -! Quite honestly, I do not care for it. That is, I should not want to live in it. It is very attractive and with their money and their furniture it will look very gay and expensive and unusual – but I do not enjoy it – I do not want one like it – and if I had one given to me I should try and sell it -! But I would not say so to her for the world and I hope you won't split on me – you won't will you, Lisa?

We spent as much time as we could on Wednesday packing, though Doris' idea of packing for a move is very sketchy and nearly drove me hairless. The first vanload went down in the afternoon and we went down with it and unpacked china and glass all afternoon and then went down to the Rose and Crown in Elham for a drink and then went to bed early.

Thursday I had a cup of tea in bed about 7 a.m. – my second since you left! Then packed up beds and bedding. The men came at 8 a.m and we went solidly at it all morning. But the time was taken up with packing as the men literally had to pack everything except the clothes – which I packed! And the silver and cutlery and food! She left soap and flannels on the basins and toothbrushes. The whole bally lot! I never SAW such moving, and of course it took the men hours. However, the last load came in about 7.30p.m. and we got to bed at 11p.m. dead beat.

On Friday Mrs Regamey came down in the morning to help and she had a little weep. I felt so sorry for her, poor dear, and when Doris took her home I went too to see Mr Regamey. They send you their love. Oh! On Thursday we were invited to lunch with a Mrs Farmer, quite nice but very correct and formal. She gave us steak – so tough I could not masticate it, and had to deposit the lot in my handkerchief – underdone carrots and overdone greens. Silver polished marvellously and a wonderfully polished table, but we would rather have had a good cup of coffee and a nice tender ham sandwich.

By the time Cuth arrived on Friday evening we had got the sitting room very liveable and four bedrooms in reasonable order. On Saturday we managed to hang most of the downstairs pictures and get the airing cupboards and larders sorted. Cuth took us to the Rose and Crown for supper, nice tender meat and vegetables and a nice bottle of wine this time and we were in our beds by 10.30 p.m. Bliss.

March 3rd Back again in East Ham and the eternal routine. I got herrings for lunch and mustard sauce, carrots and 'tatoes, and apple flop and custard. I had cleared it all up by 2 p.m. and then dashed off and bought rabbit and bread and some bacon for tomorrow's breakfast and then – I WENT TO THE PICTURES! I did. All alone I went – and to see a film that I shall remember all my days, and one that you MUST see – it is called The Kidnappers. There are two little boys in it who are so natural that they tug at the heartstrings. The whole film is beautifully done and simple, it quite restores one's faith in J.

Arthur Rank. I was home by 4.40p.m. and Rupert behaved as if I had just come in from the Everest expedition.

Monday March 28th I went to dear Josie for a haircut. She says it looks so much nicer, not being set, just washed and placed, that in future I will just go for a cut and trim once a month. I suggested I have a trim once a fortnight, but she said she COULDN'T trim! Once she got the scissors in her hand she couldn't stop, and at the end of six weeks she would have got 'down to the canvas'. And as I did not exactly want to look like Peter Lorre I concurred.

April 11th, Palm Sunday 1954 We had an invitation from a friend of Bishop Henry Wilson's, a Miss Potter out in Great Waltham, asking us to supper on April 27, to meet the Wilsons. Gates and his wife from Wanstead are invited too, and will transport us, so it is all laid on. Daddy had his airs about it and said it was the night of the borough council meeting and, as Mayor's Chaplain, he could not let the Mayor down. -!- I said B,,,,,, the Mayor, I never had the chance to meet any one but jumped up Council Officials, and I expected him to accompany me, and I wrote and accepted straight away. Daddy in a very bad temper, but cornered.

Thursday May 5th Oh! Woe, woe and more woe! I caught my little toe a clonger on the dog's basket and knocked it back. I hopped around howling with pain and rage and finally got dressed to find that   I could not get my shoe on. I was determined to go to the tailoring, and managed to cram my foot into my oldest most misshapen court shoes. I was determined to get there and I did and finally got home again hobbling worse than Gran!

Friday My toe is now a beautiful black running into purple running into maroon, and so is my language. Pooler tells me she knocked her toe up years go and it went on for WEEKS. So helpful.

Saturday The day of the great thirteen hundredth Anniversary in Chelmsford Cathedral of the coming of St Cedd to the Saxons! We HAVE to go, says Daddy! My hair needs washing and my face looks haggard, but my foot is painful and accounts for that. However, I decide that I can't look young and beautiful, so I will look DISTINGUISHED and go all out for it. And when I was ready, I didn't look so bad! I wore Doris' good black wool and the black and white check coat, a good pair of gunmetal nylons, my diamond earrings, YOUR antique agate bracelet, my Rabbi pillbox hat, my fighting cock brooch and new black gloves. And I got my foot into my best suede courts, well steamed over the kettle. Luckily we were taken all the way in the Mayoral car, as all the Mayors and Mayoresses were bidden. It was a good do in the Shire Hall; all sorts of high up people were there. It's Daddy being a Rural Dean that got US there. I found a table by the wall and sat and watched until time to come home in the Mayoral car. I WAS glad of it. The Deputy Mayoress said SHE had hurt her toe some years ago and it took WEEKS to heal!

July 8th I got the bit in my teeth and was determined to go to the sales. I went up to Regent Street and tried on countless weatherproof coats and didn't like any of 'em, so saved my money. Then I went round Dickens and Jones, and Liberty and Robinson and Cleavers snooping for material. By this time I was faint for food and wanted a lavatory badly, so I walked down to Piccadilly and got into the Lyons Corner House Salad Bowl queue.

There was a charming young man behind me. I'd noticed him in the lift, about 21-22, I suppose. He tapped me on the arm and said, "I say, what happens and how much does it cost? I've never had the nerve to come in one before and anyway I don't know what it's like, we don't have one in Edinburgh." So I told him all about it and said to follow me, and get as much as he possibly could on his plate! He prattled on until we got to the cash till, and then I smiled and said Good Bye, and his face fell and he said, "Oh! Can I – Are you – May I -?" So I said, "Yes, do come and sit with me if you want, but I am SO middle aged." He laughed out loud at that which was most complimentary! And we settled down to a most hilarious lunch.

He was a medical student at Edinburgh and was on his way down to Devon for a holiday. He had travelled all night by coach and was continuing by train from Waterloo. He had only been to London once before, with an aunt, and he thought London shockingly expensive. Said you could get a good three course meal in Edinburgh for 3/- and he had been in a Fortes here and had a cup of coffee and a sandwich and it had cost him 2/4!! He was a pet. He was very interested in the American quota, and by your going to America by that means, and about the forms you had been required to fill in, and about your being required to say if you had ever kept a brothel! He hooted with mirth and was full of fun and nonsense. I had to bid him good-bye very firmly or I should never have got any shopping done!

I felt thoroughly rejuvenated by the whole encounter and set off for John Lewis where I bought the red underslip material for your organza cocktail frock and some very fine grey viyella stuff for your two winter shirt blouses.

August 26th Our wedding anniversary. We set off early evening and went to the Northumberland Arms and I had some shandy and then into a dear little pub called "The Two Chairmen" off Cockspur Street and more shandy, and we had our photos taken for you by a man in the street, and then we went to the Haymarket Theatre to see A Day by the Sea. It was a most successful evening and a lovely play. I chose it simply and solely for the cast. I did not know a thing about it but it had John Gielgud and Ralph Richardson and Harcourt Williams and Mary Jerrold and Megs Jenkins and Irene Worth. Good enough, I thought! It's a charming play full of philosophy and gentle humour. Daddy was very appreciative. Gielgud I thought superb as his was a very dull part, but the changes of mood were beautifully portrayed. Ralph Richardson was a retired doctor – a ne'er-do-well too fond of the bottle. Harcourt

Williams was an old chap who sat in a garden chair most of the time. He looked as if he was so old that his elbows and knees would snap!

Afterwards we went to the Lyons Corner House Brasserie, and got home at midnight to a deliriously happy little dog. Nearly went cuckoo with joy!

Sunday Sept 5th I woke up 49 years old – and felt it – but not more – which was useful. Your dear little card came on Saturday afternoon and Johnnie G. had sent the most heavenly bunch of flowers, bronze and yellow chrysanthemums and about a dozen assorted gladioli, you never saw such profusion. I fond a new Vogue pattern book with the Sunday papers, an unexpected treat. Nadia gave me a pair of nylons and Daddy gave me £5!! I nearly laid an egg! I only did the essential chores and then indulged myself and went and sat in the garden and knitted my black cardigan. Josephine gave me Atkinsons lavender water and Creeps gave me Elizabeth Arden soap. Gran then gave me a vile pink apron with jade binding and a face flannel!

On Tuesday I put on my black wool dress and my diamond earrings and Daddy took me to the Aldwych to see Edith Evans and James Donald in the Christopher Fry play, The Dark is Light Enough. I thought it was superb. You must read it and so must I. There is far too much to absorb in one hearing. The setting was by Oliver Messel. And as lovely. The second act of the old house stable was in subdued monotone like an old print, an aqua tint. I hope it runs long enough for you to see it. Then we went to the Charing Cross Brasserie again and got home by midnight to a mightily relieved Rupert. He had been lying in the hall waiting.

The next morning Gran told us she had been to see The Robe at the pictures. She said it was about a very fast young woman who threw her skirts up and enticed a nice unsophisticated young man and she couldn't think why it was called The Robe! We told her the Robe was not coming till NEXT week. But she said she jolly well knew it was the Robe! RIGHT! So we left it at that.

October 3rd I have been so exasperated with Mrs A. this week, and with Gran, I had got to the stage I wished never to see any of the whole set up ever again. Talk about a home help – Mrs A. is a dead weight, I shew her time and again how to do the simplest tasks and she is useless. Johnnie is here, thank God, and today he said, "Come on out of it." So we got on the first bus that came along and it was going to Woolwich! So we went over the ferry and it was a lovely, breezy, sunny day. We had some lunch at a nice pub and then got on a bus and went to Greenwich and spent the whole afternoon at the Naval Museum. It is a MARVELLOUS place, the middle of it is a summer palace built for Anne of Denmark, and later Henrietta Maria. I could have spent days in the building. I think Johnnie was fed up with it after a couple of hours. Then we went back the way we had come, and that was grand too; the sun was setting and there was a foggy misty haze all over the river, so the wharves and warehouses and boats and power station chimneys all looked as if they were made of smoke or grey chiffon, all bathed in this soft diffused pinky glow. The water was beige colour. It was sheer poetry except for the smell. What they pitch into the river at that point I will not try to conjecture!

Oct 13th 1954 On October 22nd we have an Old Girls Meeting of the Norwich High School in London and Miss Broughall wants to do a reading of Laurence Housman's one act play El Greco and has cast me as Jusepe, The Fool! It's a nice little part and ought to be quite fun. I got the play out of East Ham Library; it's one of Eight One Act plays of 1938. It was ages before I ran it to earth. That is a wonderful Library.

Tuesday I scrubbed the kitchen floor and was planning to start on the back kitchen floor when the phone rang and it was Doris. She was up in London, and could I go to lunch? I said no, but she could come to tea if she wanted, and she said yes, so I abandoned the scrubbing and did the flowers in the sitting room and made some scones and a filling for a sponge and changed, She came about 4p.m. and looked SMASHING, in a black costume, white blouse and the most fascinating, expensive little turban hat in dull grey green with little sequiny feathers or leaves. She looked absolutely super. She talked and talked, and said she had had a charming letter from you, and we shewed her your birthday snaps, and she said she would give you a 21st birthday present next year, so keep her to it. Daddy came in and was most agreeable. She and Cuth have got a small flat off Great Portland Street which is much more convenient for Cuth than lodgings. She had come up for a business dinner and was going back next evening. She went about 5.45p.m. and unsettled me for the rest of the evening.

Friday   Johnnie G. is here, and is preaching for some Mayoral Do on Sunday evening. He and Daddy and I went to see Romeo and Juliet at the Odeon at the Boleyn. I can't think when Daddy last came to the pictures! Laurence Harvey and Susan Shentall were the stars. The scenes were breathtaking and the costumes lovely and it is the only Juliet I have seen who gave the appearance of extreme youth. She was gauche in her movements and yet had the promise of charm and grace. I think I liked it more than the men did. Flora Robson as the Nurse was wonderful.

Tuesday January 17th 1955 I had a letter from Elizabeth asking me to go to Switzerland with her, at her expense, from July 11th for three weeks – and saying that you approved, and would look after Daddy and Gran. I must say that at first I was inclined to throw the whole thing into the wastepaper basket. I haven't the clothes, it means packing in the M.U.Council in Bangor, etc. etc. And the far greater consideration being that I shall miss three whole weeks of my Lisa which I don't want to do. However, I decided to sleep on it, and the next day I wrote and told her that a) I had no head for heights, so if she was contemplating mountaineering I would not suit and b) I had never flown in an aeroplane so had no idea how I would react to that! But if she was prepared to risk both counts I should be delighted to go! However, I should quite understand, blah, blah.

After I had thought it over I came to the conclusion it was no use moaning about never having a holiday on the one hand and having everything handed to you on a plate and refusing it with the other. I know full well I do need a holiday, and there I should only have to fetch and carry for Elizabeth and should not be expected to wash up ANYWHERE! At the moment I am still moaning about missing three weeks of your holiday. But I have not had a reply yet, and she may prefer a less timorous companion.

March 13th I woke feeling cold and headachy, but went to the tailoring class, and then went straight from there to the Mothers Union Council up at Westminster. OH! So dull. There was another meeting after that one but Mrs Owen and I couldn't stomach any more. We had a cup of tea at the Westminster Lyons and came home.

When I got in I felt awful. I was as cold as death and my neck ached and my head ached and my belly ached and my back ached and my calves ached and I didn't feel at all well! I couldn't face setting out again to the Soft Furnishing class, so I stayed home. I tried to cut out the pattern for the box seat cover, but by 8.30p.m. I had had it and went to bed. Daddy brought up Rupert, and Pooler brought up hot milk and whiskey, and it was lovely. I was SO glad to get into bed. I put the electric fire on and lay in the dark, and watched the rosy glow lighting up the furniture and the walls, and it reminded me of when I was about six years old. When it was winter they lit a ruby lamp in my bedroom at bedtime – a big thing about two foot high with a brass oil container. It was all so rosy and warm looking and so much nicer than the little flickering gas light that used to be left on warm nights, a nasty, niggly, little mean- souled light – cold greeny bluey yellow – goblin light!

April 11th 1955 I've had a frustrating week as my left hand has gone back on me, and knotted all my muscles in the palm and wrist, so that I can't bend my fingers, and it aches like toothache most of the time. Rheumatics? Old age? General creakiness? I had a bad night of it on Monday and Tuesday and had to come down for hot milk and aspirins. So Daddy sent for Dr Ollie Thomas and he has given me codeine, which has helped, and some nasty white medicine which has had no effect at all. I can't grip anything, so I can't knit, nor hold a fork even.

Thursday May 8th I went to Tailoring, and stuck it until half time, but although my hand is very much better, it doesn't like holding heavy material firm for long stretches at a time. I got back by 11 a.m. just as Doris rang up, reclining in bed at the Berkeley, if you please, and saying languidly could I go up and have lunch or tea with her and Cuth? I said somewhat tartly, no, I couldn't, and it was nice for some people! They were up for the Business International Fair. But in the evening I changed into my new pinstripe self-tailored costume, and white blouse, and the yellow silk scarf I made out of the Duke's nightshirt, and went off to the Old Girls Meeting of Norwich High School. I enjoyed it very much, and after it was over I went to supper with my dear Miss Broderick and her sister at the Cowdray Club, and got home about 10.30p.m.

Monday May 17th Daddy and Johnnie and I had a very inferior lunch at the Charing Cross Corner House and then went to the Warham Guild to see about a new altar frontal. Then Daddy went home and Johnnie and I went to the Passport Office and got my passport fixed up with a nice picture of me, looking British and proud of it. The thing is, is Britain proud of ME?

Monday May 30th Elizabeth has arrived from New York for the summer and is safely ensconced in the Washington Hotel, Curzon Street. I posted your letter on my way up to London to have lunch with her. I wore my gray, pinstripe, home tailored suit, and my British Home Store nylon blouse and sported the Duke's yellow nightshirt scarf. Felt good when I left home, but distinctly shop soiled when I arrived. I found Elizabeth sitting in a chair of the minute foyer of the International Musicians Association, completely overpowering it with her personality and making it seem much, much smaller than usual. She was very gay – looked better than when I saw her three years ago. She had on a super navy blue suit, and a Persian lamb short jacket with grey lamb facings, and a most saucy black hat with cock's feathers. We went down to an elegant snack bar arrangement where she swung herself up, aged eighty, onto an acid yellow leather topped stool and proceeded to order liver and bacon! We talked, or rather she did, and I answered in the right places, more or less adequately, and then we went back to her hotel and I was presented with a grey costume and a black coat -! She had worn them over, apparently bought new – and was now discarding them! I was VERY pleased.

I came home and tried on my spoils. I decided the American tailoring is not a patch on English – but very nice all the same. I am not too keen on the black coat, but shall lie low for a while and decide what to do with it. It's not a patch on the one I have made at the tailoring – not a PATCH! Even Pooler says so.

Saturday Elizabeth rang up and said to come to lunch on Whit Monday. I accepted with alacrity! I suggested she should come here, but she said too far and too cold!

Whit Monday Up latish and then had a general Clear Up and put on my new blue two-piece to go to lunch with Elizabeth. It's O.K. but it creases – as does all material under £1 a yard – and as this was only 3/11 you can't have everything. Pity! We had a very ordinary lunch at her very expensive hotel, in an airless underground cavern all done up to look like a French prostitute's bedroom. I had a tiny coddled egg with ham in it, and then a slice of tongue and a slice of corned beef and a midget salad with some stewed apples. She had the same and paid 10/6 each for them! Ten and bloody six! I could have screamed!

Then we went up to her room and this time she gave me a priceless grey cashmere winter coat, and a dressing gown, and one of the large size Liberty scarves to go with the coat. I was completely overcome. I shall wear it to my death and if you are a VERY good girl, I'll leave it to you afterwards. .

Trinity Sunday, June 5th It's been a nice, sunny, blowy Sunday and Mary Jarred, the singer, and her husband Sam brought Elizabeth to tea. She looked very well and very charming, but I cannot understand why it is she wears such fabulous emeralds and diamonds on her fingers and then a beastly cheap showy brooch she might have got for 35/-! It beats me! Mary had on a navy blue wool frock I saw three years ago and a geranium red halo hat. She is bigger than ever! And so sweet! And Sam looks much smaller. Elizabeth wore a stupendous black face cloth and grosgrain coat and that saucy little hat with the cock's feathers. That is SO becoming.

Wednesday July 4th I had a whale of a morning. Mrs Jeff came and we decided to wash the gray carpet on the landing. So I threw it out of the window onto the sun patch and frightened a black and white cat to death. It was asleep under the lupins. It jumped quite one and a half feet into the air. The gray carpet was so successful that we brought out the Persian rug from the sitting room. MARVELLOUS! Except that it is now so bright that the chair covers look dingy! So we washed a small rug from Gran's room, and two rugs from the kitchen, and then sat and drank coffee in the sun among the suds. Then I had a bath and went to the London Hospital about my poor hand.

My appointment was for 1p.m. – but so were 20 other people's appointments! I was to have seen Sir Russell Brain at the Neurological Dept. I waited and waited but no Russell Brain. He was on holiday! Why is it the high and mighty so often have no manners? I saw, I believe, a Dr Croft. About 3p.m. I was told to go into a cubicle and take off everything except my shoes and pants and put on a bathrobe which was totally inadequate and gaped in all the wrong places. I waited some more. Finally, I got to see the Doctor who gave me a thorough examination and scraped the soles of my feet while exhorting me to relax. I told him tartly, "Don't talk such nonsense. I can't possibly relax while you do that. I am exerting all my strength not to scream the roof off the hospital!" The nurse in attendance looked terrified, as if I had reprimanded the Lord God of Hosts, but after looking a little shaken, the doctor chuckled, shook hands, told me to go and have an x-ray, and come back next week. He thought I might have arthritis in my neck which was causing the nerves of the arm to seize up. I was finally let out about 5p.m.

Monday September 3rd Johnny Griffiths has bought me a perfectly lovely gilt mirror for my birthday – convex – with gilt balls round it and an eagle on the top. We have put it in the sitting room over the side table and taken the print of George the Third down and put him in the dining room under the portrait of great-great grandfather. The mirror looks frightfully aristocratic!

Tuesday I went to Ilford to get a pattern for my new suit, and fell for an 8/6d, Paris Original Vogue, which I will endeavour to sketch for you on the next clean sheet of paper, and then I went up into the lingerie department of West's and bought a simply exotic petticoat, which I don't suppose I shall ever wear, and if I don't you can have it for your trousseau! Ruched nylon net with little bands of red and pink roses, quite ridiculous, and I ought to have known better! But it was because it was my birthday tomorrow!

Wednesday My 50th birthday! I woke up at five minutes to NINE! – with Pooler bringing me a cup of hot lemon! I nearly died of shock on both counts. I went to Josie this morning for a haircut and have told her I want to finish up with a crew cut on top! So she has given me a neat short crop. She says she is training their eyes to it bit by bit so it won't come as too much of a shock! I am afraid that won't help YOU much.

November 22nd I went up to Dr Levin this morning and shewed him a new crop of sores or spots or patches that have come up all round my waist, and he said it was a nervous thing, and has given me some tablets which make me half doped all day and asleep like a log all night. And some stuff to stop the itching. I said, "But I'm not the sort of person who has nerves. I don't have hysterics or temperaments!" And he said, "No! If you did you wouldn't come out in spots -! You bottle it all up and it has to come out somewhere!" THAT'S all you get for trying to lead a controlled and disciplined life! There's no bloody justice in it, is there?

After leaving him I went to Marshall and Snelgrove and met Lady Robinson – to you – and Marjorie Thursfield, as she was, to me. She is such a nice person. I like her so much. We had lunch at Marshall and Snelgroves and she paid. Dubonnet, grilled Dover Sole and cauliflower, fresh fruit salad and cream and black coffee. Heaven.

Thursday November 24th I've been to dinner at the Savoy with Rollie, whacko! I came home early from the tailoring and Jose washed my hair and placed it. I could never do it like that myself, never. Pooler said it looked like the hair style adverts in Vogue. Rollie collected me at 7 p.m. and we picked up his friends, Fat Fred and Father Seymour, very handsome in a youngest son of the manor sort of way. We arrived at the Savoy a few minutes before Lady Roll and her daughter, Dr. Ball, and I felt I looked quite as nice as they did, but I could not compete with the furs and the diamonds. Lady Roll had on a mink shoulder cape, beautifully worked skins, and Dr Ball had on an ermine and sable shoulder cape, absolutely fabulous. She was very friendly but did nothing but knock things over from start to finish. She knocked over two glasses of dinner wine, one after the other, She then won a four pound box of chocolates and insisted on opening them, and we lost a good three pounds of them under the table. Then she mislaid her diamond brooch and we found THAT under the table. I won a bottle of vintage wine and a very nice Irish linen tablecloth with four napkins. I presented these to Lady Roll for her Church Bazaar and Rollie said, "You don't want those, Mater. We need the money more than you do," and took them off her again. He, Rollie, won a brassiere! He said he was going to give it to his housekeeper, Miss Cottee, but we persuaded him not to, I think. I hope.

We had a heavenly meal, of green turtle soup, and dover sole and tournedos of beef with french beans, and a heavenly sweet, all peaches and ice cream and sugar fluff. Princess Marie Louise was there, looking not unlike Gran, but not so decrepit, with a tiara on one side and very tottery. The Marquess of Milford Haven was there, and Lord Mancroft and all the nobility and gentry. The clothes on the women were simply stupendous. It was a very wealthy crowd, and many of the dresses must have cost hundreds of pounds each. Momma's red lace and tulle that Doris gave me that had been new in 1938 didn't get a look in, but it passed in the crowd! We came away after the cabaret about midnight. And then –

Friday   Up at 6.45. Fish pie and rice pudding for lunch! Back to normal! Boo Hoo!

December 18th 1955 Chrissie Sparshott rang up last week! She sounded exactly the same as she did when I last heard from her in 1920 – when she was about fifteen. We arranged to meet by the bookstall on Charing Cross Station today at 11a.m. I was simply terrified I should not recognise her, and so I got there very early, scanning every middle aged fair skinned woman I could clap eyes on – and suddenly Chrissie walked into view. Quite unmistakeably Chrissie – rather bustling and teacherish – but quite unmistakeably Chrissie. Just as scatterbrained and yet oddly efficient in short jerks! We had lunch at the Egg and Bacon at the Lyons Corner House and it was fun. I heard all about her family. She told me she got my address from Peg Gittings at a Fancy Dress Party up at All Saints Church in Whitstable! She said they all had to go as witches. I said, "Did you go as a witch, Chrissie?" and she replied, "Well, actually, I hadn't got a costume, so I went in a nightdress with a nylon stocking over my face. Nice and anonymous, you know!" I said, "What sort of a nightdress?" She said, "Oh! Wincyette with frills!" I remember years ago when Daddy was first sweet on me, and I had just moved to Norwich, he sought out Chrissie and said, "What can I give Margot for Christmas?" and she replied, "I should give her a nice face flannel!" He has never forgiven her to this day. He says she is a fool of a girl!

January 15th I was due to go to Lyminge as Doris and Cuth are having a grand party there, but on Wednesday I woke with a snorting cold. Glands in my neck as stiff and swollen as tennis balls, and swallowing was an unrefined torture, so I got Daddy to ring up and say I could not go. She was very sweet and said I must go and stay later. But I would have liked to have gone NOW! I obviously went to too many parties in a former existence.

March 5th A while ago the Old Girls of Norwich High School asked me to give a talk at their next meeting on "Being a Vicar's wife". At first I thought what could I possibly say, but as I thought it took shape and in the end I enjoyed putting it together, though most of what I REALLY wanted to say I thought I had better not! However the day has come! I spent most of the morning turning out the big bedroom as we are going to have a spate of visits over the next few weeks. Then I spent most of the afternoon getting ready for the Old Girls Dinner. I had a bath and put on the black and white suit with the red lining and the new skirt and it looked very nice, but by the time I had gone up to Charlotte Street on the bus it had creased, and I had a neatly pleated skirt horizontally. Still, never mind.

I had very bad stage fright before the speech – but, just as always, once I was on the stage I forgot all about it, and though I say it as shouldn't, it was the speech of the evening. They rocked with laughter from beginning to end. And Diana Gillon, who has written a successful novel with her husband, said they would give me an introduction to Punch if I would only write it down and do a series! I ask you! I was SO glad I did not make a fool of myself. There were a nice lot at the meeting and it was a nice dinner, and we had a few drinks to get things going – it was a very successful evening.

Good Friday Breakfast at 9.30am and then chores and then to the Three Hours Service. Johnnie preached one of the sermons and Witcutt preached two. Daddy was down at St Mary's with Rollie. Johnnie's was adequate but Witcutt's were masterly. I cannot express how deeply grateful I am to be given this opportunity of listening constantly to his sermons and ideas. He is a very great mind – albeit practically unknown – and I feel it a mighty privilege to hear him so often.

Tuesday I went up to London and met Doris at the Cowdray Club and had lunch. She looked very elegant in a black wool frock, black coat with Persian lamb collar and a fascinating red turban hat that was made for her and cost NINE GUINEAS! So what! I wore my three winters' old Aquascutum coat, and a skirt of the same charcoal wool material of yours, and the charcoal cardigan that Panny sent me (for the first time) and my red Liberty scarf, bought in the sale, and considering, except for the cardigan, the whole lot didn't cost much more than the hat, I didn't do too badly.

After much lunch and chit-chatting we went into Selfridges, and had an orgy of gadget looking. I bought a tray for Johnnie G.'s birthday, black with a gold rim and black handles. Very masculine and chic looking. We had some tea at a place in Bond Street, and I got home about 5.30p.m. I spent the evening sewing the cover for the wing chair.

"…I leant on the five barred gate and gazed down
onto the common. A perfect vista. Brown bracken,
sun shone, blue smoke from cottage chimneys,
then back to the hugger mugger inside."

The Hothfield Folk

Margot's grandfather had married twice and each wife had borne him four children. The two youngest were Fanny, Margot's mother, and Jack, always known as Robin. Their mother died when Fanny was seven and Robin was five, and they were brought up by their older half-sister Hetty Betty. When they were very small they were sent to a dame school in Wantage, run by a cousin. Fanny and Robin were very close all their lives.

Fanny became a music teacher and Robin, after surviving the First World War with the loss of an arm, married Kathleen Clements and became the village postmaster in the idyllic hamlet of Hothfield in Kent.

Robin and Kath had three children, Betty, Jean and Bob, all much younger than Margot, and both Margot and then Lisa had many happy holidays staying with the Hothfield family in the 1930s and 1940s. There was very little money, but it was a cheerful, welcoming family full of fun and affection.

Fanny and Archie Dodman married in the tiny Hothfield church in 1904, and Margot and J.O. married there 21 years later in 1925. Their names appear in the same wedding register, separated only by one page.

Thursday night, November 3rd 1953 only 10.35p.m. and in bed! Oh! Magnifico! Or Spanish phrase to like effect. The reason for this is that Johnnie Griffiths and I are going to Hothfield tomorrow to see "the old 'uns" and he is going to help me take a whole lot of clothes down there and we have to make an early start.

Friday   Got up early and beetled off to catch the 9.15 from Charing Cross to Ashford. Then we got a bus to the main road at Hothfield and walked down through the trees and saw the havoc at the bottom. They have built houses all round the coach road, and all the space in between is choc a bloc with houses. It looks like Surbiton! Kath is wild with delight! – "Sick of all those trees – makes a nice change!" I could kick her!

We found them really quite chirpy. From what Cousin Queenie had said I felt they were at their last gasp, but was glad to find that I was wrong! Robin had got a tummy ache, but nothing worse, so we went down to the Thanet Arms and Robin had a port and brandy to Settle His Tum. After dinner we settled down for a good talk. Betty came. She moved to Charing about ten days ago and likes it there. While we were there another old girl turned up, some church worker from Westwell. They always seem to turn up when I get there and the old fool would not go. A most obtuse old woman! We left by the 6.30 bus and got home about 10.30. They wanted to know all about you and told us Jean was expecting her third baby in March. They are going to stay with Bob next week, so they may drop in here on their way home.

June 18th 1954 I wrote letters this evening, including one to Uncle Robin saying I couldn't meet him at the Zoo on

Friday! They are coming up on a cheap day trip with Betty and the children. Betty's son Roger suggested I should meet them in the Reptile House! I told Robin I was running a Zoo of my own and couldn't leave it!

January 17th 1955 It's bright and sunny and very very cold. Letters from Kath over Christmas have not been bright. Robin has been pretty seedy; he has had a series of heart attacks and the last one kept him in bed all over Christmas, poor old boy. I will try to get down for a day when the weather is a bit better. I rang up Doris as I had not heard from her over Christmas and she said she had had gastric flu. The woman who lives in her little flat, free, to be on hand when wanted, went to Yorkshire for Xmas and had still not returned. So we all have our little worries!

Easter Monday 1955   Tomorrow Johnnie and I are going to Hothfield and I wish we weren't for it seems such a ruddy effort, but I've sent them a postcard now, so we have to go. I expect it will rain hard tomorrow too!

Tuesday We got up as the dawn cracked and caught the 9.15 to Ashford. Arriving there we did some shopping as I had said we would take the dinner. We bought ham and cream cheese and lettuce and some chocs for Kath and then we went to Hothfield on the bus and it's all rather vile. There are now 104 houses on the common where the trees were.

We found Jean and the children there. They had been

there for Easter to help out. Sarah Jane is the loveliest baby I have ever seen. She is adorable. She is at the "hotching" stage and hotches at incredible speed on her bottom. Robin was looking better than I expected and he toddled down to the Thanet Arms and back with Johnnie and Jean and me at dinnertime. They said it was the farthest he had been since November! Anyway, he managed very well and very slowly. Jean was wearing your cherry wool short sleeved jumper and your costume, dyed black, and it fitted and suited her, but I wished we had given it to her a few years sooner. Poor child, she says she never gets anything new. The children grow at such a rate and Ken has to have a good suit and overcoat for work, and Jeanie Jo has to hope that someone will send her something that fits! I've been a bit like that myself but never quite so bereft. Poor child, for one thing she cannot sew and that is a CALAMITY if you are poor! Learn to sew, my pet, even if you are going to be rich, it comes in so useful! Ken came in at teatime and he drove us to the station and Kath came too. Just before we left, Jim turned up to collect Betty. He had a sort of tin cake box on wheels – part car, part shooting brake, part dog kennel! But it WENT!

December 1st, 1955 I had a letter from Kath and one from Robin. He is better in that his heart is stronger, but he has lost all control of his bladder and his bowels and it is a great trial to them all. Also poor Ken has been in hospital again. He has a blood leak and they can't find where it is. I thought from Kath's letter that both she and Jean sounded all in – so I wrote and said I would go down this week from Wednesday to Sunday if they would like me to and they replied by return – so grateful. I was glad I had offered. I only hope it doesn't turn too cold as they never have enough on their beds.

December 4th I got to Ashford at 12.34 and humped my bag up to the High Street and bought a few groceries and then had lunch at that place we had coffee at. The nasty Adams Apple-y man was still there and the Burne Jones waitress. A perfectly FOUL lunch. I can't think how they made everything taste like tepid rain water – meat – sprouts – gravy – coffee – dismal! The only palatable things were the biscuits and butter! The cheese was plastic. I waited a small eternity for the Hothfield bus. It was early closing day and Ashford a dead place.

Got to Hothfield round 2.15 and found Robin very frail and Jean looking the picture of dreariness. Sarah Jane the most adorable scrap, all smiles and good humour, and Ken just the same. Andrea and Michael are really nice children and I spent the afternoon settling in. Betty and Jim came over after tea. Roger is a real poppet and so handsome. David is another little white rabbit! Just like his mother was at his age. Betty looked most aristocratic. She improves with age. But Jean looked dreadful. I know she is not well, and very tired, but all the life has gone out of her, I think she has given up trying. She droops like a piece of fading chickweed. I feel so sad for her. Anyway, I cut out a frock for Sarah that Kath had bought the material for and got no further. I put the markings in, and got everybody a hot drink for supper, and did all the ironing and went to bed.

Thursday It was a lovely day. Jean did a donkey pile of washing and I put it out on the lines and then I walked up to the end of the garden and leant on the five-barred gate and gazed down into the bogs of the common. It is the one vista that has not changed and it was perfect. It was crisp and clear and the sun shone on the brown bracken and the blue smoke rose from the cottage chimneys and there was a heavenly smell of damp earth and wood smoke – it was sheer elixir. I then went back to the hugger mugger inside!

Poor Robin has lost all control of his bowels and his waterworks, and the washing and work is indescribable, and he cries and cries so about it, as he is fully conscious and it does grieve him so. I do hope he will die in his sleep soon. It is heartbreaking for Kath and she really is a perfect brick and stands up to it like a stoic. We had dinner and washed up and then Ken and I took Sarah into Ashford as we had to get some sleeping pills and I spent the evening sewing the frock and ironing.

Friday Not such a nice day, but fine and cloudy and muggy. I did the beds and cleaned upstairs and saw Goody Smith, who sent her love to you, and I got the mid morning coffee. Ken did all the downstairs housework and saw to Sarah. Andrea got breakfast and got herself and Michael off to school, and Jean drooped round like a faded lily and said she was so tired; and I lost my temper, and said, "I CAN'T think what doing! For it's now 11 o'clock and as far as I can see you have made no contribution to the running of this family whatsoever this morning!" Dead silence -! Whereupon I took Sarah's frock and Sarah off into Grandpa's room with the coffee I had made, and Kath came in and said, "Thank you, Margot. That's needed saying for a long time, but she will take more notice of you." I felt mean after I had said it. But still!

In the afternoon Ken, Jean, Sarah and I went over to Betty's for an hour. We were away from the house for about an hour and a half all told and when we got back Robin was beginning a heart attack, so Jean went in to her mother and I gave the family their tea and kept the children quiet. Ken helped and they were quite happy and very good. Andrea and Michael always wash up the tea things together with no argument and no grizzling, and when I showed concern that Sarah was not house trained at eighteen months, it was Andrea who said, "Ought she to be, Auntie?" I said, "Yes, indeed, six months or more ago," and she said, "How would you do it?" and I told her, and she said, "I'm not here all the time because of school but I will try when I am at home." I hugged her. Next morning around 7am she came into my room and said, "She's done it in her pot, Auntie, I sat her on as soon as she waked up"!

Robin got over his attack.

Betty's house in Charing is very small and compact and pretty and they have made it all charming.

Saturday Was a heavenly day. Bright. Clear. Sunny

with lots of wind. They ran out of milk so I got up at the crack of dawn and got some for breakfast. Jean made a Christmas cake and did a pile of washing and dinner was not until 2.30pm. in consequence. Ken took the children to Ashford to get haircuts. Robin had a threatened heart attack so Kath went for the brandy and found Jean had used the last in the Christmas cake! I ASK you! So I went up to the Thanet and bought 'em a bottle of brandy and then I reduced Jean to tears. I was simply COLD with fury. Anyway, I guess she was glad to see the back of me. But she could not say that I did not pull my weight. I rang up Doris in Rhodes Minnis and she said she would come over on Sunday and take me to the station. Goody.

Robin was much calmer on Saturday evening and I sat and talked to him and sewed most of the evening after I had ironed for about two hours!

Sunday I went to church with Ken and Andrea at 11am. Then after dinner I sat with Robin until Doris came, but he cried so bitterly when I said goodbye that I could not take Doris in to see him. Her little dog Boofy was in the car and was most welcoming. We went into Ashford and had a most civilised tea at the Saracens Head and I got home about 7.15pm. Rupert went delirious with delight.

Sunday December 14th Last week I decided to take that reversible mac out of Rupert's basket, and have it cleaned and reproofed for Andrea! It came back yesterday and looked smashing, so I have put new buttons on it, and shortened the sleeves and spent the rest of this evening packing it up. It looks most classy!

Thursday February 14th 1955   Jean rang up to say that Robin had died at 2p.m. I had had a letter from her in the week to thank me for Andrea's jersey and skirt, when she had said that Ken was in bed with a bad ear and that he was in great pain, but that Robin was much the same. So I had not been expecting to hear of his death so soon.

She sounded so terribly grieved she nearly made me weep. She and Kath had been up all night. He had had a haemorrhage and they were distracted and the doctor came out and brought a specialist and they sent him straight to Maidstone Hospital in the morning. Bob was there. I said did they want me to go to the funeral or would I be a nuisance, and she said, "Oh! Do come. You will be such a comfort to Mother!" So what can I do but go? Robin is being cremated at Charing on Tuesday, so I'll tell you more next week.

Sunday February 19th   Mass   8am.   Snowing   and freezing hard. Decided that I shall freeze going to Hothfield. So go and get down the fur coat I bought for 5/- in the last jumble sale and spend the entire morning and afternoon lining my tweed coat with it. I put it on to go to Evensong and everyone must have thought me about seven and a half months pregnant, but I was mighty cosy! Absolutely pneumatic, I look.

Monday I put on my fur lined coat and Daddy's socks

inside my boots and my thickest scarf over my head and set off for Ashford by the 11.15 train. It was so damn hot in the train I had to undo my coat. And my knees sagged it was so heavy – still, it was lovely to sweat in the train.

The snow was piled high at Ashford. I had lunch in the café with the Burne Jones waitress, and then caught the bus to Hothfield. I got there through the most beautiful white world. It really was enchanting.

I went in through the back door and found Jean and Bob washing up and Kath in the dining room. We had cups of tea and Kath was magnificent throughout. Jean had arranged to take Sarah and Andrea over to stay with a friend at Willesborough to stay the night. Then Bob would fetch them home after the funeral. So they set off and Andrea was very cross because she wanted to stay with me! But she is a good child.

Then the flowers began to arrive and that kept Kath busy. Poor Ken is in the Maidstone Hospital with still no knowledge of what is the matter with him and he is in great pain with his head. Acute pressure on the brain. Poor children. I am so sorry for them.

Bob went over to Willsborough to collect Jean and returned without her. Sarah had developed an earache and was howling her head off, so Jean stayed the night. I slept with Kath and she was very grateful.

We got up early in the morning. Jean's host brought her back by 8.30 and we all set off for Charing Crematorium. The British Legion had turned out in force when we got to

Charing. Robin was evidently the oldest member, but Kath said he seldom went to a meeting! However, they were all there, banner and all.

It was a lovely morning, bright sun on the snow and the Crematorium was very pretty and the chapel was bright and sunny and full of flowers, not wreaths but big bowls of flowers. So I must say it was the least harrowing form of funeral I have been to. And as Kath said, it was warm and sunny and she could not have borne to have had him lowered into that bitter, bitter ground while we stood and got chilled to the bone.

We came home about 11a.m. and had hot milky coffee and then lunch and then Bob drove me all the way home. We saw Ken on the way in Maidstone. He said he had been x-rayed all morning long and was fed up with it. He was to have an operation on his ear the next day, but that was nothing to do with the pain in his head which they had still to diagnose!!

It was the night of the Mayoral Reception here, but not on your life for this old baby. The very thought of walking half clothed along that tarpaulin covered freezing passageway between the Town Hall and the Swimming Baths was enough to give me pneumonia. I wrote a very nice letter to the Mayoress and excused myself on account of a death in the family. Robin will be delighted to have been of service, I know. So poor Daddy sallied forth alone, but I did warm his dress clothes before he went!

Mothering Sunday March 24th Daddy brought me some lovely daffodils for Mothering Sunday and I put some palm pussy willows with them, and I got a lovely bunch of yellow and pink tulips, and blue iris, and orange fat narcissus, and I put all those in the old yellow bathroom jug on the kitchen dresser and they all look LOVELY.

After lunch I went up to Charing Cross to meet Kath off the train. She is coming for four or five days. When I saw her I nearly died. She had two very heavy cases, bulging FULL, and a scarf, and a short fur coat over a woollen frock and she kept dropping her handbag! Her face was literally pickled cabbage colour and she was ready to have a stroke at any minute. By the time I got those two suitcases on the Upminster train I was in a like state!

Wednesday Kath is having a lovely quiet time, breakfast in bed and has dozed nearly all the time. She has months of sleep to catch up on, poor old darling, and I am glad she CAN sleep now. I took her to church at St Bart's on Sunday evening. I must dash now and get the shopping and then go for a slow march up the High Street with Kath. She is too slow for a funeral, so I like to get the shopping done first!

Sunday June 17th It's so damn cold I am off to bed with a hot water bottle. Flaming June. I rang Hothfield last night and said I had a load of old clothes for them and was there any chance anyone could fetch them as they would cost pounds to send by parcel post. So today, Ken, Jean, Andrea, Michael and Sarah all came over in the car this afternoon, had early tea and went home around 5.30pm. The children were all very well behaved. The only one who wasn't was Rupert who did not like his nose put out of joint and barked and snapped and was altogether a nasty, spoilt dog. Ken is waiting to go into Guy's Hospital for his head and he looks very strained and ill, I thought, but he is a nice lad. After tea I shewed them the church. Before we came out we all knelt down in the front pew and said our prayers in a row and Sarah Jane (next the centre aisle) put both hands together and said loud and distinct, "Dod Bless Auntie Mardo" and then was so pleased with her effort that she rolled on her back in the aisle and chortled with her legs in the air! She IS a poppet.

"Daddy came in from the garden
and said in shocked tones,
'Have you seen next door's washing?'"

East Ham High Street

Although East Ham got more than its fair share of bomb damage during the war, the buildings around the cross roads in the centre of the Borough had come through remarkably unscathed. High Street North and High Street South were intersected by the Barking Road, Barking and Dagenham to the East, Poplar, Stepney and the City to the West. At that crossroads, the Town Hall and the Library stood on one corner, a huge police station, with barracks, and stables for police horses on another, a large Co-operative Department Store on a third and an old fashioned drapers, Hawkins, on the fourth. It all looked pretty drab. No painting or redecorating had gone on during the war years apart from white distemper, inside, and brown paint, outside. No other colours were made apart from camouflage.

High Street North contained the shopping area and the markets. High Street South led down to the Docks, passing the little church of St Mary's on the way. St Bartholomew's was a hundred yards from the Police Station along the Barking Road.

Life had been a struggle during the war. Even if your house had not been damaged, it was more than likely to have an outside loo and an old fashioned cooking range. The coal fires mixed with the river mists to form dense smogs that left the roads filthy when they lifted, and any washing left out inadvertently overnight was grey and smelt of ash and had to be washed again in the morning.

Food though, was not in such short supply, and

clothing was beginning to brighten up. Furniture still bore the Utility label, but furnishing fabrics were about. Slowly, slowly, variety and colour began to appear in the East Ham shop windows, and people began to look forward to PARTIES! And Dressing Up!

Wednesday Gosh, but I'm tired after traipsing round London looking for rugs for the church. And patterns and samples for altar frontals. I got back to East Ham and went into the British Home Stores for a snack; my usual wholemeal bread, two pats of butter, one portion of cheese, one dish of beetroot! And there was such a hoo-ha going on at the counter by the tea. Now that sugar is off the ration they put it in bowls on the tables, instead of doling it out to you as you need it. But people are so used to being given sugared or non-sugared tea, that they kept on saying "tea with" or "tea without" and to each one a lean weary carroty server with protruding teeth replied – very adenoidal – "It's Orl the Sime nar – it's Orl The Sime – there ain't no DIFFRENCE – ther sugar's on the Tables – it's ARN THE TABLES – Cor, Ain't they AWFUL – IT'S ORL THE SIME!" No one else seemed to think it was funny.

Monday November 14th I went and watched the Remembrance Day Procession to the War Memorial from the Town Hall yesterday morning. My oath, you never saw such a frightful lot! They get worse every year. Only Daddy and the Rabbi looked anything at all. I stood by the wall of the police station with one of the C.I.D. men and said, "Aren't they awful?" and he replied, "Yes, Mrs Nicholls – a little bit of Hitler's Germany wouldn't come amiss with their marching!"

Monday Dec 21st 1953 My sweet. Oh! I shall be glad when this Christmas lark is over. Why it should always mean this awful kerfuffle I cannot imagine. I went straight up to London this morning to get another consignment of pills, and posted your letter in the huge Post Office at Charing Cross – much easier to get to that counter than the East Ham counter – I think I shall go up and post everything there from now on! It's murder in the East Ham one, a solid block of evil smelling humanity. The little writing counters are full of women with enormous posteriors writing out Xmas cards. What a place to do it! One – larger than the rest – was saying to her companion "Where shall I put it, Lil, on the back or in the inside?" and Lil replied, "Oh! For Gawd's sake, what does it matter? We've got all vese to do – we shall be 'ere all night at vis rite"– and from UNDER the counter where there were at least eight or nine children belonging to various mothers, came a little wail, "Mummm – I'm orl we-eeet!" which, according to the little streams which were there as proof, was all too true. The mother said, "Shut up, can't you, you'll get us turned out -!" Now, at Charing Cross!

Wednesday Dec 23rd Well! What a day. I don't know what the time is, but it's Thursday for sure and I don't feel strong enough for a shock so I'm not looking at the clock. I've wound it up with my eyes shut.

I went into the Tip Top Cleaners today to fetch Johnnie G's fawn weskit and the girl there made me laugh. I asked her if she was going home for Christmas. She said, "Yes, of course, but reely, my Mum tikes the biscuit. I've sived up and bought 'er a new frock and a new cardigan and a littul box of chocklits and I took 'em over 'ome during the week a'cos I thought she'd like to wear 'em for Christmas, and wot do you think! She sat in her chair and frew 'er apron over 'er 'ead and bleedin' well cried!" I said, "For Gawd's sike what 'eve you got 'a cry over?" and she said, " 'A'cos you are so good to me!' Di'nt 'alf touch me, it di'nt!" There she stood with her thin little body clothed in a costume with enormous lapels – all a size too large for her, though I expect it was the smallest one in the shop, and her hair in lank ringlets and her teeth all bad – she's a nice good hearted girl.

Friday New Years Day It was a beast of a day, bitterly cold. Cold enough for Daddy to suggest having the radiator on in the hall all day. And all night. I changed the sheets and sorted the laundry and did a bit of washing and ironing and went to the sale at the Co-op and bought some very attractive hankies for 4d each. All ready for next Christmas! This cold paralyses me and I did very little all afternoon except knit Gladys Riley's sock and write a couple more Xmas thank yous. I put a hot water bottle in Rupert's basket and then had his and mine in my bed, and when I lowered him in he had a lovely surprise and gruntled himself into the warm spot and I never heard another sound from him.

Saturday It isn't so cold and I stupidly promised Jessie I would go and help with the big Post Office Party in St John's Church Hall. I got up late and scuttled round like a scalded cat and went to Matthews the florists to get the church flowers. Eucalyptus leaves and big daffodils and white jonquils. I was frozen stiff by the time I had arranged them, so stiff that I nearly cried when I washed my hands in warm water after dabbing about with cold stone vases and buckets of cold water. There were some lovely lilies left over from last week, so I cut some laurel to go with them and my big bowl by the High Altar looked like a fairy Spring wood. Then I came home and had a grilled herring and a dollop of rice pudding, wholesome but not inspiring.

Then I changed into my home made tweed costume and beetled off round to the Church Hall. Muriel Middlebrook and Netta refused to help Jessie. They said they were not going to put up with her ANY more. So you can guess there must have been a grievance if Netta struck! I was afraid no one else would turn up, but Topsy Porteous came, and Mrs Ives, and Mrs Crocker, and Mrs Wates and Pat. Two girls from St. Mary's also came and were very useful.

It was a proper non-stop eating effort. Two hundred children sat down to tea, and we ran a running buffet for the parents and adults from 4p.m. till 6p.m. They were a very rough lot but pleasant and jovial and appreciative. We held it all downstairs and the buffet was next to the kitchen. They comprised the whole East London Area Postal Workers, so they came from Whitechapel, and Poplar, and Stepney, and

West Ham and "orl round the bleedin' place". We gave them smashing eats. Ham sandwiches, paste sandwiches, meat patties, jellies and cream, fancy cakes, buttered scones, jam tarts, coffee, tea, orangeade, buttered buns, bread and butter, cheese sandwiches, cheese rolls, chocolate biscuits, doughnuts. We got it all washed up finally and left at 10.45p.m. I don't know what time the dance finished, but we shut the bar at 10p.m. And was I tired? But Jessie had been as sweet as honey and as smooth as butter all day.

Thursday Feb 5th 1954 Well! We've been to the East Ham Male Voice and Ladies Choirs' combined effort of a dramatised version of Mendlessohn's Elijah! And really we behaved very well, considering the orchestra was excruciating and we sat on top of it! The Choirs are very well trained for local Choral Societies. The tableaux were a big mistake. Daddy says the costumes were authentic, but one of them definitely got into the wrong parcel, for it was the dress of an English peasant girl of the 15th century! Elijah was played by a gormless youth of about eighteen, with a ready made beard two tones darker than his hair, and he wore his praying scarf wrapped around his neck like an undergraduate's scarf. And every attitude he made was like a scarecrow in a gale.

The child that was raised from the dead looked as if it had fallen head first into a bucket of Condy's fluid. I've never seen such a colour for makeup. It looked like a Red Indian with high blood pressure. Its mother was the normal pink and white colour. They must have used a mixture of iodine and cocoa powder. Jezebel was a bit of a tata! But I can't think she would have done much damage in these enlightened days. She looked like a battered Brunhilda complete with Viking helmet and fair plaits.

The two lady soloists were worth notice. The contralto was taken out of the ranks of the contraltos and was feeling her feet. Her stance was superb. She had one foot in front of the other and her chest well out and her arms outstretched as far as they would go holding her score. – with long white gloves and a grey silver brocade (not heavy) evening gown with a pink rose tucked into her bosom. The top was rather tight so the shoulder straps cut in rather. She had a face like the back of a coal cart, and when she sang she sort of pursed up her face and managed to show both top and bottom teeth all the while, a tricky business. The soprano was a demure little puss of about 49 summers and evidently a big hit at Masonic ladies' nights. She was plump and petite, and wore a gunmetal brocade with an apple green velvet stole and apple green long gloves, and she had to stand on tip toe to get the high notes and nearly fell off the little rostrum to get rid of the difficult bits.

The male soloists were up to the Male Voice Choir standards, none of them special but all very competent and pleasant. The trombone was a quarter tone sharp and most of the woodwind was a quarter tone flat and the timpani was half a tone flat so it was a bit difficult to tell what the others were like. Now I am off to bed to dream of Jezebel and the priests of Baal. The frenzied dance before the altar was like a Keep Fit class at Butlins, and the people would bow to the altar solemnly in a most High Church fashion when passing it. There was a bullock on it covered in straw.

Tuesday I took my shoes to Little John's the cobblers and the girl there always asks about you. She said she had no coal and had had none all through that bitter weather. She said, "Me and my husband used to eat our teas over the oil stove and then go to bed." I said, "I can't think how you had the courage to get up." And she said, "We nearly Never!"

Maundy Thursday After the Maundy Thursday service I went to Wo Pangs with Daddy in the evening. I had chicken chop suey and he had I See Nits or something – but really – as I observed – we were both eating exactly the same thing, only his gravy was white and mine was manure coloured. The clientele was quaint. Two youths, one in Edwardian rig with sideboards, and the other in a brown suit and a white teeshirt with scarlet poppies all over it, and royal blue socks with jelly bottom suede sandals. There was a very respectable couple – man with mac and trilby and white scarf with fringe – girl with a tight perm and little hat with a fluffy feather, and a fitted coat, who crooked her little finger and said, "Oh! Bert! Do stop it?" when he read out the menu. They had sausage and chips and peas and fruit salad to follow. Why go to Wo Pangs then?

Monday I did the usual chores and then went to Josie to have my hair cut. Josie was slimming and had got some amazing American diet which lasted a fortnight which she had got from the Mayo Clinic. It was very rigid but guaranteed the loss of a stone and she had made her poor husband go on it too. They had just completed a week and he had lost eight pounds in four days and came in while I was there. He said, "Mrs Nicholls, it's murder. I'd never have bought the damn television if I'd known. Josie says we have done nothing but eat biscuits and sweets and drink coffee and tea all evening since we have had it and we must get all the weight off before Christmas." I said how much slimmer he looked and he said, "I'm depraved. I am, really. I even drink my toothpaste water. Do you know what I've eaten today? Four boiled eggs and a dollop of spinach. I DAREN'T have any more – she weighs me every time I come in to see if I've cheated!" Josie looked marvellous, but then I always think she does no matter what shape, and I said so.

October 24th Here you can't go anywhere without a whole host of little so-and-sos swarming up and saying, "Spare a copper for the Guy." Johnnie G. rang up last week and said he had just been accosted by a swarm on entering the telephone booth and he said no, he hadn't got any change, and one of them said, "What would it be you wanted changing, Guv?"

November 7th 1954 On Thursday next there is a dinner that the East Ham doctors and dentists are giving in London and they have invited Daddy and me, and I have not got anything to wear, and have suddenly woken up to the fact! So I 'm sweating on the top line trying to knock that red lace and tulle thing into something approaching modernity. I have cut the sleeves out and altered the top and made it ballerina length and bought a full net waist petticoat and I hope it will pass. But now I have cut it I have to hem it and there are three layers, the crepe underslip and the tulle and the lace and I reckon I've got to sew about twenty yards round the hems.

Thursday I managed to finish it! And at 6p.m. I swep' out of the front door with Daddy, and there at the gate, was one of the longest, flashiest, blackest cars I have ever seen come to collect us. Marry a dentist, say I!

We were taken to the Abercorn Rooms near Liverpool Station, a very nice place. It was very comfortable and nicely got up, cream and gold and mirrors and crystal chandeliers, and really we had a very good evening. We met countless doctors, dentists and eye specialists and others. Dr Stanley Thomas was a very attentive host. His wife was a tall woman in a pale blue taffeta frock with rhinestones round the halter neck. Also on our table were Reg Slater and his fiancée of twenty five years standing. She wore orange chiffon velvet. She was good fun. I liked her a lot. Another of Stanley's guests on our table was an old girl of about sixty -six summers, called Miss Packer, who, believe it or not, had a grey ponytail! And a black taffeta frock with royal blue stripes.

The lady of the evening was the wife of the Recorder of East Ham. She was very striking with gray, near white, cropped hair, and a   masculine face in a thin bird like way, an interesting face, well bred and intelligent. She wore a lovely frock of queer green, pale goldy lime – a lovely colour, soft satin, slim and draped in the skirt, but the top looked as if it was falling off, strapless and most unshapely. She had lovely skin, golden tan, and a perfectly beautiful necklace of big yellow and deep red uncut stones which MADE the dress, but quite honestly the top looked so sloppy and loose I was sure it would fall.

We had plenty of short drinks beforehand. I confined myself to gin and tonic – two! And we had a very nice dinner, hors d'oeuvres, baked sole with a nutty sauce, chicken and roast potatoes and cauliflower, and then iced pudding with glacé pears, dry white wine, black coffee and liqueurs.

Daddy will have told you about the speeches. And after a dull cabaret there was dancing. I made Daddy dance the last waltz with me and he didn't do at all badly, and because the lights were low he looked much more efficient than he actually was! I enjoyed the evening and we got home just after midnight and I made a cup of tea and we went to bed.

Saturday Hammett's the butchers has now been taken over by Dewhursts (Mr and Mrs Ayres are still there) and the shop has a new front, so that where Hammett's door and Down's Cooked Meat shop door were side by side, now they are apart and it naturally looks very different. Also Hammett's has now got "Dewhurst" over the shop front, and a woman was wandering up and down the other day and all of a sudden she grabbed my arm in a frenzy and said, "Where the bloody 'ell's 'ammetts?!"

Wednesday Josie had to go into hospital last week to have a cyst taken off her back. I rang her up today and she said she was home again and felt much better. She said the East Ham Hospital was filthy! And the whole while she was there the bathroom basin was stopped up with dirty scummy water! It was like it on the Monday she went in and was just the same on the Saturday when she came out! She could only conclude that no one washed. She got a bowl and washed on the floor when she was up, she said! She said the Sister was run off her feet and was sweet, but the nurses were absolute sluts and couldn't care less!

March 18th Our nice Mounted policeman, Skipper Hawkins, has won first in all England at a horse show in Aldershot! He has also got you two tickets for the Police Horse show at Imber Court in July when you come home.

Oh! I was on the bus to Manor Park this morning and there were two women pouring out their most intimate family details to each other at the tops of their voices, and as I got off I caught the bus conductor's eye and he grinned and said, sotto voce, "They ain't 'alf spring cleaning their pedigrees, ain't they?"

Thursday Thick fog, a real smog, very tricky to breathe in. I rang up the Tailoring class and gave my apologies. Miss Otis regrets she's unable to tailor today. I got panicky because it made me cough so. It tasted so vile. I'm determined to get a smog mask if it continues. Gran was housebound solely because she saw the headlines, "Killer Smog" and I think she thought it was a Jack the Ripper effort and not just the smog itself.

Saturday Bitterly, BITTERLY cold and smog with it. Feel I shall commit hari kari and fall on my sword, but face it like a true Briton. I went shopping to get some cushion ticking to make Johnnie Griffith's chair seat and while out must have dropped my little half specs out of my coat pocket, for when I got home I couldn't find them anywhere. I have an exhaustive search through the house, knowing all the time I must have dropped them in the street. Around 3.30p.m. I put on layers of coats and scarves and went round to the police station to notify their loss – and there they were! Oh, I was so thankful! So then I came home and bought fifty Players and took them to the man who had found them and by this time it was 5p.m. and dark and bitter cold. Home, triumphant, and drank cups and cups of hot, sweet tea.

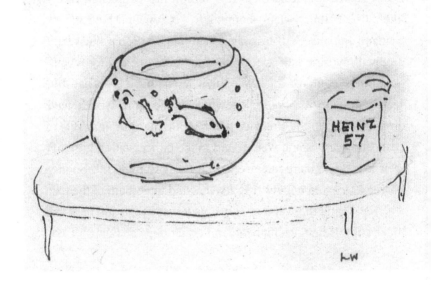

"Lou came with two goldfish in a soup tine. She
says she is calling them Mercedes and Benz".

Lou

Mary Lou Weaver was a young cousin of the great family friend Johnnie Griffiths. Born and brought up in the years of the Depression in the Black Country, Lou had a tremendous zest for life and would have a go at anything. She said that when she was taking the scholarship exam for the local Grammar School one of the questions was: Finish these proverbs. Lou had no idea what a proverb was, but had a go anyway and finished the proverb 'It's a long lane' – with 'Willenhall Lane is'! I am pleased to report that the examiners awarded her the scholarship. But her parents could not afford to pay for the uniform nor have her not contributing to the family before she was sixteen. She began work aged fourteen in a factory but her employers luckily recognised her talent for artwork and design and she was moved to a job in the office. Just after the war she got a job in a surveyor's office in London and Johnnie Griffiths asked Margot to keep an eye out for her. Margot found her lodgings nearby and Lou became a part of the family; she was generous and ingenuous and enthusiastic in her likes and her dislikes and kept us all amused with her exploits and wit. In her late thirties she was courted by a master bricklayer, Charles, a very quiet kind man whom she married in 1953. She came to stay at East Ham Vicarage for the ten days before her marriage.

Wednesday 16th 1953 Daddy posted the first letter to you today. Since then Lou came in unexpectedly, having had a crashing row with Charles last night, because his sisters want to have the reception in the Peckham Mission! Poor Lou! She says it will be nothing but a knees up with beer and sandwiches and had told him so, and then came here all remorse -! I said good on her, and to keep it up and whose wedding was it anyway? And finally she felt better, poor Lou.

September 22nd I went up to London to try and get some decorations for Lou's cake and to look at some Oriental rugs – for the church – that the Civil Service Stores were advertising. Then I met Lou at Whiteman and Bass. I got some not very nice decorations after going to several places.

Then I went over with Lou to the house in Brixton that they are going to live in. I think the sitting room and the little kitchen and bathroom are all very neat and attractive and cosy but the bedroom is a bit of a sick headache. Lou let it be known that she wanted it green so everybody has given her green things for it and she has bought a green carpet. Unfortunately every article is a DIFFERENT green and she has bought a green lampshade and you know how depressing that can look; and what with the bluey green carpet and the sage yellow green bedspread and the apple green silk cane stools and the beigey green curtains and the bloody awful green lamp shade, it's a bit much. Also the furniture is a sort of greeny fumed oak with oxydised 'pretty' handles. Still, she is the one who has got to live in it.

Charles brought us home in the car tonight. How on earth they are going to get to Eastbourne on honeymoon in that on Saturday, I know not. I thought it would disintegrate in the East India Dock Road on those cobbles – and I almost thought I might, in the back. At the least, I thought I would have to spend the rest of the evening sorting out and tidying up my intestines!!

September 24th Then tonight Lou came in and said, "No Mission!" so that's the first battle won. She then proceeded to tell us what Charles had done for his brother Spen's daughters, and Pooler and I collapsed. Lou had not thought it funny until we laughed. It appears that some time back in the war one of these daughters was coming down to stay with her father and mother with an illicit black market pig in the back of the car – dead – or rather, killed! And she got about halfway between Huddersfield and London when her car broke down late at night. So she rings up Charles to go up in his car to locate her because she daren't go to a garage because of the pig! So Charlie set forth in the dead of night and found her car and transferred the pig, and when he got it home he had to cut it up with a scout knife as they couldn't ask anyone else to, for fear of being locked up! And, said Lou, Spen's other daughter has had a pretty hectic life, her husband was an undischarged bankrupt and they were afraid the official receiver was going to come and take the furniture, so her husband bought an old double decker bus and they piled the furniture on it and set off one night for Sheffield, taking it in turns to drive. I think this wedding will be worth going to!

September 26th I am TIRED tonight, I've been going like a steam engine all day. Pooler went out and I began the dinner and Lou began to sew her tan skirt. After about ten minutes I heard a loud and significant sigh from Lou. "What's up?" I said. "Oh, DEAR!" says she, "I don't want to do this skirt." "Well," said I, "I don't want to do this dinner." "Now, I'd LIKE to have a go at the dinner," said Lou. So we swopped and I worked on the skirt till about 3.30p.m. when we went in to Barking and I bought her the little copper coal scuttle from the coppersmith. Then Pooler and Lou and I went over to Wo Pangs and the food was good and the china tea was lovely!

Pooler iced Lou's cake very prettily, little pink posies all over with some yellow and mauve balls in the centre and tiny silver balls scattered about in rings.

Saturday night Whew! What a day! Lou's wedding day! To begin with, darling, another letter from you came the first post and I began to think I would not get to the wedding at all – I would not budge until I had read it through. Anyway we got off to the wedding in good time and it was a perfect day, warm and lovely sun all day after a misty mushroomy morning. She wore the beautiful pale brown grosgrain dress and had a spray of creamy roses that fixed her stole by the shoulder and that stunning big brown hat. I wore my black dress and Bishop Henry Wilson's hat – not literally of course – NOT a battered grey trilby over one eye – but that fedora shaped hat – and had some white carnations as a button hole and white gloves and took my black and white coat in case it was chilly coming back. Johnnie G. had a beautiful grey suit and a white buttonhole! We got to the Camberwell Town Hall, a LOVELY building- most impressive – MUCH better than the Caxton Hall – and there on the steps were Don and the two Young Ones from Lou's Office, and a lot of very old men in tweed suits who turned out to be Charles' elder brothers. In the foyer a lot more men came pitchforking out of nowhere and finally Charles.

Then I got ushered into a little waiting room where at least twenty women were sitting on hard chairs with their backs to the wall. They looked exactly as if they were waiting for ration books, handbags on laps, and knees nice and far apart for comfort! I ploughed my way through the lot, beginning at the door and they were nearly all brothers' wives, and all the blokes in the hall were either brothers or sister's husbands. It was bedlam. Everyone mentioned in the Tables of Affinity were there on Charles' side! We then all filed into a large sunny room, everyone including Mr and Mrs Mainwaring, Lou's boss, and the signing and the ceremony proceeded. All over in ten minutes.

We went out on the Town Hall steps once more for photos and confetti, and then everyone packed into the cars and we all went round to a charming little house in a terrace, three up and three down, and a built on scullery, I'd guess. Very early Victorian, or Georgian, with a fan door with a fanlight and big front window. Lovely. The sister in law Nell was a good sort, and had got a very nice spread awaiting us, very dainty sandwiches and mince pies and sausage rolls. Pooler's cake was much admired and they handed round most generously. Lou had organised the drinks so there was something for everybody. I stuck to Dubonnet, but I noticed that Green Goddess was much in vogue with the younger brothers and sisters.

I could go on forever. But suffice it to say that one of the elder brothers, aged 64, shewed off his prowess by turning upside down on the table with his nose on the cloth and his feet nearly on the ceiling – it was only a low room – and then he challenged me – as a "young woman" – to see if I could do likewise! I said I would rather try in my working clothes! Nell was furious with him, but it made the others laugh Anyway after a bit I managed to get Lou off to the house and to pack her bag for her as she changed. She went away in a very pretty brown wool frock, almost the same colour as her wedding one, and had bought a big brown coat, plain but very nice, and I lent her my grey and brown Liberty scarf. We finally got them off in that ramshackle car for Eastbourne about 2.15.

March 19th 1955 I posted your letter and had lunch, and about 3.p.m. Lou turned up – full of affection and enthusiasm to everybody and everything under the sun. DEAR Lou! She stayed until about 8p.m. We had high tea with Daddy about six and they rattled on to each other and got on well. The cream of the visit came when Lou announced triumphantly, "We are going to Paris, Charlie and me, in August week." Then she said, "Do you know what the French for parrafin oil is?" I said, "No. Oil is 'huile', but I don't know what parrafin oil is." "And

I shall need to know the French for methylated spirits is as well," says Lou, as serious as a judge. "What the hell for?" said I. "Because we are going to take the primus," said Lou. "Are you going camping?" asked Pooler. "NAW," said Lou, "But the French make lousy tea." I laughed and laughed and Lou was most hurt, the tears started up and I felt dreadful, but I could not help it. The thought of Lou and Charles in that hotel bedroom pumping up the primus was too much for me. She's going to take a pound of tea and a tin of Nescafe. I daren't ask any more questions for fear of breaking up our friendship.

Monday May 2nd 1955   A nice sunny day but a Southerly gale blowing. Lou arrived early afternoon and Pooler had the day off. While Lou was here I turned out Gran's room to save old Mrs Jeff on the morrow, and Lou reclined on Gran's sofa, and knitted, and regaled me with her nonsense, and suddenly convulsed me by saying dramatically, "MY GOD! If you had only turned your energy and dogged will power into the world of business you would have ROCKED Wall Street – you would REELY – you would have ROCKED eet!" I was just by Gran's commode as she said this – and I felt it was a pity I hadn't! Anyway I finished the room and got the tea and helped Lou to conquer her pattern and then Poo came in and we all had coffee and talked and so to bed.

Monday December 4th 1955 I posted your letter and lit the dining room fire and sewed nightdresses for the Bazaar in the afternoon, and then Lou arrived, complete with two goldfish in an old soup tin she had just purchased from the pet shop. So I had to find them a pyrex dish they could swim in until I got them a large Kilner jar to travel home in. I suggested she call them Debenham and Freebody, and Pooler suggested Porgy and Bess, but Lou said no, she was calling them Mercedes and Benz. I have since heard that Charles was heard addressing one as "Hiya, Merk!" And this probably did not suit Lou, so I expect they are something else by now! We spent a quiet evening by the fire, I sewed, Lou knitted, Pooler tailored, and Gran banged her stick, and we had high tea with Daddy, and coffee later, and Lou went home around 9.30p.m to get the fish settled for the night!

Lou was making a geranium pink jumper. She said she hated the colour of it and what did I think? I said I hated it too, and she was cross! But Lou is neither the colouring nor the shape for that colour and neither am I and neither are you – in fact I don't know who IS!

February 6th 1956 Lou is thrilled to bits. She is finally going to have a baby, in September. She is very well, and not bothered with morning sickness so far, so she may get away with it. Such good news.

Monday March 29th I posted your letter this morning and when I got back Lou had arrived already to start making her navy nylon suit – I was adamant and refused to be drawn into the actual laying out and cutting – I was going to be there in a purely advisory capacity. She sighed several times and looked helpless, but I just said, "Pin it all on and then ask me BEFORE you cut." She managed quite well in the end. She stayed to lunch. We had planned to go to Wo Pang's, but she said she had had a bilious attack the day before, so I advised against it, thinking cold meat, potatoes in their jackets, carrots, and apple charlotte were better than Yah See Min and banana fritters which she had last time! After lunch she continued cutting out and putting in the markings, and then went off to the Bargain Shop for some interfacing. She went off home about 5p.m.

Monday June 4th 1956   It was a lovely hot day. Lou came and I gave her the choice of ham salad or curry, and she chose the curry! So we had curry, heat wave or no heat wave, and she took the remains home with her in two jars – one with curry and one with rice! She is very well, as indeed she ought to be. She was given a supply of vitamin pills from St. Thomas' Hospital, and told to go and see them again in the maternity department in three months. She had to go to another department last week and while there she told them she needed more vitamin pills. They said, "Surely you don't want any more?" She said, "I do, I've only got four left!" And she had eaten three months issue in under one month! She's BUSTIN' with vitamins. Lou told Gran she was having a baby and Gran said she wasn't at all surprised as "she was wearing a little loose jacket!" So Gran is not as simple as she makes out.

"Pooler has brought in a packet of the most
revolting herbal tea called Yerbama which does
EVERYTHING to you, she says!"

Pooler

Annie Pooler was widowed in the last months of the war, and for a while worked as an auxiliary in a mental hospital in the Midlands. Then she became a housekeeper, and for some months she had a post with Lewis Shirlaw, good friend of Margot and J.O. He was a partner in his family's solicitors firm, and had a pretty house in the country in Shropshire. She was an excellent cook and got on well with her employer, but found life very lonely there, with no car and hardly a bus service, and Lewis away all day at work. So she came to live at East Ham Vicarage, and took over all the cooking and food shopping and the care of the two huge kitchens, for full board and £3.10.0 a week.

Wednesday October 14th Yesterday Pooler decided to do something with all those grapes from the sun patch. There are masses this year. She thought grape jelly because of all the pips and because it would be nice to eat with mutton instead of redcurrant jelly. The result was nearly five pounds of the most heavenly jelly, perfect champagne colour and flavour. It's wicked to leave them to rot and the birds are at them already.

The cat Spitie was sitting on the washing basket, and Pooler was running the liquid off the spoon to see if it had thickened. This fascinated Spitie who sat on her hind legs in the basket and watched intently. Pooler called me to watch. I came. Spitie overbalanced and put a paw on the stove to save herself and YOWLED. I picked her up to put bi-carb on her paw and she was having none of it and turned and jabbed her left hook into the fleshy part of my shoulder, and I yowled too and dropped Spitie, and Pooler dropped the spoon, and in the general melee we lost half a pint of ambrosial jelly because it boiled over!

Pooler has also joined a Red Cross Class – New Phase – to find friends – interest – and gaiety. Last week she came home and said she wished she'd never joined, and this week she said she wished to hell she hadn't said she'd go, and she came away early, so I don't think it will last somehow!

Tuesday night Pooler has made a blue grosgrain hat from that pattern that goes with the velvet bag I made you, and has put two little feathers on the side front. Oh dear! She looks like a very thin streaky cat playing at Puss in Boots. And she has made it so beautifully. It looks smashing in the hand. It needs someone young and fluffy to wear it.

23rd November 1953 Pooler has brought in a packet of the most revolting herbal tea called Yerbama which does everything to you! It tones up your muscles, and frees your urine from deposits, and cures sleeplessness and gives you energy, and is a laxative, and cures obesity, and stimulates and has a good effect on the heart. The only thing it does not do is taste nice. But she says we must take a course of it to see, and had better begin by having it middle morning instead of coffee. Well, I'm up at Mary Sumner House tomorrow and Thursday on Mothers' Union business, so that lets me out for two mornings.

November 30th Old Gran has nearly sent us frog eared about your Christmas presents. She has bought you a fearful pink nightie. Pooler said, "Just don't send it," so we are not going to, but you have to write and thank her for it! She also wants to send you £2.00 and has got a sheaf of forms from the P.O. which poor Daddy is sorting out for her. Pooler said, "I never knew a woman balls up good money like it!" I was bound to agree with her.

December 7th Daddy had been up to Mowbrays bookshop to get some Baptism cards. He had come back on the train and had sat on the end of a row of four seats and opposite him sat a little well-meaning man, and at the far end of the row sat another man. Daddy put his gloves on the seat beside him and read his book. When the train stopped at Bow Road the man at the far end got out, and the doors shut, and quick as a flash, the little man opposite got up and picked up Daddy's gloves and hurled them out of the window onto the platform, yelling, "You've forgotten your gloves!" Whereupon Daddy looked up and said, "Now you've thrown my gloves out of the window, you stupid dolt!" The little man was most apologetic – but Daddy had to get out at the next station, and go back to Bow Road – but the gloves were in the stationmaster's office!

When Pooler came home from her day out tonight, I told her, and she said, "Oh! That's nothing. He was a free agent. I got in the train at Kensington High Street and there was a crowd inside and I only JUST got in, and then I found my coat was caught in the doors and the girl next to me said, "Where do you want to get out?" And I said, "Next station." And she said, "The doors don't open this side for the next three stations!" So poor Poo had to go on until she could get her tail free!

Saturday night Pooler inadvertently trod on Rupert's tail tonight while I was out and she said he didn't let out the usual – ow – ow – owow – ow noise, but turned round at her and let out what Pooler called a lot of "filthy swears". I wish I had been in.

Pooler and I have been having a fudge making session and have made some smashing concoctions, but alas, it just wrecks our waistlines. We made coffee fudge, and walnut vanilla fudge, and tomorrow we are going to have a go at white fudge with cherries and almonds, and the next day pink with almond flavouring, and then mix them all up and send a box to the Hothfield cousins and a box to Pooler's sister Lottie. Rupert adores the coffee sort and sits with his feet splayed in and his little teeth shewing and BARKS for it and then BARKS again.

January 11th Pooler spent her day off at home. She has a nasty cold and feels lousy. She attempted to clear out her chest of drawers and got the bed about three feet high in wool and materials and then felt so exhausted that she wanted to lie down and COULDN'T!

Wednesday night Darling, you will, I know, be as shaken as I was to hear that Father Roll's Brown Owl's Uncle has died! He came in looking most distrait and, when asked why, said he was looking for an undertaker as his Brown Owl's Uncle had died. Apart from this distressing occurrence there is nothing desperate to report. Pooler went off at 2p.m. for a perm and, MY GOD, I hope she never has another as long as she remains under my roof. She came home and behaved exactly like a naughty child. She tied her head up in a scarf for the rest of the evening and grizzled and GRIZZLED. It really looked very nice, and a damn sight better than it did all wisping about in her neck and droopy, but she thinks it's too short and too curly and she looks a sight and has gone on and on until I shouted at her and said, "For God's sake. Pooler, behave like an adult. I had no idea you were so vain. You must have thought of yourself like a modern Helen of Troy. "She shut up after that! Poor Pooler!

April 11th 1954 Pooler went to Croydon for the day with her sister in law. She is very moody and discontented, and I should think the sister in law had a treat!

In the evening I settled down to read for a few minutes before the fire before I went to bed. Daddy was out. Pooler was drooping in the chair opposite, when she suddenly said she felt so wretched she felt she must leave and go somewhere where she could just REST! (I have not breathed a word of this to Daddy, so have a care), so I am afraid I did not mince matters. I told her roundly that if she would only pull herself together she was as fit as the next; that she didn't know what hard work meant; that she was utterly selfish and she would always be lonely (one of her piteous cries) if she did not forget herself in service to others; and that I reckoned I had been about as kind to her as anybody she had ever come across and she had better start in on looking after me for a change! She is quite hopeless and I expect she will go, but I'm not thinking about it any more at the moment, and as long as Daddy doesn't get wind of it I can bear it! But once he starts bellyaching over it, I shall commit suicide – murder – or something drastic. Spitie had two kittens while this was going on!

Wednesday General scuttle round to tidy up for the Bishop of Chelmsford who comes to supper tonight after the Ruri-Decanal Conference Service in St Bartholomew's. I buy red tulips for the dining room table, and yellow and white iris for the big bowl in the sitting room. The coal man comes, of course, this afternoon and also Pooler takes the opportunity to tell me that she thinks she must really leave and go nearer home! I answer her very kindly though it was only by the grace of God that I didn't knock her front teeth in or kick her in the stomach. But I felt it would be more of a blow to her to seem not to mind!

Sunday morn Woke late at 7.15 and woke Daddy who had also overslept. Give up all hope of early church and go to 9a.m. Over a solitary breakfast of haddock and poached egg I see an advertisement for a German woman cook general in my

148

newly acquired copy of The Lady. I read this out to Pooler who bursts into tears and says she doesn't want to go! I tell her I won't write to the woman till tomorrow!

Sunday May 1st Whew! What a non-stopper! Up and dash around and get to 8.a.m. at St Bart's, home for breakfast. Raining all day on and off. Chilly. Pooler was packing like mad, first she meant to catch the 11.10a.m., then the 2.10p.m., then finally left to catch the 4.10p.m. I tidied round, changed the sheets, got the coffee, cooked the dinner. I said if I got anyone very suitable I would let her know, but I wasn't going to really get cracking till the end of July – I expected her to let me know one way or the other what she was going to do then – and so we parted on good terms – but she is a fool, for she will never find a better billet than this.

The next six months turned out to be a nightmare for Margot. A Russian lady, Mrs A., came to take over Mrs Pooler's duties, but proved both lazy and unable to cook! And a MUCH worse hypochondriac than Poo! Details of coping with Mrs A. are to be found in Section Thirteen.

The Christmas festivities were back breaking for Margot that year. Winter was always a hard time, with the constant journeys down into the cellar carrying buckets of coal and coke. And besides having to cope with the housework, she was expected, not only to attend many of the parish functions, parish socials, carol services, civic parties, looking smart and cheerful, but also to provide food for them as well. Christmas

meant extra people dropping in for a drink, of coffee or sherry,
and all the extra provisions for the festive period had to lugged
home with countless extra journeys up and down the crowded
High Street. And this year she had to all the cooking and the
washing up, the one household task she liked least. So it was
with great relief that she wrote to Lisa on January 9th:-

Sunday 9th January Cold, and inclined to be foggy.

Sweet darling Lisa, I am writing this in comparative ease
on a Sunday morning. POOLER IS COOKING THE
DINNER! Yes, she came back on Friday night for a spell, I
don't know how long for, I don't ask and I am not interested!
But as long as she is here I shall be grateful and when she goes
– even if it is next week – I shall try not to care one jot, or whit,
or tittle! But as is always the case when the works run down a
bit after doing overtime, the old body tends to feel a darn sight
more tired than it did when still on the go and I tend to fall
asleep all over the place and wake feeling 'like death!'
However it's gorgeous to let go for a bit. She came back last
Friday; she looked very well and I think she was just fed up
with the set up at Brownhills. But it was nice to see her and she
is just the same! And I think she is very glad to have someone
to talk to for she never stops at the moment. I hope it will wear
off in time! It is a joy to have someone competent again, you
have no idea how grand it is. We made a night of it and had
gins and Dubonnets and Daddy came home early and joined us
and all was light and joy and peace.

February 12th Sunday morning Cold, cold. Snow, but with a bit of sun to enliven the scene. I hate it. It makes my hand ache and I can't face slimming in this weather. I am sitting on a stool on top of the dining room fire writing to you. If I was any closer I'd be on it. Daddy at Matins; Gran not up yet, and Pooler crying her eyes out with self-pity in the back kitchen. She says she is cold and she doesn't feel well and no one in the world cares two pence for her! And when I told her to take a hot water bottle and go back to bed, she said, "Don't be beastly!" I said, "Hell to that for a tale. I'm cold too and my hand aches like an exposed tooth, and I got up hours before you, and went to church, and I have been up hours before you all winter – and I'm not being beastly, and I prefer you to go to bed to getting hysterical with self pity over the sink." So she has shut up! And so far she has not gone to bed! I regret, but she is spineless!

March 9th Pooler seems much more cheerful. She has just gone out wearing her new suit, which she has made beautifully and it looks VERY VERY nice. I am green with envy over her figure – she really is a nice shape now and I am like a cottage loaf. Boo Hoo. Perhaps this has something to do with Poo's joie de vivre!

Thursday I go off to the Soft Furnishing class in the evening, and when I come home naughty Pooler provides me with sausages and fried apples and a coconut pyramid and I scoff the lot!!

April 2nd Pooler's well-being has run out with a vengeance. She is as miserable as hell. Her chest is bad, her throat is bad, her head is funny, she is depressed, her heart palpitates, and she is too tired to live and doesn't want to but I notice she has bought new material to make up for dresses for her holiday to Italy in June. If I felt as bad as that I should knit myself a shroud in dishcloth cotton, nice and quick on big needles.

Monday May 7th Pooler hasn't gone away yet. She's gone to bed with the flu! She went round to the doctors, ostensibly to get enough medicine to go home with and she came back and said he told her to go to bed as she had flu! So she went, and I rang up my old friend Chrissie and cancelled our lunch date for the third time! We don't seem to have much luck with our dates, Chrissie and me!

Tuesday I get up about 8a.m.and find Poo down in the kitchen reading the paper over a cup of tea! I get the breakfast and take some up to her! I buy fish and spinach and get the lunch. Take some up to Pooler who eats the lot.

Wednesday I did the chores and went shopping and cooked pork loaf slices in toad in the hole fashion and we all ate it with salad. Pooler was down for all meals in her nightgown. I wish she would either get up and go home or stay in bed!

Thursday Pooler staggered down around 11.30 but

hasn't done a hands turn, and has been lying down since 3p.m. She is supposed to be going home tomorrow but I doubt it. They won't look after her there like I do, and she knows it! They've got more sense. On the other hand she has still got two and a half dresses to make before her Italian holiday and she hasn't got the face to sit downstairs machining solidly while I do all the work!

Pooler learnt this morning that she will only have her overnight case for the first FOUR days in Italy, not her main case! I must say, I think that the tour company could be a little more efficient. Am strongly reminded of the time Mary Eaves read that there was to be clothes rationing! Pooler is considering losing the £50.00 and NOT GOING! SODS! BITCHES! COWS! And MEAN THINGS!

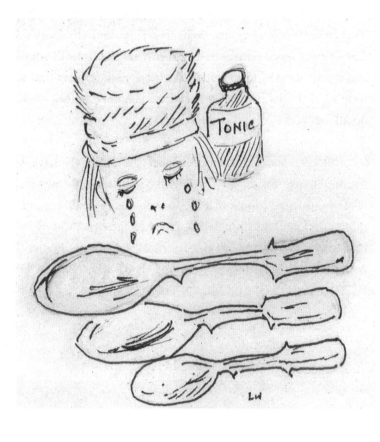

"When I told her to use a heaped
tablespoon of flour she said, 'Which size?
Zey are ALL tablespoons!'"

St. Mary Magdalene, Norman Church,
East Ham in the 1950's.

St. Bartholomews,
East Ham in the 1950's.

Doris Greig, Margot's best friend, 1955.

Lisa and the 21st birthday
charm bracelet, 1954.

Lisa, Westhampton Beach,
Long Island, USA, 1955.

Robin and Kath Wiltshier.
'The Hothfield Folk', circa 1950.

Father Witcutt, Margot, Father Roll,
Mrs. Gilson. 'The Staff', 1956.

J.O. Nicholls, East Ham, 1950.

R.J. Griffiths, "Johnnie".
Walsall, 1940's.

Lou and Charlie Coles wedding day, 1953.

Mrs. Pooler, Mr. Parrish and Margot.
East Ham, 1956.

J.O. and Margot, 'On the Spree', 1954.

Lewis Shirlaw. Wednesbury, 1950.

Mary P, Old Gran, Johnnie G and
Margot, 1954.

East Ham Vicarage, Front Door.

East Ham Vicarage, East Side.

Margot and Rupert, 1956.

Coping with Mrs A.

There were very few ways of earning a living for working class women in the early years of the twentieth century. There was farm labouring, laundry work, factory work in the new industrial areas, but the most common of all was domestic work. Keeping the house and family clean, fed and clothed was hard and unremitting work, and a house servant was by no means confined to the houses of the gentry or the prosperous professions or trades people. In those places the work would be parcelled out between a small army of servants under the control of the housekeeper and the butler; kitchen servants, cooks, parlour maids, chambermaids, nurse maids, dairy maids and so on. But by far the most common were the maids of all work, who came to help out in the small houses alongside the housewife. Together they worked on the scrubbing, washing, polishing, cooking, in the days before electric irons, washing machines or vacuum cleaners.

All through Margot's childhood in Whitstable the maid had been Alice Tilley, one of the seven daughters of a fisherman living in Island Row, Whitstable. Often the bond between maid and housewife was strong and friendly, and though the wages were small, the contract between fair employer and trusted maid went on for decades, only broken by ill health or the maid's marriage. Often, if the family moved, the maid went too.

When Margot and J.O. married in 1925, they lived on a curate's income of £190.00 a year in two small rooms in

Wednesbury and she had to do her own housework. But when they moved into the Vicarage at St. Paul's Wednesbury, on twice the amount, Hetty arrived to do the rough cleaning, and Hetty's niece, Evelyn, came, aged fourteen, to be the live-in maid and help look after Lisa. Evelyn, or "Eba" moved to Pitsea Rectory with them in 1939 and stayed until she was called up into the W.R.N.S. – the Women's Royal Navy.

She was replaced by Mrs Charvil, a small tough, rough woman with a gentle simple minded giant of a son called John; he worked in the great Rectory garden. He had perfect manners. Mrs Charvill saw to that. They ate their midday meal with us, but she refused to let him eat at the same time as us – "Tain't fittin'". So his enormous helping had to be kept for him over a saucepan on the stove.

Two women came to clean for us at St Elisabeth's Becontree. The first was Hallie, a mournful woman with chronic ill health caused by a poverty stricken upbringing, and then, when she had to give up work, a cheerful smiley little person called Clarkie, who loved polishing the "pretty furniture" and scolded the air raids and the anti aircraft guns as if they were noisy children. Her daughter Joan and Lisa were good friends and often stayed the night with each other to give each other's parents a night out.

At East Ham they found first a lazy woman left over from the last Vicar's employ, and then a woman who was very pleasant until she became drunk more evenings than not. And then, when Old Gran came to live with them, Mrs Pooler arrived to take over the cooking, wise old Mrs Jeffery arrived

156

to help with the twenty-three rooms and Mr Parrish came to cut the grass and trim the hedges. With Margot they were a good team. The only fly in the ointment was Pooler's hypochondria.

July 28th 1954   At the end of July I had a letter from Pooler which made me hopping mad. She had said she would come back to me, but she could not come until 25th August as her mother had been ill gain, but she would come on the 25th. BUT – she had arranged to take a holiday in Teignmouth in September, so would go again, "Perhaps for one week, perhaps for two!" I felt it was a gross imposition and at I really could not be kicked around for another person's convenience like that, especially as I was paying HER to help ME! I exploded. And Daddy said surprisingly, "Well, there is that Russian woman Mary Eaves has mentioned, she would be only too pleased to come!" I rang up Mary Eaves and asked her what she thought. She said she would get hold of her that evening and ask her, and that she was working in a factory in Birmingham, and hated it, and was living with a sister in law who wanted her out of the way. She was fifty or so.

I didn't say anything about it to Gran, or to Lou when she came for supper. I held my hand. In the evening Mary Eaves rang back to say that Mrs A. was thrilled and would like to speak to me, whereupon a very deep voice and VERY broken English said, "Mrs Nicholls, I will be very subservient and obedient and to please you only will I try!" This sounded all right on the face of it! So they arranged to bring her down to

East Ham for the day on Sunday.

I decided I must write to Pooler straightaway, as even if Mrs A. did not come I should find it hard to forget Pooler's treatment. So I wrote her a very NICE letter, but I told her I felt that I must have someone I could rely on as I was VERY tired and could not face the winter wondering if she was going home every few months to her mother! I am sorry about it, but she does not give me a thought, and although she is a good sort and I find her a congenial companion, I am afraid that's not enough. I went to bed but was too churned up to sleep much.

Thursday After lunch I cut out and made up new curtains for Pooler's room or whoever will inhabit it. And I HUNG THEM UP. I had about six yards over so decided I would have a go at re-covering the armchair in that room and I spent the rest of the evening on it.

Saturday I shopped all morning and made a bed cover of some yellow stuff and also a cushion cover for the chair in yellow. And finished these by teatime. Then I turned my attention to the Sunday lunch, and I baked a damn great chicken and a damn great piece of bacon and a quart honeycomb mould and laid the breakfast in the kitchen and the table in the dining room and cleaned some silver and finally washed some stockings as it struck midnight. To bed – "healthily tired!"

Sunday The Eaves and Mrs A. turned up about 11.30.

Mary had on one of the prettiest dresses I have ever seen her in. Dark gray cotton, very fine like silk, with spiky mauve flowers and black flowers, a very pretty shape. Mrs A. was a very tall large woman with a sallow complexion. Very Russian – in that she is all tragedy one moment and gaiety the next. Mostly tragedy, I think. I should think she will be very willing. Whether she can do any housework I am more doubtful. Anyway she has had so much kicking about that it would be sheer cruelty to turn her away without letting her try. She wants to come desperately badly.

She speaks French as well as Russian and I am determined to avail myself of the former, at any rate. She wandered about the place like a mournful mule, saying to herself, "Nooo – it cannot be. It is Tooooo goooood forr mee" – She has her lighter moments though, and when I informed her that there were five more rooms in Mrs Gilson's bit of the house she said "BLIMEEE!" That came straight from the Birmingham factory I felt, as did "Bad Bugger" an epithet that she attached to her sister in law, and that, Kenneth Eaves said, is more than justified. I gave then a smashing lunch. She can come on Wednesday 25th August, so we await developments.

They went at 3p.m. and it took until 5p.m. to clear away and wash up and then I lay on the sofa for half an hour to get my second wind.

Monday I had a VERY nice letter from Pooler saying how sorry she was to have been so selfish and she felt that her mother would in all probability need her more often from now on. I am sorry about Poo. If only she could forget about herself a bit she would be so much happier. Heigh ho. Have a feeling this one will be all the things Pooler wasn't but as irritating as hell!

Wednesday August 25th Daddy fetched Mrs A. from Euston and we sat on the sun patch and had tea, and then I cooked curry and we had high tea at 6.30p.m.

She unpacked as much as she could as her boxes have not yet arrived. She is very overwhelmed with kindness; has had very little of it. Very Dostoevsky. She is most willing and, I hope, will become competent in time.

Thursday 26.th Our 29th wedding anniversary. A cup of tea brought up to me at 7.30a.m. Goody, goody. Your letter on the mat, wonderful. A lovely morning. Daddy went off to the cricket and I shepherded Mrs A. Both Rupert and Tiggy have new names. She calls Rupert "Pouchok" the Russian for "Powderpuff". And Tiggy rejoices in the name of "Morrrcha" which means "Mary!" Poor Tig! – no balls – but does not relish a change of sex – perhaps he thinks it is the name of a brave Cossack! I am not going to attempt to spell her own Christian name. She says it is Nadine – as then people call her SOMETHING!

Sunday 29th Up 7.15a.m. Mrs A has a bad pain – oh lor'! – in her back and has obviously been crying. I think it's some kidney trouble. I comfort her and go to church at 8a.m. I supervised the cooking of the joint and taught her how to make a baked custard. So far, so good.

After Evensong Mrs A. was still in pain, so I said I would take her to the Doctor in the morning.

Monday I took Mrs A. to see the lady Doctor. She said she thought it was kidney trouble and gave her some medicine and told her to go back on Thursday and that she need not go to bed.

Nadia Mihailovna nearly pulverised me. She was admiring my silk suit and she said, "You buy it at Marshalls?" I said, "No, I made it myself." Whereupon she devoutly crossed herself and said, "Kyrie Eleison" in tones of complete amazement.

Sunday Sept 5th Mrs A. cooked the lunch until it came to the gravy, when she went all to pieces, so I took over! It is difficult, though, when you've been used to litres and kilograms, to be told half pints and tablespoons. When I told her to use a heaped tablespoon of flour she said, "Wheech size? Zey are ALL tablespoons?" We then went through- salt spoon, teaspoon, dessertspoon and TABLEspoon – by which time the gravy had assumed the proportions of the White Sea and she felt she could not control it! She learns so slowly, though she is certainly most obedient. But it is rather like saying, "Will you put the gas on for the kettle?" And then after a while, when a strong smell of gas permeates the entire building, you remember you did not also say, "And put a match to it."

Sept 8th My Lisa's 21st birthday and NO LISA! Never mind, see you soon. In June. It was Nadia A.'s day out, and after breakfast she and Gran went off up to London together. Granny was thrilled to bits to find someone fool enough to go with her and Mrs A. was thrilled to find someone who knew the way! I breathed a sigh of relief to see them go! They came waltzing back at 5p.m. waving their purchases with triumph. Mrs A. had bought an exotic sponge from Maison Lyons in Piccadilly and two aubergines! She was deliriously happy over these, not having seen any anywhere in Berrrrmingham. Granny screamed with laughter every time she looked at them.

Then we had to see Granny's purchases. Another cake box all tied up with string. I offered to help cut it, but NO! Alas! She tipped the whole she-bang face downwards onto the coconut matting. Four cherry tartlets, all cream jelly and fragile pastry. Well! Gran shouted and groaned and Mrs A. dashed for a TABLEspoon and scooped them up, and indeed, retrieved far more than was there originally. Unfortunately, both Rupert and Tiggy have been moulting recently. What with Granny's anxious moans and Mrs A.'s Russian wailings alternated with Greek foul language, we had quite a colourful interlude. I wouldn't have missed it for worlds.

We had a slap-up meal in your honour and then we had coffee and Gran rose to her feet and with a full cup began solemnly to propose a toast to your health and fortunes and poured the coffee all over the table and pretty well scalded her chest. But we all had to stand up and then mop up later!

Tuesday 15th Mrs A.'s day off again, so she and Granny set off again together by bus and reappeared about 5.45p.m. They had had a whale of a time and both were "exhaust". They meant to go to Oxford Street and then go to Hyde Park but they got on the wrong bus and then had to change at Aldgate. Gran had a good row with the conductor. They then went into the Aldgate Lyons teashop for a reviver. Then they got on a train for Tower Hill. Mark you – steps DOWN to trains, steps UP at Tower Hill. Then they got on a boat for Westminster – steps DOWN to boat, steps UP to Westminster Pier – Granny now 80 and very lame. They then had more revivers at Westminster Lyons and went off round Westminster Abbey! GOOD look round the Abbey!! And then two busses home.

Thursday I went shopping after breakfast and Nadia Milailovna was dead stupid all morning. So stupid you would not believe it possible. I nearly screamed. I don't know if she was not feeling well or if I was not speaking loudly enough or what, but no matter what I told her to do she either did the opposite or asked if she should do something quite different. And Daddy needed lunch at 12 sharp. So I cooked sausages and apple crumble top and tried to cope with it all and her too. And Johnnie G. is here and he began to paint the kitchen mantelshelf which meant he wanted everything off the shelf, and all the chairs away from that side of the room. I'm very obliged to him but I wish he would do it after midnight!

I ended up snapping at all of them. After lunch I left

N.M. to wash up on her own – she has to do SOMETHING to earn her £3 a week. I washed and changed and carted Johnnie off to the pictures to see The Robe. It wasn't half bad – by which I mean that half of it was VERY bad. But as a portrait of Christian loyalty it was excellently put forth! Both the hero and Jean Simmons died for the Faith and that should be enough to make converts for a start!

Sunday 3rd Oct I've got a fearful cold off Gran who sneezes and drips over everybody. I woke all bunged up and headachy. Did not go to church and dressed and came down about 8.15 to find N.M. preparing breakfast. I said, "Have you taken Mrs Nicholls' breakfast up to her room?" "Nooo," she said. "Well," I said, "It's Sunday, isn't it? And for the past three Sundays she has had her breakfast taken up by 8a.m. in time for her to get to church at 11a.m. and each time I have explained to you why – haven't I?" and she said, "Yes. But you said nothing about it today!" And then I blew up and told her that for the same money, Mrs Pooler did ALL the cooking and ALL the shopping and ALL the catering, and kept both kitchens tidy and clean and that I had nothing of that to do at all. Whereupon I had tears in the eyes and sullen all day long. Well, I'll give her another month – but I think she is quite hopeless, for, unless you tell her just what to do all day long she stands and does nothing, not because she is not willing, but because she is too damn stupid to know what to do next. I COULD SPIT BLOOD!

Anyway, I have made up my mind I am not going to

164

carry another lunatic on my back. I had so hoped I had got someone at last to share the burden but we have just got another dead weight to carry as well as the rest. I expect by the time you have got this my cold will be better and I shall not be in such a selfish frame of mind, so don't take too much for granted.

Tuesday Mrs A.'s day off again. She was to go to meet some Russian friends in Kensington, but after breakfast she got all temperamental and said she could not go as she could not find the way. Would we send them a telegram? I told her that as she had somehow managed to find her way from Russia to England via Cyprus, Egypt and Yugoslavia, I thought she could get from East Ham to Kensington on the District Line! Daddy also shewed no pity. So she went. We were in no mood for fools.

Thursday In the evening I went to the Soft Furnishing class and certainly learned a lot. We had a demonstration of cutting a cover which luckily was not finished, so we have another week's grace before we have to wield the scissors alone in our own homes. Terrifying thought. By the time I got back N.M. and Gran had both gone to bed to avoid me. Nobody loves Momma. N.M. looks at me as if I was going to blast her out of existence any moment and Gran gives me a clear berth if she gets the chance. I am getting very irritable, but serve them right. Miserable Ditherers.

Sunday Up early and went to church at 8a.m. A lot there. The Clergy Wives Tea Party is looming up so I spent the morning making sponge cakes for it. N.M. cooked the dinner alone and made a batch of ginger nuts so she is coming on.

Monday Help!   A whole sheaf of acceptances for the Clergy Wives Tea Party on Wednesday. Twenty one so far. Each one I get brings me out into a sweat. However, I decided I must get 'em into one room for their teas. I pulled the table nearer to the door end of the dining room and put all the armchairs the window end, and got 14 places round the table and grouped the armchairs round the trolley, so got another seven nicely stowed away there. Then went to bed.

Tuesday I rose early. N.M. went off to the Doctor's first thing. She had been pretty stupid, but I determined to bear with her a while longer – and when she came back from the doctor she had a note to go to the London Hospital and had to make an appointment with the physician there. She told me this as I arrived in with the flowers from Matthews for the house (Leaves and gladioli, orange and lemon yellow.) Daddy said he would like some coffee, so I said gaily, "Oh, J.O., you will help Mrs A. find the number of the hospital, won't you?" and off they went together. Then I heard such a commotion going on in the hall – but I curbed my wicked curiosity and got the coffee. Presently I heard her say,"I CANnot, I CANnot" and then heard him say, "Fiddle di dee!" so I quietly shut the door and got the cups out! Then she came in very red in the face and said, "He has been OARRFUL to me." I said, "Oh! Dear! I AM sorry. Did you make the appointment? " "Yes," said she. "Thursday, 11.30, but I DIE with shame, he bin so OARRFUL to me." I forbore to ask for details and poured out coffee! Soon after she retreated to her room and then went out to find the Victoria and Albert Museum to see the Russian jewels in the Queen Mary Collection, and she did not return till the evening.

In the afternoon I went to the M.U. Annual Meeting and presented my report and then I got out all the china for this ruddy Tea Party and laid the table and the trolley and got Gran's supper. Then Mrs A. began:

She was no good. "You, Madame, need someone capable. You are Veecteem. You keep me from peety only, etc, etc." I had it off my chest there and then and said I was certainly not going to keep anyone out of pity, I had neither the time nor the strength, but I thought that if only she would pull her socks up and learn to be more self reliant it would be better for both of us. I also said, "If you learn what I teach you and if you are not happy here, you will have a better opportunity to get another post in the spring, but at the moment it would be wiser for you to stay here and put up with me!" This sunk in after a bit and she said she would try. But I did not let her make any cakes for the party!! She has really tried since and I think I may make a go of it yet, but if I do I reckon I ought to be the matron of a home for mentally deficients. By 10p.m we finished this conversation and she went to bed and I began to make another cherry cake and to ice and fill four sponges! I got to bed at 1.a.m.

Saturday I buy liver for dinner and teach Mrs A. how to cook it. This she does very well and I am distinctly elated by result! She has to go to the London Hospital again on Thursday to find out the result of the x-rays. She made me laugh when she came back last week. She said, "They laid me NAKED on table under great apparatus and she turrn a scrrew and the whole thing fall PLUMP on my Barre stomach – HEAVY it was! I say to herr – BLIMEE!! NOT to keel me before to know what I suffer from!" She can be very funny at times. Tonight Daddy was talking about Father Witcutt and the way he stands in the vestry after weddings and never says a word to the wedding party, and, says Daddy, he never seems embarrassed or annoyed, he just STANDS there. "Maybe," said Nadia Mihailovna, "He does not weesh to disturrrb heemself!"

October 17th 1954 Workmen arrive at 8a.m and begin to take up the floorboards in the kitchen under the cupboard because there has been a woodworm at work! We had an early lunch and I went shopping and fell for some perfectly fascinating Italian pottery in WOOLWORTHS! Most seductive, thick white rough pottery with cabbage roses. I went berserk and bought about £2.00 worth – so whenever you get married you will at least have a fruit set!

Then I came home and wrote some Mothers Union letters and a long one to Pooler. Mrs A. came into the dining room where I was writing at about 5.45p.m. and said she was going to bed with a bad back. I am afraid I hardened my heart and said that was alright as long as she came down about 8p.m.

and got Gran's hot water bottle an got her some coffee. This didn't go down very well, but it sunk in. Then I made scrambled eggs for all and then went to the Parish Council Meeting, and when I got back they were both legging it upstairs to bed. WHOOPEE!

Tuesday It was Mrs. A.'s day off so her back was much better. I attacked the kitchen floor after the workmen had gone. I got it looking smashing and then I got the bit between my teeth, and I washed all the dresser shelves and all the china on it, and cleaned the copper, brass and pewter and the place looked a picture. I sent Gran out to lunch, which she likes; she goes up to the cafeteria at the British Home Stores and they are nice to her and carry her tray and give her extra cups of tea. Mrs A. spent most of the day in her room and had gone to the Co-op for lunch. Mrs Jeff came to do the silver and had a good talk to her. I made some tea for us all and then left them to it, with Mrs Jeff rubbing away and apparently she told Mrs A. that she thought she was very well paid for doing very little, and didn't know when she was well off. But you can't put more than a half pint into a half pint pot, and Mrs A. thinks I am very fussy and particular, and why not put all the silver and brass away and have linoleum! Mrs Jeffreys told her why, which saved me!

Friday Early breakfast and a hot sticky morning. Mrs A. had to go to the London Hospital for treatment and I had a great pile of buns to make for the parish Sustentation Social this evening. I had promised to go and help cut up the sandwiches, and was just setting out when Mrs A. came back, and cried, and carried on, and said she felt Soo Eel and Soo Oarful, and what was to become of her? So I comforted her and left her with a pot of tea, and dashed round to the Church Hall. At 5.30p.m I came back and had another session with Mrs. A. and finally rang up Dr. Hewson and told her I was sending Mrs. A., and to give her a damn good tonic with some prussic aid in it! This she did – the tonic, not the acid! I iced all the buns and washed and changed while the icing set, and then Mrs A. came back. She has some trouble with her spine, not a slipped disc, but something, and has to go to the hospital twice a week for treatment, and MUST NOT SCRUB! Well! I'd sooner scrub myself, anyway, as she is as much good as a pig with a broom.

Saturday October 21   I got up so late that I was disgruntled. We had lunch early because Nadia Vladivostock wanted to have her Russian friend to tea. I decided that I was not going to be in on this one, so I said I was going to Ilford to do some shopping. This was a lie as I have to be there on Monday. But she said the friend would be coming around four, so I decided I would get back about five. I sneaked off to the Gaumont Cinema and saw the most fascinating minx called Audrey Hepburn in a sentimental Cinderella story called Sabrina Fair. It was pure escapism and I loved it.

I came home about 5.30p.m and found Mrs A. with a face like doom and she said, "She has not COME!" I said it

170

was a big pity and proceeded to get myself a cup of tea. No preparations for tea for the said guest seemed to be in evidence at all. No trolley. No bread and butter. No cake. Sure enough, the friend arrives soon after, and was placed alone in the dining room by N.M. who came into the kitchen to get the tea. It ended up with me cutting some Polish bread thick with caraway seeds onto which she dabbed some ham she had bought. I met the friend before she went, a young, small, white-faced plump woman with black hair and the most lovely black eyes. She spoke fluent English with a slight foreign accent accompanied by Cockney vowels. The effect was fascinating, but I did not stay longer than to shake hands and smile.

October 24th 1954 It is really chilly, so I decided we must call it a day and light the boiler for the first time this autumn. We have been very lucky as it had been alight for over a month last year.

To look at Nadia Mihailovna's face you would think I was touching off the atom bomb. She threw her apron over her head and gave little gasps of incredulity when I lit the gas poker and pushed it inside the boiler – and the fact that, once alight, we have got to keep it alight by FEEDING it, with coke from the CELLAR, and raking it out, simply AMAZED her. She nearly passed out with amazement. I had to restrain myself from relighting the gas poker and shewing her where else I could put it.

Monday A bright breezy morning with bright sparkly

sun. All my love, chicken. I get so bored and stale without you; it's not because there is nothing doing, it's because they are all so dumb and so DULL! Mary Eaves comes to stay next weekend and is being fetched by Kenneth and Lindon John on Monday, so that means a huge meat bill. Gosh! How that man can eat meat! And Johnnie G. arrives on Monday too, so I needn't bother about airing his bed – Mary can air it for him!

Tuesday I scrubbed the front kitchen floor and was just about to carry on the good work with the back kitchen when the phone rang and it was Doris. She was up in London and said could I come for lunch? I said, no, but she could come for tea, and she said yes she would, so I abandoned the scrubbing and did the flowers in the sitting room and lit the fire, and made some scones and a filling for a sponge and changed. Gran obligingly went out for lunch, which was helpful. Doris turned up at 4p.m and looked wonderful in a black costume, white blouse and the most fascinating expensive little turban hat in a dull grey green with little sequinny feathers or leaves. She looked absolutely super. She talked and talked and said she had had a charming letter from you, and said she would give you a 21st birthday present next summer. So keep her up to it!

Saturday October 31st At the moment Mary Eaves is here for the weekend and has hindered me all day by talking to me! I had to tell Mrs. A. off this morning because she hadn't cleaned the silver properly, and she flew into a temper and said I was impossible to work for – I was so particular. I said it was the first time any employee of mine had complained of that; and then she said that I scolded her terribly and NEVER had she been so scolded; I replied that if she never had anything worse to bear than my scoldings, which were at the most an irritable outburst of about ten minutes duration, she must have led a very sheltered life, and I had not much sympathy with that. Oh, dear, oh dear, she commit SUICIDE, she DIE, she very very EEL, she not stand it, she go to BED etc, etc, whereupon she went upstairs into Mary's room – Mary lying in bed like a true lady at 10a.m – and gave Mary a bellyful which did me the power of good! Poor Mary! She didn't know what it was all about, and looked as if she had been hit by a hurricane when I went in to see her about half an hour later! Mrs A. had said she could not stay with me another MEENIT, I was OARRFUL, etc. Anyway she went to bed with a bad temper all afternoon, but told Mary she would stay "a bit longer" before supper. She won't be any good. She is a complete incompetent, but she is kind to Rupert, and she can see Gran doesn't fall in the fire, and that's all I can hope for this winter. It means I can never go away at all, but I can go out for a few hours at a time, so I have much to be grateful for. Without her I should have to pack in all hope of my sewing classes. Daddy took Mary out to supper and I went to bed early.

Sunday I got up early and coped with the fires and the mop-dusting and got to church at 8a.m with Mary. Mrs A. vouchsafed me a grunt in reply to my Sabbatical greeting. I made a sponge and some biscuits and then tried to write to you but Mary ruled that out by talking so I attempted to do a bit to your blouse, and got that wrong, and unpicked that, by which time it was 4p.m and raining hard, and I went over to church to clerk seven baptisms. Home for dinner which was fairly successful, and then I said firmly that I was going to write to you, and went into the kitchen and write I did! Mary and Mrs. A. sat in state in the sitting room and talked about what a swine I was, which cheered up Mrs A. and made a little change for Mary from saying what a swine Mrs. A. was!

Monday Well! I never want to live through another morning like that! There were eight persons for lunch – Gran – Daddy – Mary - Mrs A. – me – Ken – Lindon – and Johnnie G. She had no idea what to give them and I had to do everything in the way of coherent thought myself. I even had to say what saucepans were to be used for which vegetables – she was too dumb to realise that we needed a great many more vegetables and potatoes than usual and so on and so on. I broke my large Denby ware casserole in my agitation, in stopping her from putting the dish for the COLD meat into the HOT oven, while the dish for the HOT stew sat stone cold on the scullery table. You simply could not credit it. I disgraced myself saying to Mary, "Oh, for God's sake shut up about her!" as she went on and on about her like a broken down record. However, she is a dear, and bore me no ill will.

Anyway, we had a decent lunch in the dining room. We had stewed steak and carrots and potatoes, and cold mutton, and treacle tart and fruit jelly, and cheese and biscuits and cups of tea to follow. The Eaves went off around 3.30p.m and I helped La Morgue to wash up and put away, and by 4.30p.m I lay flat out in an armchair in the sitting room and stayed there for an hour.

P.S. Gran thinks the Democrats are on the same side as Mr. Churchill, and the Left Wing isn't as bad as it used to be! Attaboy!

Saturday I got up early and scrubbed the back kitchen floor. This took me exactly one hour, but before this I came down and found Mrs. A. in front of the boiler with a face as white as a sheet and perspiration all over her forehead. "Whatever is the matter?" "OUT!" says she, in tones of deep sepulchral despair. "Rright out!" So I say cheerfully, "Never mind! Take it all out and light it again." "But I have," says she, "And it OUT AGAIN! Nearly box of metches hev I done in." So I say nonchalantly, "Oh dear, is the gas cut off then?" "GAZZ!" says she. "It izz firrre not gazz," "But", said I, "you only need one match to light the gas poker and the poker lights the fire for you. We always use it – you have watched me light it now three times, haven't you?" "Oh! Ze pokerr! I had forgot ze pokerr!" Considering she had to move the poker before she could get to the coke shute, you would think it was difficult to forget it – but she isn't very bright! It's a wonder I am still sane – or am I?

Gran excelled herself today by asking her if they had great excitement at the Armistice of the First World War! As the Revolution was raging in Russia and she had lost three brothers in it, the answer was not what Gran expected – but still – determined to keep her end up, Gran went on to say, "Oh well ! Our Dean is helping to put all that right." I had to explain, somewhat tersely, that unfortunately the Dean was on the side of the people who murdered her brothers! Whereupon Gran said that she couldn't pretend to understand it, but in St. Alphege Church Whitstable, she knew they would have had every seat filled and all up in the gallery as well, and then probably have had a debate on whether the gallery was safe afterwards. I simply can't keep up with it as a lunchtime conversation, and I do try!

I got up and scrubbed the kitchen floor, went shopping and cooked some more spam fritters for lunch. Mrs. A. went out in the afternoon to the Diaghilev exhibition with her friend. I had great difficulty making Gran understand that he was not a ballet dancer. Also, today we had been speaking of Communism and the Churches, and Gran had woken up to the fact that there was something connected to the subject which was "Not Right Up!" So she turned to Mrs. A. and said, very solemnly, "Doesn't your Russian Church believe in God, then?" I thought Mrs. A. would spit in her face! She turned to me and said, "Really, she is imbecile, she can't understand nothink at all." And turning to Gran she yelled, "God! Yes – we believe – Naturrally – why not – I ARRSK YOU ! TTTTTCHAH!" I get some quiet enjoyment out of them when I am strong enough and sane enough to stand them!

Rollie has invited me to one of the fundraising Balls he

likes to go to at Christmas at the Savoy. I must look out one of my creations from my extensive wardrobe! I'm looking forward to a really civilised evening for once. It's so good of him to include me.

Monday November 23rd The whole day was taken up with the washing and the shopping, and in the evening there was a very dull Parish Council meeting. A little boil on the inside of my thigh began to be painful, so I gave it a hot fomentation.

Wednesday It was a lovely day and I dressed in my heavy tweed suit and mustard blouse and set off for the Mothers Union Central Council at Wesminster, but my boil was so painful I came away early. I was beginning to limp. When I got home I had to prepare tomorrow's lunch as Mrs A. was going to the hospital. Mrs Jeff was going to come and hold the fort while I was gone to the Savoy. I dressed my boil and felt miserable. Daddy helped me upstairs and I knew in my heart I would not be able to go.

By three in the morning it was all up and I was well and truly sick. Daddy was kind and good and helped me back to bed and said, "There! There!" and got me another bottle, and phoned for Dr. Ollie Thomas first thing in the morning.

Thursday Ollie came before nine, bless him, and said to stay in bed, and sent a district nurse with penicillin injections. I needed no second telling to stay in bed, and Rupert stayed too.

177

In fact, Rupert stayed for two days in his bed with my abcess. He never left me except to be taken down by force for sanitary reasons and his supper. And as soon as he was done he would bark at Daddy to bring him back up. He was a great comfort, no trouble and a dear little dog. Mrs Jeffreys was golden, and kept me sane.

At the end of the morning Mrs. A. returned from hospital and came straight upstairs and sat in the chair and said, "Oh! I am terribly EEL. I am MUCH ze WORRRST." At this point the worm turned and I said, "In that case you must go away at once into the hospital for there is only room for me to be ill here." Then I felt a pig, but really it was sheer hysteria, and she had got the wind up about not being able to cope. I simply didn't care. Rupert was with me, Daddy had promised to fend for himself, Gran deserved all she got, and they could just see how uncomfortable it was without me for a change. I turned over with difficulty and firmly shut my eyes. So she moaned and sobbed her way downstairs and ate a very good lunch, which Mrs Jeff and I had provided, my Cornish pasties, and Mrs Jeff's vegetables and pudding!

Friday I knitted and slept and read and nothing happened except that the lady doctor came and she is so nice. Before the district nurse came I went downstairs to get boiling water etc. to poultice my leg. Mrs A. was in a deep sulk, and said she felt "Terribly Eel". I said, "Then you must see the Doctor, and if he says you are ill, you must either go back to Birmingham or to Hospital, but it is my belief that you are just plain scared stiff of doing a bit more work." And with that I dragged myself off. One does miss the advantages of a dramatic exit on these occasions! She said she could not do the shopping and I said, "You must tell the Vicar, then." This she did not want to do so we have heard no more of it, and I have not made the mistake of asking her how she feels.

Sunday I am up and about again, but I have not been out or to church. Gran is actually relieved to see me, but the house is very cold as Mrs A. has not felt equal to lighting a fire in either the dining room or the sitting room. Still, the boiler has behaved itself and stayed alight in the kitchen, thank God. I'll be back to business tomorrow, but thank God for Mrs Jeffreys, who is older than any of us, but makes the least fuss of all.

Wednesday December 7th After supper Mrs. A. came and sat in the dining room and began to moan and carry on, so I had a good talk to her, and I told her straight it was best for her to begin and look out for something else to do as she was obviously unhappy and as she hated all and every form of housework she was no use to me. I said I was not used to people being dissatisfied when they worked for me, and why she had ever consented to come in the first place I could not think, as I had told her from the first what I expected of her, and it had transpired that she could not do any of it! She admitted she was incompetent, which was generous but self evident – and said she wanted to go but it was so difficult to find a room in Birmingham. I said she really must get cracking, as I could not keep her after the end of March and that gave her three and a half months.

Thursday I got up early, determined to go to the tailoring class. I came down and found your letter on the mat, and one for Mrs A. from her sister in law. As I collected my sewing together she came in looking confused and said, "My belle-soeur have found me a room in Berrmingham – what you tink?" I said, my heart bounding with joy, "Oh! Of course you must go at once!" "Not at once," says the fool, "I must pack up my tings. How about Saturday wick?" I said, "Oh! No! You do not want to have to pay for a room for nothing. You GO. Finish out your week here, and then have two days to pack, and sort yourself out, and then go on Tuesday." "What will you do WIZZOUT me?" she cried. So I said very firmly, "Now look here. Do you want to go or don't you?" "Yes," she said. "Then the sooner you go the better for both of us," said I. Mummy getting downright in her old age! So if nothing happens we are free of her on Tuesday. I dashed upstairs and woke up Daddy. "Wake up. Good news. The bitch is going!" "NO!" said Daddy, all big eyed and snoozily. "WHEN?" I told him and he said, "THANK GOD!" So I went off to the tailoring class with a spring in my step, and had a very good morning's work on my gray flannel skirt.

Christmas coming and no help in the house means you will get very scrappy letters I am afraid. But I want to get this one off a day early, and I hope you will get it in time for

Christmas, wherever you are going to be.

Monday I had an M.U. Committee which I had forgotten about, so rushed round cursing and swearing to set it up. Mrs. A. spent the day – a wet one – drifting in and out of the house to the Post Office and the hairdresser and to the station. She kept out of my way and had all her meals out and behaved like a disgruntled ghost most of the time. It appears she told Mrs Gilson I was cruel to her and did not give her enough to eat! She was too damn lazy to cook anything for supper and I suppose she expected me to cook it for her! Anyway, she didn't look any thinner.

Tuesday She was up at 6a.m. ready to go by 7.45a.m., but she stood up against the dresser waiting to say goodbye to J.O. when he came in from early church at 9.a.m. I had already been regaled by the tales she had told Mrs Gilson and I was not feeling too charitable towards her. I didn't tax her with it. It would have been too paltry! I escorted her to the door and bade her a very business like farewell. Once she had gone I felt years younger and as if I had been given a month's holiday. And Mrs Jeffreys and I had a large glass of Dubonnet each.

I had a letter from Pooler on Friday saying she will come back for a spell after Christmas. She says if she gets a place of her own she will go again, and if her mother is ill again she will have to go again, but if I don't mind the "ifs and buts" she will come back. I don't mind the ifs and buts, and have come to the conclusion that I would sooner do without in future than risk another shocker like Mrs. A.

"Rollie preached tonight and told a story of two
spiders who met in the aisle and chatted…"

Curate's Tales

A curate was assigned to a parish in a training and assisting capacity.

In the first half of the twentieth century there were plenty of priests and plenty of curates; even a very small parish was likely to have a curate to help with the visiting, pastoral and teaching work. Most young priests would serve a junior curacy and a senior curacy in two parishes. The first curacy would be in a learning and probationary capacity, the second probably in a larger and busier parish, where he would be given certain responsibilities of his own. He would spend three or four years in each parish before being entrusted wit his own parish. A really large parish might have three or four curates in various stages of experience. Now, of course, Church of England curates get four years at the very most in one training parish, and then are pitch forked into a parish on their own.

During the war, theological colleges were severely curtailed, the students were drafted into the armed forces ad many clergy elected to become chaplains. Those who chose to stay with their parishes, or who were too old for active service, were required to add fire fighting or leading air raid wardens' posts to their duties. By the end of the war, clergy numbers were much depleted.

J.O. was fortunate to have two older and more experienced men assist him. The Reverend Sir James Roll – Rollie – was in his early forties. He had had polio as a child which left him with a limp, so he was unfit for military service.

He had already been looking after little St. Mary's church for a couple of years when J.O. arrived in 1948. Father William Witcutt had been placed with J.O. by the Bishop of Chelmsford in 1949. He had been ordained into the Roman Catholic Church and had converted to Anglicanism after many years as a priest in the Midlands. He was an accomplished theologian and had written several books. The three men worked together for the entire ten years J.O. was in East Ham, and all left for other parishes at about the same time. There could not have been three more dissimilar men, and yet they all complemented each other's ministry. The only woman on the team, Dorothy Gilson, the parish worker, did stalwart work with the Youth Clubs and the Sunday Schools and the Women's Group, a large group for women on the edges of, and enquiring about, the Christian religion.

Margot had her own unique role

.

Thursday 17th September 1953 I found two ripe figs on the tree by the wall and ate them quick. Then Rollie came in and made me laugh. He said he had paid £10 for a Scottie dog for Father Smith for a present and every time he went to Father Smith's the dog bit him! This because Rupert was pleased to see him! "You're a NICE little dog – not like that beastly dog of Smith's!"

Sunday night After tea I went down to St Mary's for Evensong. Rollie did his duty by the congregation and preached on St. Luke. He plodded on in a painstaking way and then suddenly said, "Little more is known about this saint except that it is almost certain that he never married but died a natural death – in the name of the Father and of the Son etc."

Sunday June 3rd Up **at** 6.45a.m. and get Gran's breakfast up to her by 7.30. To Mass at 8a.m. and dash home again to get Witcutt some tea. Rollie is on holiday. Poor Witcutt has a swollen mouth from a bad tooth and has been taking M. and B. tablets. He told me he had heard that someone gave M. and B. to a horse and it became depressed and threw itself into a pond. I replied that if he was a horse, and we had a pond, we should have to be watchful! After which pleasantry he returned to the vestry.

Gran went to 9a.m. I got her up too early! Then I changed the sheets and wrote a bit to you in the garden. After coffee I set Gran to shell two pounds of peas, after which exertion she retired upstairs for a lie down!

Later Dinner was a big success and Witcutt managed to preach at evening service without hurling himself from the pulpit or hanging himself from the bell rope so he is evidently not a horse.

Friday.December 6th Heard a snippet of gossip from Mrs Middlebrook. You know that Rollie is Chaplain to the Girls' Air Cadet Corps, or whatever they call the thing. Well. Mrs Middlebrook has been trying to get new subscribers for the parish magazine and went to one house and the woman said,

"Oh! We know all about the church – our Gertie is a member of Lord Roll's Air Force."

Rollie has got a new hat, a very upstanding trilby. It's a pity his waterproof coat is torn across the back and frayed at the cuffs, for the hat obviously cost about £3.00. Very blocked and solid, not his usual soft floppy ones, almost Anthony Eden, in a nice soft gray.

He had a whale of a sermon last Sunday. He preached on Advent AND Saint Andrew, and gave us intimate glimpses from the lives of Napoleon, Nelson, Wellington and some Japanese missionaries thrown in! And at the end he seemed to get in a flap with his notes and suddenly said, "Just wait a minute. I'm trying to sum up!" Bless him!

January 11th 1954 I read a nice story in the Church Times last week about a young deacon preaching his first sermon, on the man sick of the palsy. He got up in the pulpit and began by saying – "We notice two things about this man – firstly, he had the palsy – and secondly, he was sick of it!"

I went to St Bart's tonight and sat by myself by a radiator. Rollie gave us a circular tour in his sermon, from St. Paul to Candlemass, stopping at St. John Bosco (!?) en route. The three didn't fit together very well, but he felt we ought to know about all three; but in the end he got so bemused that he tried to get old Simeon off the road to Damascus and John Bosco out of the temple and two doves out of St John Bosco's Boys Club! And St Paul back on the rails. POOR Rollie.

February 6ᵗʰ I cooked lunch, fishcakes and the remains of the Christmas puddings. I felt this was not a suitable meal for my diet, so I had boiled egg instead of fishcakes, but then I could not resist the Christmas pud! Then Rollie turned up and carted me off to se a little house in Norman Road, next to St Mary's. The first one, opposite St Mary's Hall. He wants to buy it. It is a nice little house, but although it has a bathroom it has no indoor sanitation and he would have to have it put in. I was all for it if that could be encompassed

Shrove Tuesday Bitter cold and a hard cutting wind. Pooler's day out. She went out but soon came back and has spent the day in the warm kitchen knitting, sensible woman. During the morning two dear little girls, one about five and one about three, came hand in hand, the elder carrying a little cardboard box. Daddy opened the door and the elder said, "Please would he bury their birdie as it had just died!" Poor Daddy! He had to get a pickaxe to dig the hole! The girls didn't look too bereaved as they went off skipping quite happily through the gate. I spent the day sewing Johnnie G's chair cover and I made pancakes for all in the evening.

Sunday Snowing but with a hint of thaw. 8a.m. Mass and spend most of the day making Mary's frock. I clerked the Baptisms and read the first chapter of Witcutt's new book, The Rise and Fall of the Individual. He is the most remarkable person. Here is a subject that is quite above my head and I have no learning on the subject at all – but I sat and read the first chapter with complete understanding and enjoyment and I WANT to know what comes next. He has the great gift of making an abstruse subject completely intelligible to the ordinary intelligent mind. In this he is like one Armitage Robinson, an erstwhile Dean of Wells, who had the same gift, and who preached a completely satisfying sermon in about 35 minutes on the Atonement that I shall never forget, in words of at most two syllables.

Sunday Up early and to church at 8a.m. Rupert enjoyed his birthday. He had a pork chop for his dinner and a good brush and he was a happy spoiled dog all day long. I helped with the Baptisms. Four little darlings. Three girls and one boy and two of the girls and the boy called Leslie, or Lesley, as sex dictated. What is the reason for this? Television star, I expect.

Daddy got in a pet because he told me to put the catch of the vestry door down, and put the keys on the vestry table, as I went over before him to the Baptisms. Then he came in the front door of the church and said, "I thought I told you to put the catch down!" I said, "Yes. I did." And he said, "You didn't. I couldn't get in." And both Witcutt and I said, "If you want it left open you must say, put the catch UP!" And he simply stomped off. Whereupon Witcutt said in that silly quacking voice, "It reminds me of the Frenchman and the Englishman on the Channel Crossing. The Frenchman had the lower bunk and the Englishman the upper bunk. The Englishman felt sick and leant over the side of the bunk and said "Look out!" So the Frenchman looked out and caught the lot. He shouted,

"Whyfore you say look out when you mean look in?"

Monday Rollie came to Staff meeting and wished his mother Lady Roll on me for tea. I'm very useful to him when she comes to stay with him and he doesn't know what to do with her. She is a dear, though. So I put your letter in the post and bought Marks and Spencers cake and made a sponge in the morning and iced it and did the flowers. She didn't turn up till 5.p.m. much to Gran's disgust, who was sitting in state in the "drawing" room from 3p.m. onwards. Lady Roll looked very nice in a little bottle green and brown checked suit, beautifully tailored with a green collar and cuffs and pocket welts, and a tobacco brown cashmere sweater and little felt hat to match and a nice sable tie with four skins. . All very simple and HELLISHLY expensive! I could look as nice as that if I was given the money.

She stopped until seven when Rollie fetched her away to go to the Brownies, and that, topped up by a riotous evening with Miss Cottee, his old housekeeper, must have put the seal on her evening!

Wednesday Rollie took Daddy and me to lunch at the Denmark Arms, and Lady Roll, and Miss Cottee, and Father Smith, AND Father Smith's father, AND Father Smith's father's male attendant. I wish I could draw them. The father of Father Smith was incredible. He looked like boiled sucking pig. It's no good. I can't draw him, he is too succulent for mere pen and ink. You need goose fat, and a melting wax taper to do him justice. The manservant looked like a rather battered rubber doll. I felt rather as if we were lunching with some of the characters out of the

nastier stories in my Children's Wonder Books. Even the steak and kidney pudding had the look of being cooked in the kitchen of a malevolent gnome.

Easter Day A perfect spring day, soft and warm. After morning church we bathed Rupert and he looks magnificent, and knows it. In the evening Johnnie Griffiths and I went down to St Mary's and Rollie gave out the following notice: "Please remember to turn your clock on an hour next Saturday night, because if you don't we shan't see you at the service you set out to come to!"

Sunday I woke up dead tired so did not go to church. BAD mother! I cooked the lunch for 12.30p.m. as I wanted to go and see and hear Witcutt preach at St. Paul's Cathedral. The Church of England have just cottoned on to the fact that he is now a part of it! I cooked pork and stuffing and Rupert was very pleased to find it was PORK, and after I had washed up and put away, I changed into Doris' good black wool frock and my diamond earrings and my Rabbi's hat and my black and white check coat and I set off for St. Paul's.

I sat right under the Dome and began to feel very nervous for poor Witcutt as you know what his diction is like and he would have a microphone to contend with as well.

He asked me about it on Wednesday and I told him I

knew NOTHING about it, but I felt that if he remembered to speak a little more slowly than usual, and to spit his words out, clearly enunciating the beginning of each one he couldn't go far wrong. I never thought he would take a blind bit of notice. Anyway, just before the service began I asked the dear Lord to help him and give him a clear head and a calm inside, and then I just gave up worrying.

The service began – the choir came in – followed by a verger with a poker – followed by various canons, and then old Witcutt, cool as a cucumber, walking slanting slightly backwards as he usually does. The singing was not a patch on the St. Bart's choir. I mean it. Then Witcutt was pokered to the pulpit. And he was MAGNIFICENT. He was clear. I heard every word, and it was a masterly sermon on St Paul and his influence on the Church, very simply put over and very simply spoken and distinct. I could have hugged him. When the service was over I pinched a whole lot of service sheets to give to Witcutt so that he could send them to all his friends and relations. I got home to discover that poor Hilda Spivey had thrown a fit in the church porch and they were phoning for an ambulance. I pretended not to notice and slipped in the back door.

Sunday I went to Evensong, very nicely sung. Rollie preached a nice sermon about St. Alban, and finished up by saying, "He was executed, and so impressed was the executioner by St. Alban's great faith, that he said he couldn't execute St. Alban, and would rather BE executed WITH St.

Alban. So they were BOTH executed – by somebody else!"

Sunday night 9.45p.m. In the sitting room before the fire. Grandfather clock ticking. Rupert asleep on the biggest chair! Cat asleep on the mat. Queenie gone home. Gran gone to bed. Pooler gone into the kitchen to wash up. Daddy gone into the study. Mother in PEACE!

This evening Father Witcutt preached a very good sermon. He really is masterly at it. The theme was the outpouring of God's mercy always shining forth abundantly if only we would turn our faces towards it and receive it. He said the saints were merely people who not only turned their faces towards God, but opened their arms and hearts to Him as well, and were so filled with the radiance of it that it overflowed from them, so that other people, whose faces were not turned properly to God, saw it reflected in them and recognised it as such. He said it in his funny quacky voice – but the words he put it in were quite poetic, and I DID wish I could write shorthand.

Sunday Rollie preached tonight, and told a story of two church spiders who met in the aisle and chatted. One said she thought of moving. "I live in the pulpit," she said. "But it gets on my nerves. It's all right in the week, but on Sundays the vicar gets up in it and bangs about. It's all very unsettling." The second spider said, "You'd better come and live with me. Nothing ever disturbs me. I live in the box for charitable Donations!"

"The servants of the Guild of the Sanctuary. – All shapes and sizes!"

The Church's Year at East Ham Vicarage

The Church's year begins with Advent, four weeks before Christmas, a preparation time for the feast of Jesus' birth. It moves on through Epiphany, the festival of the coming of the Wise Men, and then through the forty solemn days of Lent, from Ash Wednesday to Palm Sunday; then on into Holy Week culminating with Good Friday, the day of Jesus' trial and Crucifixion.

Easter Sunday is the greatest Festival of the Christian year, celebrating Jesus' triumph over Death, and the forty days of cleansing and self denial and sorrow are followed by forty days of praise and joy. The feast of Pentecost, which used to be known as Whit Sunday, follows on to commemorate God sending His Holy Spirit to the disciples, and the beginning of the spread of the Church throughout the world.

This in turn leads into the season of Trinity tide, when Christians consider how to grow in their faith and live according to Christian principles of love and justice.

Trinity tide runs throughout the summer and autumn, growing, fruiting, harvesting, and when November comes and the year dies down, the Church bends its mind to those who have died, to our own death, to all the saints who have taught by their example, and to those whom we have loved who have died before us.

Then the Church's Year begins again, with Advent.

East Ham Vicarage life was bounded by this calendar – Margot kept it on track and attended to the practical details!

Advent Sunday 1953 I am whacked to the wide. I have spent the entire day rushing round getting things ready for the Bishop, Henry Wilson, to come and stay. Daddy has invited him to preach at the new St. Bartholomew's, and he is staying the night. I got up not early enough, got a breakfast lunch and got Henry's bedroom ready. Then I did the church flowers. I spent a fortune on them but they were worth it. Big blood red chrysanthemums, and even bigger pale pinkey ones, and greeny gold beech leaves and some very pretty small pink sprays to lighten up and when they were done they looked GRAND! Then I did the Lady Altar, so that it should look special and put a smaller edition of the same and THAT looked grand. I know it did because Jessie was cross! That took me till about 1.30p.m. and then I started on the house flowers and that took me till about 3p.m. Then I did a spot of silver cleaning and had a bath. Henry turned up about 7.30p.m. and we spent a very amusing evening by the fire in the sitting room with sherry and Dubonnet to make weight .Sunday I got up early and lit the fire in the dining room and the sitting room. Cold foggy morning. Then Henry came to church with me and sat with me in the congregation which was nice. He was MOST impressed with the church. Daddy had got a huge bill outside advertising in ENORMOUS letters, "Bishop Henry Wilson Preaching This Morning". Henry looked at it and said, "Coo! That ought to be all right, always supposing they can read!"

He also told Daddy he ought to be very grateful to me for criticising him. He said clergy who had no wives were a mass of bad habits and mannerisms. He said, "My dear wife renders herself quite Hoarse correcting me!"

Wed Dec. 23rd After I had my hair done I went over
to help sweep the church. Father Witcutt came and helped to
polish and he stayed for about three hours which beat me! And
he brought a lot of boys who were really helpful, sweeping and
moving chairs and pews. We moved everything out and the
mess from all the school carol services was terrific. Toffee
papers and spearmint. Dirty little sods. I got in about six and
Lou came and we all had high tea. Johnnie G. arrived at 10.45
laden like a pack mule. One of the parcels turned out to be a
lovely triple mirror. I have stood it on the bow fronted chest in
the big bedroom by the window and it looks beautiful. He also
brought a superb chicken, but he says he has hidden the rest in
the garden and we have to wait and see what it is!

Christmas Day 1953 Well little one, what sort of a day
have you had? I missed you terribly, as was only to be
expected, as I was in a place where you have always been, and
you were in a new place with no associations, but I didn't
mope, even though Daddy has had one of his "Down with
Yule" fits, and "He Doesn't Like Any Of The Food" fits, and
"Why Can't He Just Have Spaghetti?" fits. One of these days
I'll give him bloody spaghetti and got to bed with a book! See
how he likes that!

The midnight mass was very well attended. The centre
aisles were both full. Johnnie and I sat right at the back next to
the Gilsons. We had a lot of drunks as usual which Johnnie and
Ralphie Gilson dealt with very promptly, but a couple of them

were disturbing. Only the back rows noticed it, I think. They have taken great pains with the Crib, but it is one of those painstakingly prim affairs that leave me quite cold. I think the most lovely one I have ever seen is the little one down at St. Mary's. Such a perfect miniature stable and such a delicious clutter, with an apple ladder leaning by the sacks at the back by the ox. Pure Thomas Hardy.

Palm Sunday 1954 Up at 7a.m. and lay the sitting room fire and get to 8a.m. Mass. Daddy was villainously slow! And as it was the Palm Sunday Gospel which goes on for pages, AND the Blessing of Palms, AND the distribution of Palms, AND the Notices went on forever, I thought we should never have done! A thick ground frost although a lovely sunny morning.

Easter Eve 1954 It has been a very well attended Lent, all things considering. The weekday Lent sermons got good congregations at both churches, and from Palm Sunday onwards good attendances every night. I went to Wo Pangs with Daddy after the service on Maundy Thursday. I had Chicken Chop Suey and Daddy had I See Nits or something – but really, as I observed – we were both eating exactly the same thing, only his gravy was white and mine was manure coloured. Lou loves Wo Pangs. She says it's the only place where you can eat hard for ten minutes and still have the same amount on your plate!

Good Friday Traditional breakfast, grapefruit and

boiled eggs and hot cross buns, then I mop-dusted and did the chores and went to the Three Hours Service. Witcutt preached three very good sermons and the time did not seem overlong, but I got colder and colder. I came home and attacked a bottle of vintage burgundy I got from the Off Licence as I felt so tired. Daddy came in and thought that was a very good idea, and so did Pooler, so that went for a Burton! And then I LONGED for sleep, but I wrote the first half of this letter, and then off again down to St. Mary's for the start of the Grand Procession of Witness.

I got on the bus and was firmly cornered by Jessie who got on afterwards. That woman sticks like chewing gum to tweed! At the first stop by the Post Office we sang, "There is a Green Hill" and at the second stop we sang it again, only two tones higher! Going down Katherine Road there was the most terrible smell of burning – soot and rags and burnt glue thrown in, and bits of the sort of smell when the Pet Shop kept the gorilla! It went on for yards and yards and I said to Ralph Gilson, "Crumbs, whatever is it?" and before he could answer, Mrs Crocker, who was walking behind, said seriously, "It smells a bit like curry, don't it?" This pulverised Ralph Gilson for the rest of the procession. He said he thought it might have been someone trying to burn their Grandma, but curry -! I decided not to go to lunch with Mrs Crocker – ever.

We fell wearily into St. Bart's and had a service beginning with – yes – There is a Green Hill Far Away – and a basinful of the most blithering nonsense from a reverend blitherer from St. Albans.

Whit Monday   Gran and Daddy went off up to the West Ham Football ground to see the fun, for it was the day of the great Diocesan Youth Rally, and the whole Diocese was to congregate up there. They had about 20,000 which I think was good, but they expected 40,000 which was plumb daft in my opinion! The Youth Organisations gathered here in St Bart's, the choirs all gathered at Plaistow, the servers somewhere else, and the Sunday Schools all came by coach from everywhere, God knows where they disembarked! Anyway, we had a smashing procession from St Bart's, about a thousand of them I should think, and three bands, and Harry Hawkins on his police horse, leading the way, and the Bishop of Barking flanked by Harold Tomlinson and Charlie Middlebrook, our churchwardens, at the end. I watched the procession go past for the best part of half an hour. But I didn't go up to the Ground where the Bishops of Chelmsford, Colchester, Barking, and Croydon (who was to be the preacher) with the Lord Lieutenant of the County and Lady Whitmore and all the nobility and gentry were assembled. I didn't think they would miss me! So I made some coconut biscuits and sat on the sun patch.

August 24ᵗʰ St Bart's Day It was Bill the organist's last Sunday, so we had special anthems and readings. All the readings, bar one, were read very badly by choirboys and choirmen and clergy, and Bill put on all the exotic anthems he cold think of, and alas! I don't think he chose wisely, as they were not up to the standard required and they can sing simpler things so beautifully. Also a boy sang a solo in a whooping cough voice, and Arthur sang another one and cracked on the high notes. So endeth Sunday!

September 20   This morning I went round to the Church Hall to help with the breakfast for the East Ham Boys Grammar School Corporate Communion. Forty-six boys made their Communion, a very good turn out. We gave them a smashing breakfast. Boiled eggs, rolls, and butter and marmalade, coffee and tea. Roy Waters, who used to be the smallest choirboy is now a giant sixth former. He made a very good speech of thanks at the end, no trace of nervousness and very neatly put. How you do all grow up.

November 2nd All Souls Day   Johnnie preached a very good sermon at Evensong, and the choir sang the Russian Contakion and they sang it most beautifully. It really was a most outstanding effort. We came home and had cups of tea and Gran was cross because of the Contakion and said there was a lot too much of it – and that what we needed was something bright! She is a DREADFUL old woman.

"Mary P's navy taffeta looks quite glamorous. I have sewn tiny blue sequin daisies with white centres, and mother of pearl daisies with blue centres…"

Mary P.

Lisa met Mary P. at school at the Ursuline Convent, Ilford. Mary was the eldest of six children. Her father a Doctor, had died of pneumonia, at the early age of forty-seven, and his wife had brought the family up with the help of her younger brother and her sister, Auntie May, who was the matron of the East Ham hospital.

Mary worked hard all her life. All the children had their household tasks and chores, but Mary's, as the eldest, were the heaviest. One of her jobs was to keep the kitchen spotlessly clean, and every week to clean the oven – oh! That oven! Every teatime she cut two loaves of bread into thick slices with breakneck speed, and slapped margarine on each slice. No sliced loaves in the 1940s.Clothes were hand downs from her mother and aunt, and as clothes rationing and coupons were still in force, the clothes were well worn by the time they got to her. The others fared no better, and the boys' shoes were constantly at the cobblers.

She was a forthright outspoken little girl, with thick fair plaits and a strong husky voice. She loved the comparative peace and elegance of the Vicarage, whereas Lisa, an only child, loved the hurly burly and racket of the Ilford house. "Do you think Mary would like it if we had lunch in the dining room?" said Margot, the first time Mary came to lunch at East Ham. Lisa said she thought she would. So the table was laid with flowers and napkins and Mary was enchanted. J.O. fell for her at once and forever. "What do you think of school dinners,

*Mary?" said J.O. "Lisa doesn't seem to think much of them."
"Oh! Mr Nicholls!" said Mary in her deep voice." The
STENCH is enough!"*

*Mary was determined to become a nurse, and to train
at St. Bartholomew's Hospital, where her father had trained.
She had to work hard to get the high grades that the Hospital
demanded for entry, and once accepted, worked and studied
long, long days and nights, living in the Nurses Home, on the
minute wage paid to student Nurses in those days.*

*Margot made her some skirts and blouses to wear
when she was off duty in the Nurses Home, and she loyally
visited Margot and J.O. when Lisa was in America. She "stood
in" for Lisa, but it was a mutual service, as she was grateful
for their hospitality and their affection; Margot was her
confidante, and she absorbed a great deal of knowledge of
design and music and literature from their times together.*

Monday night October 5th, 1953 I have been pondering
over Mary's cocktail frock. I have seen some very nice navy
blue velveteen and thought a plain frock of that with a rather
sophisticated sash of the lovely blue organza would be rather
smashing.

Friday night I went up to the bargain shop to get the
velvet for Mary, but before the girl had cut the velvet off the
roll, she said, "Wait a bit, I've got something for you!" and
dived down into the cellar and brought out a roll of wonderful
navy blue pure silk at 4/- a yard! So I threw the idea of

velveteen to the winds and bought some of that for Mary and also bought 7 yards of it for you, so don't be envious! I thought if you don't want it now it was wicked to let it go at that price. You keep saying how useful the brown poplin is and I thought you might like another one in that same pattern. If so, I can get to work on it after I have made Gran's coat. I have got a very pretty McCalls pattern that I'll sketch for you.

Monday morning Yesterday was the usual sort of Sunday. Church at 8a.m with Johnnie G. and then after breakfast the coals and fires and wash towels, etc. and I realised I had a tight cold on the chest. Mary P. had rung and said she would come over in the evening, but by the time she was scheduled to arrive I longed for bed. Legs ached. Elbows ached. Knuckles ached. I stuck it out till 9.30p.m. and then I just HAD to go to bed. This morning, after a superb sweat in the night, I feel marvellous.

Mary P. is very taken with an engineering student and he has asked her to a dance on Nov. 20th, so I must cut out that frock next week. I will begin on yours as soon as I get the chance, as it sounds from your social life that you could do with it.

Friday January 20th, 1954 Cripes, what a day! I have gone at the double all day long. Dashed round to the Bendix, changed, dashed to Barking to a deanery meeting. It has been sunny but definitely colder. At 6p.m. Mary P. turned up for the evening. She had got an awful cold. I had lent her your backless evening dress for a dance and she had got bronchitis the night after, because it was snowing that night and she had just worn the dress and a skimpy fur cape over it, because she said to wear a coat would have spoiled the effect! She was quite happily ruining a very nicely knitted yellow jumper that she had made, but not pressed, cobbling the seams together. I took it off her, and will unpick it and sew it up myself. She doesn't want you to stop in America and she thinks you ought not to WANT to, and I ought not to LET you. "Actually, it's time she was coming home, isn't it, Mrs Nicholls?"

Friday 19th February Mary P. came at 5.30p.m. wearing her yellow jumper which now looks really nice. She goes on night duty next week which she hates. Anybody she does not like she now describes as "toxic as a tick" which pleases me! She sat in the armchair by the fire and read her book and kept saying it was HEAVEN, and she ate two rounds of toast and scrambled egg and had three pieces of coffee walnut cake and said THAT was heaven and she is as slim as a wand! She said the glamour was wearing off the young man and it was Terrible trying to recapture it and failing!

Whit Saturday Got up right early and went shopping and got a good wodge of it done before breakfast. Lovely sunny morning. I did the church flowers – red peonies – white iris – and a lot of very long spikey flowers rather like a white stella maris. You know, those tall little tiger lily things we get in the summer. I took great pains arranging them and I think they look lovely. When I came back we got out the deck chairs and Johnnie G. began mending them.

Mary P. came to lunch wearing her nice costume and little white blouse. She had been on night duty and had only had an hour's sleep and was remarkably wide awake. After lunch I introduced her to her skirt and top and she looked smashing in them, considering she had never had a fitting. It was ruddy marvellous. She insisted on wearing them, so I changed into mine to keep her company, and we sat in the garden and waited for Peter Marden who arrived about 4p.m. He wore a very smart brown suit and was very debonair and friendly. He came into the garden and was introduced to everyone and Mary and Peter both knew the same part of Ireland and Cork, and Mary nearly screamed with joy, and rattled on about the Barrascales, and the greyhounds, and being sprayed for foot and mouth when she went over on the boat with a lot of cows – I couldn't make head or tail of it – but it's the "troot" I'm telling ye. I felt Peter might be Mary's brother! Well, we all had tea in the kitchen and Gran surpassed herself all about the Pope, and Russia, and the Red Dean and Billy Graham – and she said the latter "seemed to perfectly attain a vacuum" which I thought VERY profound, especially as nature abhors it! – Peter collapsed over that and nearly swallowed his handkerchief. Pooler produced a marvellous tea. Iced coffee sponge and jam and cream sponge, and Johnnie produced a Lyons Wonder Cake in the middle of the evening, and we ended up with coffee and sandwiches and Peter went off about 9.45p.m. and Mary about 10.45p.m. Gran regaled us with some nice musical items from Our Miss Gibbs, and The Girl in the Taxi, both musicals about 1902-1907 period, and then suggested a spelling game but got fed up with it when I asked her to spell asphyxiate! And then Rhododendron and Pathological and Psychiatrist. Peter could not spell ANY of them and Gran's attempt at the last was killing. This item only lasted about five minutes but was hilarious while it did. I took photos which I hope will come out, but it rained at teatime and continued to rain all evening and there was hardly any sun when we took them.

Sunday June 26th Anniversary of the Birth of your father, Joannis Godelpus Worriguts, Allah be praised. Up at 5.45 a.m. and got the preparations ready for the breakfasts and got to church and then back to take the sausages out of the oven with lots of mushrooms as a birthday treat for Daddy. Then, after changing the sheets, I wrote a bit to you, and then after coffee I made an apple pie, a gooseberry pie, a jam turnover, a baked custard, a joram of salad cream, iced the sponge, a green salad, a russian salad, some hot potatoes and we had the cold meat left over from yesterday. Just as we finished the meal Mary P. turned up for the evening. So she happily finished off the gooseberry pie, and made a cup of tea and helped me to wash up. Daddy was in good form and Mary screamed with laughter at him. She rattled on about the hospital and the students and was very good value and read your letter and said sadly at the end, "It looks as though she still likes it!" I think she has a secret hope that the Americans are going to annoy you in some way, and you are coming straight home!

Monday September 20th I have done most of the washing but there is a young gale raging and it is hard to keep the clothes on the line. Mary P. rang up yesterday. She is coming over for a few hours one night this week after which she goes off to some annexe of St Bart's Hospital somewhere in St. Albans for six months. So she will not be able to get home very often. She is browned off about this, but she is simply steeped in the nursing and would sooner die than do anything else.

Wednesday October 14th. I am longing for next June my precious. Take every care. I had a lovely letter from Mary P. this week. She is enjoying St. Albans, though the Sister is toxic, and the matron is septic, and one or two other nurses are either suppurating or cancerous! She is an antiseptic pet!

January 16th 1955 A long letter from you. I had a letter from Mary P. on Thursday to say that she hadn't heard from you for ages. I said I expected it was on its way over! The poor girl was devastated as her Uncle Tim in Ireland had died and his wife was going back to live with her people and her grandfather will be going to live with her Aunt Joan, and it means Ring House will be given up, and the bottom has fallen out of Mary's world. Poor Mary. I do feel sorry for her as that house was a haven for her and she is such a misfit in that family. This Uncle Tim was the one nearest to her, I think. She sounded quite shaken with it, poor child.

Wednesday April 27th Mary came over for the day. She is still at St. Albans and still on nights, has been on for a month now and does not come off until her birthday, July 19th. It's too long. The poor child already looks like a pale faded flower. It was a heavenly day, very warm, so I made her spend all of it out in the sun. We only came in to eat and I think it did her good. Mrs P. is over in Ireland for a while, the grandfather has died and Ring House in Ringaskiddy is sold, poor Mary. She arrived at 11a.m. and left at 10.45p.m., so she had a good day. It's nice having her and I haven't seen her for NINE months.

Saturday October 28th I spent the afternoon joining up material for the settee cover. Literally all afternoon that took. I played about with ten and a half yards, got it round the chairs and between my legs and round my neck and nearly went batty, but I got it all joined up in the end. Mary P. rang up. Jubilant! She has passed her exams and is now a fully fledged nurse. She is coming over on Wednesday. She says her mother has broken her wrist and it has shaken her up considerably, poor thing. Mary rattled on at great speed and the phone was rather indistinct. I must try to alter that pink corduroy before she comes, and get a scarf to put in the neck for being a good and clever girl.

November 18th Mary P. was to have come this evening,

but she is in sole charge of 27 patients and the ward while the Sister is away and she said she is too tired to do anything else but go to bed when she is off duty. She says she has two probationers, and it is marvellous. She tells them to do things and they DO them! She says, "I keep thinking of things for them to do so that I can see them going and DOING them!"

November 20th 1955 The only excitement this week was Friday when your letter came with the pretty snap of you in the tree and the delicious episode of the reluctant dragon and the knitting for his spikes! On Friday Mary P. came over for the evening. She brought a fearful creation that had belonged to Auntie May that she wanted me to turn into a glamorous evening gown. Lou came also, and I gave them a very good nourishing fish pie, and celery and mushroom sauce, and I had made hot scones and we had those with cups of tea afterwards. There was a nice fire in the sitting room and we all went in there after we had washed up, except Daddy who had to go to some Medical Meeting – and unpicked Auntie May's abortion and did the best we could, took the sleeves out and gave it thin shoulder straps. I think perhaps a tulle stole would help, it's a pretty deep blue, but a very poor quality paper taffeta.

Tuesday I went into the market this morning looking for some stuff for a party frock for Andrea for Christmas. Poor child, she has nothing to wear. She was wearing an old frock of her mother's last Sunday. And I also bought some blue sequins and some mother of pearl sequins and came home, and after I had got Gran her tea I began to sew them onto Mary's frock from Auntie May. It begins to look glamorous – little blue daisies with white centres and little mother of pearl daisies with blue centres. Very amateurish, but they catch the light and sparkle. It certainly looks better than it DID!

December 17th We had the joint hotted up for supper. Mary P. arrived and was famished, so it was just the job. She is still in charge of her 27 patients, the Sister is away ill and will be away all over Christmas, so Mary is doing the Sister's duty and arranging for all the Christmas festivities for the ward etc. etc. and is tired out, but supremely happy. She wore your pink corduroy and looked a smasher. We spent the evening sewing sequins onto Auntie May's dress and Mary put it on and looked very pretty in it so it was all worth it. Then she talked to Daddy when he came in over coffee about 9p.m. and finally went back to hospital about 10.30p.m. She is a dear child and so grateful for a bit of peace and a quiet chat.

Friday February 10th 1956 Chores. Fires. Bitter cold. May P. came. She looks thinner and tireder than ever, but FULL of joy and enthusiasm. She is taking me to see the Boy Friend on Monday at Wyndham's. I am going to have tea with her first in her room at the hospital, and then she is coming to supper with me afterwards. I will tell you all about it next week. She stayed to lunch and Daddy was on good form.

Monday 14th February About 4p.m. I painted my nails and put on my pewter and copper cocktail dress and two petticoats and a cardigan underneath!, and sallied forth to Aldersgate and Barbican in the cold, cold night to meet Mary P. I got to the station a good seven minutes before she came and paced up and down the cold booking hall like a confined tigress – I dared not stand still in case I froze to death! Mary came and took me to her rooms in Charterhouse Square, a charming room, and all as neat and trim as a new pin, with a dainty tea laid on the table and we sat and talked and ate Fullers cakes, my oh my, until around 7.30p.m. we got on a bus and went to see The Boy Friend. I laughed and laughed and LAUGHED. It was blissful – and incredible that I had been one of these silly young things in my youth! And I am quite sure JUST as silly. I adored it! Especially the little silly dressed as a butterfly who squiggled all over the stage, and then dashed up and down waving her wings and saying, "Oh! I am exhausted!"

After the show we walked down to the Charing Cross Corner House and had supper in the Brasserie. This was my treat. It was pretty full and the band was playing but we didn't see the little Chad Valley Man playing the double bass. Perhaps he has left, or he may have been behind someone else. We had mushroom omelette, and Mary had chips too! And cider and Wondercake and coffee, just as you and I used to do, and she came on the train with me to Blackfriars, and I got home about half past twelve. I did enjoy it. Rupert was very pleased to see me. I wore Elizabeth's cashmere coat. It is a perfect dream, so warm and light and lovely.

March 9th 1956 I bought a very attractive pattern for a frock for Mary P. She is beginning to go to a few parties after her stint in the wilderness and only has that navy silk, which must be pretty well through by now, and the blue sequin evening dress, so I decided I will give her a heavy silk dark red brocade sheath dress and a navy and white swishy skirt. She can buy herself a little white or navy top to go with it.

Thursday Went to the tailoring and got the collar on my jacket. Home and wrote out the wedding registers and spend the rest of the afternoon doing Mary's frock, which is the most damned awful pattern I have ever attempted and I'll not make it up again for ANYBODY, not even you! I'm going frog eared over it!

Palm Sunday 1956 Mary P. came in the evening and I sewed her belt. She told us what a heavenly time she had had at a party and then she had spent the next day at the young man of the moment's houseboat near Battersea Parish Church's Graveyard! Bliss. Heavenly bliss! No sleep for 40 hours, and then three and a half hours sleep. and then on duty again. Bliss and youth and more Bliss! You all do it and I must say I suppose I did, but one tends to forget ones own damn sillinesses!

"… a connoisseur of local beer and ales all over
the Midlands from Burton on Trent to the
Welsh Marches…"

The Last Visits to Lewis

Lewis Shirlaw was a solicitor in the family firm of Thursfield, Messiter and Shirlaw in Wednesbury. His marriage had foundered soon after the First World War, leaving him with a son, Andrew. He had met Margot and J.O. through his aunt, Mrs Margaret Thursfield, and her daughter, Nancy. Mrs Thursfield and Lewis became two of Lisa's godparents and friends of the family for life.

Lewis was in some ways an extremely conventional man. After his son Andrew grew up and left home he lived a bachelor existence, keeping up all the old fashioned niceties of a gentleman's code. When he came to stay his suitcase was immaculately packed. Every shoe was in its own chamois leather bag, with its own shoe tree. Every jacket was folded and packed with tissue paper. His silver backed hairbrushes and combs were in their own leather cases, his handkerchieves in their own sachet. We had to make sure the trouser press was- dusted- in his room.

He liked his breakfast in his room, and there was a set way to arrange his tray, the toast rack, the egg cosy, the butter knife, the marmalade spoon, the little flower vase, the starched but not overstarched napkin. Lisa became quite adept at it.

In his own house his housekeepers were expected to observe these details, and those he employed took pride in doing so. He was courteous and attentive, if somewhat reserved to his acquaintances, but with Margot and J.O. and Lisa he was relaxed and affectionate, with a dry wit and a sharp sense of the ridiculous. He was a connoisseur of the local beer and ales all over the Midlands, from Burton on Trent to the Welsh Marches, and he soon found out his favourite local drinking places in the City of London and the East End.

Andrew married Marie, and they had six children. Their multitudinous activities and exploits made him very proud, but bemused and exhausted him. Sadly, by 1953, when Lisa set off for America, he was beginning his last illness.

Friday May 28th, 1954 Darling – here I am sitting in Lewis's sitting room at 11a.m. with nothing to do but write to you. He rang up at the beginning of the week and it seemed a good chance to have a couple of days with him. I can't get away for the foreseeable future after this, so we fixed it up.

On Monday afternoon I went to the Bargain Shop to look for some curtain stuff for Lewis' bedroom and see if I could make them in time to take with me. I fell for **some** glazed check cotton in the most musical comedy colours, pretty and soft, orange, blue, grey, cyclamen and pink like a geometrical sunset. I also got a singing petrol blue for a bedcover. The lot including the rufflette tape only coming to £2.15/- I carried it all home in triumph and managed to run them up, except for the hems, with no problem.

I spent Wednesday evening finishing them and packed them into a parcel for Pooler to post to Perton as they were too heavy to carry. Then I packed my bag. Rupert's tail went down when he saw the bag and he looked reproachful, poor little dog.

I got to bed about 1.a.m.

Thursday Up at 5.30a.m! Yes! And crept downstairs and dressed and got a cup of tea and took some to Poo and left Rupert asleep in his basket and none the wiser for my going. I left the house at 6.30a.m. and got to Victoria coach station by 7.30a.m. and got a decent seat on the coach and set forth at 8.a.m. sharp.

It was a beautiful morning and I thoroughly enjoyed the ride. We stopped in Dunstable for a cup of coffee at about 10a.m. and then on to a pretty place called Dunster for lunch, and got to Walsall about 2.30p.m. As the coach swung past the County Court I saw Johnnie Griffiths on the steps coming out. He had no idea I was coming, so I went straight over to the little teashop by the Court and there he was. He nearly choked when he saw me. I told him I had to meet Lewis at his office in Wednesbury at 4.30p.m, so he took my luggage to his office and then parked me upstairs in the Court to listen to the cases until he could collect me and take me to the Wednesbury bus. I quite enjoyed it. The Registrar bowed deeply to me as I entered and the Judge looked at me over his spectacles. I sat at the back of the Court and just before 4p.m. the usher came to tell me that Mr Griffiths was waiting in his office to give me tea! If I had been Princess Margaret I could not have been treated with more ceremony – except that the Judge did not rise as I went out!

Then I went to Wednesbury and called for Lewis, and there was the same old office, and oh! dear! He looked so dreadfully old and ill that I was quite bowled over. However, I do not think I shewed it, and we went to the car and drove to Perton. He certainly ought not to be working and he certainly ought not to drive the car. He looks quite ninety and is very pathetic. He has got so tottery and almost senile. Still, it's no good crying over it.

We had a very good supper provided by Mrs Hallas, who is fatter than ever! But she is a cheerful little soul and had filled my room with flowers so that I felt sure I would suffocate in the night? We went to bed at 9.p.m. Lewis looked more than ready for it and I decided it could do me no harm. I read for a while, but was asleep before the clock struck ten.

Friday   A leisurely morning. Lewis went off early to Darlaston to Court and I pressed my clothes and knitted and read and wrote to you. Andrew had arranged for Colin to come and collect me and take me to tea with Nancy in their new cottage. It poured with rain. Colin came and we had a pleasant drive to the cottage, the rain had stopped and the sun came out and the wet fields and trees sparkled. The cottage is a perfectly charming place with a perfect hidden garden. The house is side ways on a hill, like Wardie and George's was, and the garden dips down and ends up in an orchard. The view across to the Brown Clee hills is superb. It is quite a tiny house but with amazing views from all the windows. We talked and had tea and about 6 o'clock we set out to meet Andrew and Lewis for dinner at a pub called the Mitton and Mermaid at a little place called Atcham in Shropshire, and had a very good meal

Poor Lewis looked like a ghost who had been made to return to earth – but we all tried to behave as if he didn't look like that that, except Andrew who didn't seem to notice! We stayed there until about 9p.m. until Andrew drove us home at TERRIFIC speed. Lewis looked all in when we got home, so I packed him off to bed and followed very shortly. It was a pleasant evening and I was glad to see Nancy and Colin again. They were most interested in all your news.

Saturday I had breakfast after early tea and a bath – luxury! It poured all morning so I spent the time taking measurements for chair covers and cushions for everything is falling to pieces. We went down to Whitwick for petrol and oil and a drink at the Mermaid before lunch. When we got out to the car again the self starter would not work! Lewis just sat there hopelessly and said he didn't know what to do. I said I would walk back down to the garage which I did – luckily it had stopped raining – and I got a man who came and soon put it right and we finally got back for lunch – but poor Lewis was devastated by this and I felt he was near to tears. Anyway, we had the most FATTENING lunch. Liver and onions and a very rich cake with lashings of ice cream. I helped Mrs Hallas wash up and I m writing this as Lewis is sleep on the sofa.

I rang up Pooler to see why the curtains had not arrived, but she said she had posted them on Thursday morning. She also said Gran had been having her airs. She ALWAYS breaks out as soon as I am out of the house.

When Lewis woke up we went over to Wolverhampton

to have tea with Marie and Andrew. They have six children now, the new baby is called Mary Gerard, so they have three of each. Marie had told Benjy to be a good boy because if so, he would see Auntiemargot tomorrow, Grandpa was coming to tea and was bringing Auntiemargot. He was vastly intrigued and said, "But what IS it?" I must have been a dreadful disappointment to him when I arrived as he was evidently expecting a deep sea monster or a new sort of Meccano set. However, they were all most welcoming and natural and perfect pets. They're all exactly like each other except Sarah, who does not belong to this robust rambunctious family. A gentle wisp, who smiles vaguely when they make earsplitting noises and picks up her sewing card and laboriously goes on with her "Bebroidery".

Grandpa had a cup of tea by himself in the sitting room and we had tea round the kitchen table. Barny informed me, "We have got scones AND biscuits today because of the visitor." I said, "Am I the visitor?" and he said, "No! Of course not! You are Auntie Margot." So I don't know who the visitor was. Marie was as adorable as ever and Andrew had bought a knitting machine and was knitting jerseys for everyone at great speed and very badly. But Marie said it kept him happy and was better than nothing.

Sunday afternoon I am sitting on the steps in the only bit of sun we have had since I came. Mrs Fletcher's bicycle has broken up after fifty years of hard work, so I could not go to church this morning as I could not walk five miles there and back. I got up leisurely and knitted after breakfast and read the papers and then we went down to the Pigot Arms and saw the Sexton Rowley and the usual old locals who were all very welcoming and friendly. Rowley said, "'Ows yor dorter in furrin' parts?"

We then came home to a sumptuous lunch of roast lamb and mint sauce and onion sauce and sage and onion stuffing and roast potatoes and damsons and cream and I felt absolutely blown. I helped wash up and then walked down to the end of the garden – rather like going down Mucklows Hill, Halesowen – for my figure's sake, and took some photos of the house. The garden is overgrown and neglected, but very lovely all the same. A cuckoo was bursting itself cucking, and a father blue tit was working overtime feeding worms to his family over my head.

I am having a restful time here, but am distressed about Lewis. He is so ill and old and despairing and I wish I did not live so far away or that the prospect of the outlook without Pooler did not make it so hopeless to get to see him more often. I can only ask the Good Lord to take care of him. He worries so about being so helpless and about the garden going to seed.

Later We spent a quiet evening and now I am in bed. I have packed my bag for the morning and shall be glad to get home to your little dog! I am SO thirsty and would love some Eno's Fruit Salts, but I don't know where to search and if I stir out of the door Mrs Hallas will appear to see if I am "hongry". She asked me after a colossal supper if I had had enough. "For iff not zere iss zom dripping cakes wizz jam and cream eef you LIKE?" She has a 48" bust. That comforts you, doesn't it?

Lewis is so pleased with the letter you wrote him. He carries it round with him in his pocket, very battered, but I don't think you will ever get a reply, poor old chap. The effort of producing notepaper would finish him.

March 13th 1955 I had such a sad letter from Andrew saying Lewis was desperately ill and in a nursing home and had been there five weeks and had collapsed on the very day he was to have been discharged. He feared there was no hope for him. I don't think anyone knows this outside the family. He gave up the house when he went into the nursing home and said he would go and live with Andrew and Marie as it all worried him. The garden, and the water softener, and the car, and all! Darling Lewis, it is such a shame. I don't think he has very long to go. I will try to get up to see him before Easter if I can and stay with Johnnie G, as Lewis' house is no longer available. Andrew says that he is so unhappy and in such a pitiful state that I hope he goes soon, so it has been a mouldy day.

Friday March 24th 1955. Rushed around in the morning and packed my bag to go and see Lewis, and finally left the house in time to catch the 4.10p.m. from Paddington for Wolverhampton.

I thoroughly enjoyed the journey, but had difficulty keeping myself to myself, for when I got in the carriage there was one very ordinary mousey working class woman in one corner and an enormous woman in the other, fat and tall with a lot of brown hair done in plaits on top with a brown turban on top of that. She was about 50 and wore a green and brown mottled stockinette skirt, very badly bummed in the seat and a very nice brown twin set and on top of that a shocking pink quick knit jersey, very pulled – as if cats and dogs had slept on it for most of the winter. And on top of all that a duffle coat with a hood. She proceeded to pull out a large napkin filled with large nourishing sandwiches and to munch happily and with gusto.

She was in the corner facing the engine and Mousey in the other corner facing the engine nearest the corridor, and I sat back to the engine facing Mousey. Presently in swept a prim puss about 55 – 60, grey lamb coat, blue feather hat, grey skirt and jersey, pearls and very pale face with no lips but lots of powder. Cold, steely grey eyes. She at once began to organise the carriage. "Fearfully stuffy." Clang! Opens the window ventilator at he top. She then throws off her fur coat and upsets Duffle Coat's sandwiches on the floor. Profuse apologies from Gray Lamb. Hearty. "Oh! It doesn't matter – true I have had no lunch but I expect I eat too much anyway," from Duffle Coat. This was so self evident that it needed no comment from Gray Lamb, who settled comfortably into her corner, spreading her books and bags all over the seat, covered herself up with her fur coat and shut her eyes.

This contentment proved too much for Duffle Coat who had been baulked of her feed and was feeling sore. So she ups and begins o throw off duffle coat and manages to knock grey fur awry in doing it and to sweep two magazines on to the floor. "Oh! Dear! Now I've done it to you! I am SO SORRAY!" "No matter," says Gray Lamb, looking daggers and composes herself again, and all was peace for three minutes, when two girls enter the compartment having caught the train by the skin of their teeth. They have to sit between Mousey and Duffle as Gray Lamb has eyes firmly shut and has no intention of moving books and magazines. Also, she has managed to strew one suitcase, one small holdall and one cloth coat all over the rack, so the girls tried to get their luggage on the other side.

The Duffle began to be helpful. "Let's push yours just a teeny teeny this way and yours a teeny teeny THAT way and there will be room for my poor battered little traveller. Oh! Now Donald Duffle has fallen on your velour coat. How naughty of it. Velvet coat must go on top of Donald Duffle – he's such a heavy old man, but SUCH a comfort." And she beamed at me and I smiled vaguely and looked out of the window. I tried to look good tempered but not very bright,

At the next station a young man came by the door and looked longingly at the place strewn with Gray Lamb's belongings and said, "Excuse me, is that place taken?" and I said loudly and assertively, "NO!" which made them all jump and Gray Lamb open her eyes, so she gave me a dirty look and began to half heartedly draw them towards her and I helped energetically to clear the seat AND the rack, after which sudden burst of activity I subsided into a vacant stare at the landscape. Gray Lamb looked at the young man and said, "This is a NON smoker." And he replied, "I don't smoke, Madam." I beamed at him and winked and went back to the landscape.

Gray Lamb asked Duffle to please move her picnic basket on the floor as she had cramp and needed to stretch out. Duffle got the needle and said, "I too need stretching space, so if you put your feet there and THERE just a teeny bit wider, and I put mine HEAH and HEAH, all our little bothers can be sorted out." Gray Lamb snorted and pulled her feet under her again. Cramp evidently over.

Then the man came in for the tickets. Gray Lamb had to look in one of her bags on the rack and in doing so lost her spectacle case. She kicked up such a fuss. She knew it was on her lap. It must be on the seat, etc. The young man had to get up and shake himself. I refused to budge and shut my eyes determinedly. Duffle said, "See if upholstery has eaten it. Upholstery simply GOBBLES up spectacle cases and scissors." Gray Lamb snapped that she had had it in her hand or in her lap and it didn't get anywhere near the crease in the upholstery. So she swished and flapped and shook her skirt and I got weary of her and said, "Look on the rack," and she did and there it was. "How did you know?" she asked accusingly, and I said very quietly, "I used my intelligence. It's very simple really." And Mousey opposite laughed out loud to everyone's complete surprise, as we had all forgotten she was there.

I got to Wolverhampton at 7.10p.m. and Johnnie met me. It was dark and cold. We went home to Willenhall and I phoned Andrew. His sister Edith had had a good tidy up and my bedroom was quite civilised, but the rest of the house is

227

like a bear garden. Johnnie hates it and is in it as little as possible and I must say it is very dreary. Edith had made some very good soup for supper. It was very tasty, but there must have been everything in it except rhubarb. You never knew what was coming up on the spoon next! We talked for a bit and then I went to bed and left him looking for his sermon for Sunday morning!

Saturday I got up late and leisurely. Johnnie had gone off to work and I had a cup of coffee and caught the trolley bus to Walsall and had a good snoop in the Walsall market. There are some lovely crockery stalls on the steep market street. I called for Johnnie at the Court and he took me out to lunch at the Picture House and we had boiled mutton and onion sauce. I went on from there to Andrew's house in Penn Road and he took me to the Nursing Home. Lewis has grown a beard, being altogether too feeble to shave! He is just a shadow of himself and mortally sick. He seemed quite pleased to see me but spoke very little and I sat and held his hand and told him about the daily round and Gran, and he just nodded and listened, or not, as the case might be.

Sunday Johnnie went off to Princes End, Tipton, for the day preaching, so I got up after he had gone about 9.30a.m. and decided I could not spend most of the day in this higgledy piggledy room so I turned everything round and turfed two chairs and a footstool out altogether. I then took a dislike to the sideboard and took the back off that and the room looks

MUCH better. Then I had a boiled egg and a cup of tea and went to see Lewis again.

He was more talkative today, but inclined to be weepy and it is difficult to pump hope into a person when you know there is absolutely none. But he has no idea how ill he is, he is just despondent because he is not making progress. It is quite devastating. Andrew took me back to tea with the babies, Loosy and David are away at school now so there were just Barney and Sarah and Benjy and baby Mary G. all rolling on the floor like puppies. He took me back to Willenhall. I left early as I didn't want to let the fire out and I JUST saved it. I just got the kettle on before Johnnie returned and he went straight into the sitting room and saw the "improvements" and I heard him say, "Ber-luddy hell, what's all this?" Anyway he was quite amusing over it and I think he likes it and is going to leave it. It looks a damn sight better to my mind, anyhow.

Monday I went into Walsall and had a cup of coffee with Edith at Chattins and we nattered. Then I went to the Court and picked up Johnnie and had lunch and then went to the Nursing Home to see Lewis. He was asleep when I got there but then woke up, but he seemed so muddled and weak that I felt it was kinder to go and leave him. He was trying to make an effort and clear his brain and the effort was too much for him. So I just kissed him and told him I loved him and would come again soon and he said, "Thank you for coming!" And shut his eyes and I left him. I rang Andrew at night when I got back home and said I had been and he said, "I wondered if you had as Lewis said he didn't know if you had been or if he had dreamed it." Poor Lewis.

Friday. October 7th Andrew rang up to say that Lewis had died on Thursday night. So I was not in time with my letter and am eaten up with remorse because I didn't write as often as I ought to have done. I cannot but be thankful he is free from that miserable existence but I shall miss him badly. It was Pooler's day off which was a good thing as it kept me busy. Andrew rang Daddy about taking the funeral on Tuesday and Daddy told Gran Lewis had died, whereupon she started to bombard me with ghoulish questions. I could have choked her. I bet she did a spot of rejoicing though, for she couldn't stand Lewis. She was scared to death of him and he once said she was "devoid of every womanly attribute" which just about puts it in a nutshell!

Monday October 10th Up late, a heavenly morning again, and walked round the dew sodden grass with Daddy in our dressing gowns. It is the sort of morning Lewis would delight in. I HOPE he can share it. His cousin Marjorie rang to say was I going to the funeral and I said, "No," but we have arranged to meet in London soon. Daddy set off mid-afternoon for Wolverhampton. The funeral is to be in that charming little church at Pattingham. We shall send two dozen roses for Lewis, and I shall put a card with "with love from Margot, J.O. and Lisa" on it.

Tuesday Go to Mass at 10a.m., home and coffee and feel miserable about Lewis so go back into church and get over it. Daddy comes back about 7.30p.m. I got him some supper and we heard all about it. He said the church at Pattingham looked lovely and that it had been a perfect sunny day. I think he was more shaken up than he thought he was going to be, poor Daddy, he had to give a short address which must have been a great strain. Lots of Wednesbury people were there and police people and lawyers and court officials. Johnnie G. went to represent the County Court. And Nancy and Colin were there and Alan Shirlaw and his wife Eva. Lewis could not abide her! J.O. said it was FEARFULLY sticky at the Wake afterwards! As you can imagine I listened to all this with mixed feelings and so did Pooler, as she had been his housekeeper for some months and had a great respect for him. Gran said, "Well, what I want to know is, has he left YOU anything? Or Lisa? THAT'S what I want to know!" One of these days I shall bash her head against the wall – several times.

"…going frog-eared matching checks. Mr
Molyneux doesn't have to make for these
shapes, I bet!"

Sewing for the Family and Friends

The sewing machine sat in the East Ham kitchen near the ironing board. The ironing board was never put away. The sleeve board and the frilling iron, a very slim early electric iron, sat on the shelf just above it with the cloths that were used to damp and press skirts and seams and starched items kept in a bag to stay clean and soft. The radio sat on the shelf too.

In Becontree Vicarage the sewing machine had been one with a treadle. The electric one was new to East Ham. It had many attachments for button holes, rick rack, gathering, applique, and countless extra bobbins with different coloured threads. Under the dresser sat the Button Box, the Elastic Box, the Braid and Ribbon Box, The Hook and Eye box; most of their contents had been saved from garments going back several generations, minute mother of pearl buttons for babies' petticoats, Swiss braid from an Edwardian coat collar, all lovingly unpicked many years ago, awaiting the garment of the future for their reincarnation. They were the perfect playthings for rainy afternoons for Lisa and her friends, sorting them into patterns and sizes.

The war and clergy salaries between them meant that the family wardrobes were dependent on jumble sales and make do and mend. The Nicholls family was lucky in that Margot had several friends with both money and good taste, so that the garments handed down were well made and of good quality fabric. But her flair and excellence in dressmaking and tailoring was the greatest advantage, within and outside the family. She could not be generous with money; so she was generous with her time, her ingenuity and her patience.

Sept 21st 1953 Monday night in bed. My most precious, Are you really in New York or still tossing about on the ocean outside the harbour in this gale? We have thought about you such a lot and Daddy has said, "Do you think she is all right?" so many times that I feel I ought to turn it into his theme song.

I went out shopping to the Bargain Shop – fatal – and bought some very attractive everglaze check cotton for your attic bedroom curtains. I also got a five yard remnant of pure silk in dark rusty red with a large paisley pattern for 25/- The man said his wife took a lot of it when he had it first, and she didn't use it so he put it back into stock.

Tuesday night, 9p.m. in bed I cut out the red sitting room curtains tonight and made one pair, double lined. I seem to have treadled about six miles and I hemmed the sides, they look so much more professional that way.

Wednesday night in bed Oh, I am tired tonight, I've been going like a little steam engine all day… Lou is here now until her wedding on Saturday. Pooler went out and I began to get the dinner, and Lou began to sew her tan moygashel skirt. After about ten minutes I heard a loud and significant sigh from Lou. "What's up?" say I. "OH dear," says she, "I don't want to do this skirt." Well," said I, "I don't want to do this dinner." "Now, I'd like to do the dinner," says Lou. So we swapped and I worked on the skirt till about three.

Thursday I didn't go to the Tailoring class and did as little mop-dusting as I could and began on the eternal treadmill of the curtains and finished them about 4.p.m. Pooler helped me to take the others down and to clean the paint and then we got them UP. They look quite magnificent, rather like the Hall of Fame! But they will soon fade. They look like the velvet ones when they were new, and THEY went a lovely colour in 20 years' time!

I then had another pot of tea and thoroughly hoovered the sitting room and the sofa, and after supper I began to sew the clean cushion covers back on. I got in a fearful kerfuffle over that as I couldn't find which ones fitted which – one long one and two oblong ones on the sofa and three square ones on the arm chairs and one very big one and one long one on Gran's big chair, and no cover seemed to fit any cushion. I put 'em on and changed 'em round and took 'em off till Gran thought I had gone daft. "Stuff 'em in and sew 'em up – Right Up There!" said Gran, and it was the most sensible thing she has ever said! Pooler nearly screamed with frustration but we managed to knock them into shape somehow and they look quite normal in the chairs.

Monday 28th Sept Mary P. came about five and Rupert went wild with delight. I think he connects her with you. Mary was thrilled to bits. I read her out lumps of your letters and she was amazed at the length of them. I have promised to make her a cocktail dress for Christmas and she kept on, "Oh, Mrs Nicholls, you are kind, how super, how SUPER! I've never HAD one –" until I told her if she didn't stop I would withdraw the offer. She replied, "Oh, Mrs Nicholls, I will stop, but you ARE kind, it's super!" and spent the rest of the evening poring over the Vogue pattern books. Also, let me know if you would like a navy silk frock for Christmas.

Tuesday night. In bed It's a very self conscious, frenchified little attic tonight. It's got its new bed cover and curtains and chair cushion and it looks most Montmartre. It has taken me most of the day.

Midnight Gran's coat has got a collar on and both sleeves and I have bought some bright scarlet crepe for the lining and some buttons and a white towel rail for the attic for 6/-. While at the Bargain Shop Ena fished out three yards of very attractive crunchy pure silk in dull blues and greens, so I got it to line my black grosgrain suit, and to make a matching blouse. It only cost 12/6.

Wednesday night Dear child it is past midnight and I am sick of sewing. Mary came yesterday and tried on her frock. Very little alteration needed to the bodice, navy silk. Today I houseworked and sewed all morning and got the zip in. I did it very neatly close to the edge and put a very chaste oxydised silver buckle with marquisite bits and it looks very expensive. I spent the whole evening hemming the skirt, six yards of it, and made a red and blue silk sash as an alternative to the belt. I'll do the same for yours, my pet.

Friday night November 28th Auntie Kath came for the day. Bob brought her over. She let out that Jean was so grateful for your green winter coat as her own was quite unsuitable for her pregnancy and that your green angora dress was the only warm frock she could get into. So I thought how miserable it must be to only have that green frock and be that shape; so when Kath had gone I raked out that curtain remnant with all the woodland colours and have managed to cut her out a smock from your pyjama top pattern. And I'll make her a black maternity skirt and send it for Xmas. It looks SO gay – all sort of Tibetan and very, very expensive. She always was on the exotic side.

Only a week before the bloody Bazaar. I have been virtuous. I have cut out and machined three petticoats and hemmed the bottoms and have only the straps and lace to put on. I have one more to do tomorrow. I was all evening doing them, so it wasn't bad going.

Thursday December 9th I started to cut out your navy silk frock and have cut out half the bodice. It's a queer pattern and looks like a combination suit for an octopus when laid on the table. Gran can't make head or tail of it and looks me as if I am just buggering about to befogg her – and to tell the truth it was some time before it made any sense to me. But now it is all light and joy and peace and I can get on with it in the morning.

January 15th Bitter, bitter weather. Snow. Ice. In the afternoon I went up to the Bargain Shop to get some of that nice curtain stuff, like the red in the sitting room, in a nice sea green , enough to cover the two chairs of Gran's in the dining room. They must have loose covers, they are filthy, but when I shall get the time to make them I know not. While there I fell for 6 yards of golden yellow silk with little lozenges on it. 6/- a yard. It will do for one or other of us at some FUTURE date.

Friday Up at 6.30 and darted around. Pooler is a lot better and came downstairs yesterday and cooked dinner today, thank God, so I went shopping, and came back with meat and vegetables and some very pretty crepe de chine with roses on to make you a nightie.

April 13th 1954 I attacked the dining room for Spring cleaning. I took down all the curtains and took off all the loose covers. I go to buy rabbit for the animals and meet Ena, the Bargain Shop girl, who tells me they have some marvellous cotton stuff. I buy some lovely embossed glazed seersucker, browns and reds and I shall wash the green curtains in the study and line them with the seersucker and they will look grand. I also bought some pillow ticking at the Co-op and made two pillows, and filled two of them with feathers from two busted ones. I do this in the new coal house and don't make much mess.

May 2nd Yes darling, you shall have the watch for your

21st, and we can wait till you come home to chose it. We will give £15 - £20 for it – but no more. Now, how do you want the red and black organza made up? A cocktail frock? Or an informal ballet length dance dress? ANSWER ME! With sleeves or without? That very pretty cross over pattern must be about somewhere. It had a halter neckline in front, bare shoulders, high neck at the back.

May 16th I never knew anything like this perishing climate. We have been sweltering in sun frocks at the beginning of the week, now it's fires and cold feet! Early this week I bought four yards of stiff cotton to make myself a summer skirt and a black top. Only 12/- so it was hardly extravagant. Pooler suggested I made my skirt circular, so I did, and tried it on, and you should have SEEN it!

However, I finally put the most smashing pleats in it, and it really looks a cinch.

May 17th Pooler's day out Another lovely day. Went shopping early after breakfast for bread and rabbit etc. and went and told Ena to cut off 20 yards of dull green curtain material – for new covers for dining room chairs. They still had that for 3/11 a yard and I'll never get anything cheaper and Daddy said I could have it. I have already got 10 yards of it upstairs. The material I have got in that attic cupboard is quite shameful. But it will all come in useful over the next twenty years! I have decided to go to the Soft Furnishing classes this autumn at the Technical College and learn to make loose covers properly.

Friday Early breakfast, I did a spate of ironing and was still so elated over the black skirt that I decided to get some more stiff stuff and make a skirt for Mary P. so I bought some very pretty glazed waffle cotton, pale pink with green hats and little red bows. This will give her a gay outfit for her visit to Ireland. She doesn't know about it yet.

Monday In the afternoon I decided I would get some curtain stuff for Lewis' bedroom and try to make them up before I go to stay with him. So I sallied up to the Bargain Shop and fell for some glazed check waffle cotton in the most musical comedy colours, pretty and soft, orange, blue, grey, cyclamen and pink like a geometrical sunset. I also got a singing petrol blue for a bedcover. The whole issue and rufflette tape and all only coming to £2/15/0. I felt very pleased with myself and carted it all home.

Wednesday July 10th I spent the evening removing all the stacks of unmade up dress materials that I have accumulated from the attic cupboard into that old wardrobe in Daddy's dressing room. The old sewing room is in an unbelievable state of filth, soot, dust and moth, and I got the wind up about the moth, so I shook it all and refolded it, and liberally mothed the cupboard with Para-di-chlor- benzene which is a foul smelling stuff and always reminds me of Sister Smith, who reeked of it! But I can't afford to get moth holes in all that.

August 1ˢᵗ 1954 Old Auntie Kath and Uncle Robin have come to stay for a few days. It rained and rained all day. After lunch I attacked my blue Molyneux dress that Elizabeth gave me last year for Kath. I decided to give it her so I had to alter it to fit – let out all seams and cut about three inches off the bodice as her waist is under her armpits and she hasn't got a waist anyway! And let the hem down and shorten the sleeves. Mr Molyneux doesn't have to cope with people this shape, I bet! But she is such a darling old brick.

August 15ᵗʰ The Singer Sewing Machine man came as the machine seized up on Monday night and I CAN'T HAVE THAT! He was a competent pleasant man who took pains and got it rattling along a treat. He brought two small nephews to help him and they were very nicely behaved! Lou came, and she and I went to Wo Pangs for lunch and then to the Bargain Shop and she got 4 yards of black moss crepe for 8/6 the lot! And 4 yards of navy grosgrain for 7/6 the lot! And I got 4 yards of red and white spot silk rayon for 8/-! And we came back flushed with victory. Lou's was the biggest bargain though, for the moss crepe is worth at least 15/- a yard!

Thursday September 29ᵗʰ 1954 I have signed up for the Tailoring class again and for the Soft Furnishing course. They are both on Thursday, morning and evening, so I spend most of my day either here or waiting at bus stops. I spent all afternoon finishing the cutting and planning of my paper pattern for my room chair. I was very bucked, as my pattern was a damn sight better than any of the others and needed no alterations. One girl said, "Cor! Are you an Archy Teck?"

Saturday Newspapers and buses on strike. Lou made me laugh. She said, "What a life! At the beginning of the week there were no papers to read on the buses, and at the end of the week there are no buses to read the papers on!" In the afternoon I cut a pattern for your blouse from the top of a frock pattern and the sleeve from another. I am getting quite good at this, but I do wish I could get at you to fit it and if you continue to ignore my requests for your waist and hip measurements you shall not have the very expensive skirt that we have decided to buy you for Christmas and I shall send you some Marks and Spencers handkerchiefs instead. So sucks to smelly you!

Thursday I got up late and found your letter on the mat but no time to read it. I had a good morning on my jacket at the class and finished it bar the final pressing. Came home and cut out my loose chair cover. This took me all afternoon and then I went off to the soft Furnishing Class and here was great triumph, for mine was a good effort and we got it all pinned together. BLIMEE!

Wednesday January 26th 1955. I got up and did the chores, and as it was a nice sunny morning I decided to go into Ilford to get a pattern I liked, as I saw it was being withdrawn

242

from circulation. I called at the Bargain Shop on my way home – alas - ! Fell for a whole lot of slate blue silk tweed that they had got for 4/- a yard. I've not seen it ANYWHERE for less than 12/- a yard, so I bought up 12 yards! Enough for a long summer coat and frock and short jacket. Not for this summer, I fear, but mayhap for next. It's a pretty middle aged blue, so not kittenish, and you can't call it expensive, £2/8/0 for twelve yards.

Wednesday. February 2nd In the afternoon I began to cut out the slate blue duster coat. Couldn't resist it. OOH dear! I think I have bitten off more than I can chew. I cut the bloody thing out from 2.30p.m. till 6p.m. and Lou came and we had supper and I went on cutting after supper. My knees were so sore and my back ached and I cursed myself for an old fool. The thing is in four separate pieces and I had to put in all the markings each time before I could use the pattern again. The room was festooned with slate blue material and I was heartily sick of the sight of it, and then Pooler decided she would make a jumper suit of it too! So we shall be like the Houston sisters and it will be a slate blue summer from what I can see of it.

March 13th 1955 A bitterly, bitterly cold day. Spent the day at the Mothers Union Study day in Caxton Hall and spent the evening cutting out a red wool frock from a couturier pattern. Felt awful.

Saturday Had a hot and tossful night on Thursday and a

temperature on Friday, so managed to stay in bed most of the day; Pooler and good old Mrs Jeff held the fort. Today, Saturday, I felt better but decided to take it easy over the weekend, so I got on with my red couturier dress and Pooler got on with her off white chunky coat and we did nothing but unhook each other's cottons off the machine and grab the iron off each other till bedtime. We listened to the Saturday play while we fought amicably.

April 25th I went into Ilford as I wanted some buttons for my blue paisley frock. I got some nice blue glass ones in Moulton's, but they were 7d. EACH! Ruination! Then I saw some lovely grey lace – 17/11 a yard. So I bravely turned my back on it and went home. BUT the next day I decided I would pawn everything, so I went back to Ilford and bought it! Terrible extravagance and I felt guilty all the rest of the day. Daddy and I have been invited to a Civic Dinner in the Town Hall soon and I felt I really could not wear Doris's old red lace and tulle AGAIN.

Thursday I should have gone to Tailoring class, but I sent a note saying I couldn't, and cut out the gray lace and lining all afternoon all day

Tuesday They all went out, goody goody, so I sewed Gray Lace all day and made the cape stole and lined it with rose coloured net, very tasty! And Wednesday I spent the evening putting in the zip and made the belt and I tried it on and I looked VERY NICE INDEED!

September 20th I got up latish and pottered around most of the morning and then went up to Singers and paid them for your dress form. I have been waiting for it with impatience so that I can REALLY fit your winter skirts. And by the time I got home Ralphie Gilson tapped at the window and beckoned me to his front door and as I went round to his steps he said, "There's someone waiting to see you!" and there stood your new green shape! We decided it would be more decent to transport her through the landing door than round by the dustbins! So I went into the kitchen and Johnnie Griffiths was standing there, and I said, "Will you help me quick and help me to manage Lisa in through the stairs door? She is looking frightfully green!" You should have seen his face! I put her in the little dressing room and put your dressing gown on her to keep her clean and decent, and later on that evening Johnnie went up there for something, and he came down and said, "My God! That Sarah Porter did give me a fright -!" So I decided she must be called Sarah Porter from now on.

Sunday October 2nd 1955 I sit here at 11.15 a.m. in the dining room amidst a welter of muck and muddle on the table. Writing paper. Material for my new suit. Sections of paper pattern for your clerical grey skirt. Sections of skirt half tailor tacked, piping cord of chair cover materials, pins, hooks, and eyes, string and bits of Daddy's summer coat on the floor. Oh dear! Too much started at once, I am afraid.

Wednesday Around teatime Poo was going out shopping for bread etc., so I said, "Come round the market with me and see if you can get me a piece of suiting for a skirt." So we went round to HER favourite stall and went inside behind and you never saw such MOUNTAINS of stuff! I nearly went berserk. I came away with a small piece of suiting just like your skirt and another length of flannel grey suiting with two large flaws in it – four yards of it to make me a street frock to go with the cashmere coat that Elizabeth gave me in the summer – Attaboy! The whole lot only cost the price of one yard in a West End shop! I was thrilled to bits. Am now completely broke. All my wedding certificate monies gone and all my birthday money too, but am well content.

October 27th It poured and poured and poured, and I could get on quite well without going to the Tailoring class, so Poo went on her own and I spent the morning cleaning round and then in the afternoon I spent joining up material for the sofa cover. I played about with ten and a half yards, got it round the chairs and round my legs and round my neck and nearly went batty but got it all joined up in the end.

Friday Poo had the day off on Friday, but it rained knitting pins so she stayed home and made her niece Anne's frock, a browny Donegal tweed which looks grand. I cooked them all dinner, fresh haddock, boiled celery and mushroom sauce and stewed gooseberries and cream, and all were satisfied. Then I got the urge to sew the settee cover, which I did for the rest of the day, very much like making a siren suit for a hippo.

Tuesday December 12th. Mrs Jeffries came and did the washing. I went to the Bargain Shop and bought curtain Lining and some stuff to make Andrea a party frock for Christmas. Poor child she has nothing to wear. She was wearing an old frock of her mother's when they came last Sunday. She is big too, not yet eleven and takes a 34 bust and a 28 inch waist. I also went into the market and got some blue sequins and some mother of pearl sequins and began to sew them onto Mary P's evening frock. It begins to look glamorous – with little blue daisies with white centres and little mother of pearl daisies with blue centres. Very amateurish, but they are far apart and just catch the light. I hope she will like it, it certainly looks far better than it did.

Friday Chores. Fires. Bitter cold. Mary P. came and was thrilled with the frock. I spent the evening making up a piece of thin blue corduroy into a skirt for Andrea's birthday. I shall give her that blue jersey I spent all last winter knitting for myself. I never liked it and have never worn it.

Sunday Snowing. No Baptisms this afternoon, so spend the evening on Andrea's blue outfit and make her a little sweater scarf out of your dressing gown material – I fringed the borders and it looks very smart. I've packed it all up and will send it off tomorrow. I do hope she likes it.

Friday March 9th Kath is coming to stay for a few days, so I can't spend much time this week writing to you. I bought a smashing remnant of navy and white striped, thick, stand alone, cocktail silk, and thought it might make me a suit. But when I got it home, try as I might, I could not get the pattern out of the material. So I am making a pencil slim cocktail frock for Mary P. She only has that navy silk, which must be pretty well through by now She is coming tomorrow for a fitting.

Thursday Spend the end of the afternoon doing Mary's frock, which is he most damned awful pattern I have ever attempted and I'll not make it up again for ANYBODY, not even you! I'm going frog eared over it.

Tuesday March 29th. Holy Week We've had Canon Styler staying over Palm Sunday. He is good company. I went up to the Bargain Shop and bought you 5 yards of the tan poplin for an Easter present, then came back and made the backs of Johnnie's cushions for his new flat. The backs are tan poplin, and the fronts are those handsome hand woven orange and yellow wool scarves we got in the market a couple of winters ago.

Thursday. Maundy Thursday Mrs Edwards came in the afternoon instead of Good Friday morning. I had a fit of generosity and gave her my gray and copper cocktail dress! I must have been mad, but still, I did it! I then went all virtuous and attacked the old wing chair and cut a paper pattern of the beast. It really is rather a formidable proposition. However, I began at 2.30p.m. and I packed it in at 9.30p.m. and I had done all but the back which is the simplest part. So I feel I have done something worthwhile. Learn to sew, darling, even if you marry a wealthy man it is always useful, and if you marry a poor man it is vital. It means you can finish things off properly and risk cutting good material and you can always feel in the swim. And I reckon I've saved hundreds of pounds over the years. I reckon I can make ANY garment you like to mention for 35/- -!!!

"Johnnie has arrived, laden like a pack horse, with a large chicken, some rhubarb roots, and a superlative mirror with gold balls and an eagle…"

Johnnie G.

R.J.Griffiths – Johnnie G. – became a friend of the family when J.O. was a curate in Wednesbury, and Johnnie had just become a lay reader. A lay reader is a person who has taken a course of training in the Church of England to enable them to preach and teach. There is no salary attached and lay readers continue with their own jobs – he was the Recorder of the Walsall County Court – and can be sent to various churches in the Diocese to help out. Johnnie G. lived with his parents in Willenhall in the Black Country, looking after them until their death. He was very close to his sister Edith, who married and lived close by.

When J.O. and Margot left Wednesbury he would come to stay, and in the end he spent all his spare time with them. All three of them looked forward to the evenings out at various pubs, or evenings in with a quart bottle of beer, a quart bottle of cider, and a bottle of Tizer for Lisa. His weekday job was exacting, his weekends mostly taken up with preaching, his home life dutiful and grey. He loved the wide-ranging conversations with J.O. But Margot was the light of his life.

He was a kind and generous man with his feet firmly on the ground, and a great handy man; he loved to "fix" things, and relished the chance to bring about some imaginative scheme of Margot's in the house or garden. He always arrived with some mirror, or china, or some nuts and bolts to refurbish and mend some bargain she had discovered. One day they found a large Victorian wicker backed chair commode in the cellar at East Ham and dragged it out into the light of day. It was black with coal dust and green with mildew. They scrubbed and sanded, and let it drink a quart of linseed oil, and today, sixty years later, it stands here with its bright piped cushions in pride of place.

During the war years he always arrived with some unobtainable goodies, usually wrapped in his pyjamas. One night in 1944 he was stranded in Barking during a particularly vicious "doodle bug" raid and took shelter in the Police Station. They took him in and gave him a bed in a cell and a couple of blankets and a cup of tea, and he slept gratefully with a large Black Market ham in his suitcase as his pillow.

Whit Monday 1954 It was windy with some fitful sun, but the sun was pleasant while it lasted. Johnnie G. is here for the weekend. He decided to paint the little square garden table white, so he nailed it all together firmly and then proceeded to paint it. Jut as he got it finished it rained. I got proper tea and washed my hair and Johnnie filled in a dip outside the back door that gets a big puddle in and wets Rupert's feet. Rupert very disappointed at the disappearance of puddle. I then iron five sheets and get supper and go to bed. Exhilarating day full of GAY ADVENTURE!!!

June 26th 1954 Johnnie G. sent a parcel and when I undid it I found it was a superlative mirror. Mrs Jeffery had an old sideboard with mirrors in the top and her son wanted the bottom of it to make a cabinet. She was going to chop up the top too. I said, "Don't chop up the mirrors, they are sure to be bevelled edges and good glass." She said, yes, they were, and a few days later she brought me one of the mirrors, and Johnnie carted it off. He has had it put into a heavy gilt frame, and made it stand up like a photograph frame, and it looks smashing. I've got it on the bureau in the sitting room and it looks most handsome, and rather like Buckingham Palace.

August 10th Daddy goes off for a few days' holiday in Birmingham with the Eaves. His train passes Johnnie G.'s who comes for our protection until Thursday! He couldn't come over the weekend as he was booked up with preaching. I would really rather have done without him, as I could have got more done, but Daddy bellyached about my being alone with Granny. He is an old fusspot and it is a damn sight easier being alone with Granny than having to get meals for a couple of men. I got Johnnie's bed ready, and made a sponge, and got dinner for me and Gran, and he turned up at 3.30p.m. and I had to get dinner for him. See what I mean? I would MUCH rather remain unprotected! He also brought half a garden of rhubarb roots and catmint and it took all evening to plant them.

Sunday October, 1954 This has been a mixed bag of a week, but not as bad as last week. Mrs A. was still sulking after the bust up we had had, and Gran was particularly exasperating. Johnnie said, "Come away out of it!" I had got to the stage where I wished never to see any of the whole set up ever again. I also didn't know what I DID want! So we got on the first bus that came along and it was going to Woolwich. We went over on the ferry and it was a lovely day, breezy but sunny. We had some lunch in the town at a Lyons Teashop and then got on a bus to Greenwich and spent the whole afternoon in the Naval Museum there. It is a marvellous place. The middle of it is a summer palace built for Anne of Denmark, and then Henrietta Maria lived in it. I could have spent days in the building. I think Johnnie got a bit fed up with it after the first two hours! We had tea there and went back the way we had come and that was grand too, the sun was setting and pinky and there was a foggy misty haze all over the river, so that the wharves and the warehouses and boats and power station chimneys all looked as if they were made of smoke or gray chiffon, and all bathed in this soft, diffused pinky orangey glow. The water was a beige colour. It was sheer poetry except for the smell! What they pitch into the river at that point I will not try to conjecture!

December 18th Johnnie is coming on Thursday night for Xmas and says he is bringing a bird. I do hope he means poultry and not a blonde as I have not ordered anything, and as we are only four in the family this year I thought a good joint and a piece of boiling bacon would suffice. Anyway there will still be time to dash out and get one on Friday if it IS a blonde!

He is very pleased as he had applied for a flat in a small complex Walsall is building for single professional people, and he has just heard he has been successful. They won't be ready for several months. I said I would help him furnish it and I really look forward to doing it.

Sunday February 27th To 8a.m. Mass. Very cold morning. Breakfast. Papers. Change sheets, and put the feather bed to air before the gas fire in the big bedroom as Johnnie G. comes tomorrow for a week. He has had all his teeth out last Tuesday, and has got the new ones, so I'm going up to meet him tomorrow to get the big laugh over before we get back to East Ham.

Monday A bright morning but cold, cold, cold. I went up to Paddington to meet the train and got there just as it came in. I was standing around looking for him as the people streamed off the train and suddenly someone slapped me on the back, and a man's voice said, "Hello, Margaret," and I turned round to see a complete stranger go puce in the face. He stuttered and apologised and I laughed. I said," You got the name right, anyway!" Then along came Johnnie with his face all muffled up and his nice new teeth. They don't look any different from his other ones so there was no need to laugh! But they hurt him a good deal and eating was a torment, poor chap. Still – he persevered.

We walked back through Leather Lane Market, where we had a good look round the stalls and I found a LOVELY big decanter, cut glass stopper neck and base, and the rest square and plain, a very big one and old. It caught my eye and I got it for 3/-. I gave it to Johnnie for his new flat.

Friday September 20th   Johnnie is coming to preach for Rollie's Harvest Thanksgiving. After tea I changed and went to meet him off the 7.15p.m.train and we had a drink and some supper, and got home about 10.15p.m. He has brought me a perfectly heavenly gilt mirror for my birthday – convex – with balls round it and an eagle on the top. We have put it in the sitting room over the side table, and taken the picture of George III down and put him in the dining room under the oval picture of great-great grandfather.

He told us a lovely story about a drunk on the top of a Willenhall bus, very merry, singing at the top of his voice, and he said, "Now then, I want all yow bastards to sing with me. Come on." And one man was mad and said, "I'll 'ave yow know I'm not a bastard!" So the drunk said, "All right then, Yow needn't sing!"

December 22nd 1955 Thursday. Shop, shop, shop. Begin to make Johnnie's Xmas present, i.e. kitchen curtains for his new flat. White ground with red, blue, green and black utensils, very gay. I finished them about midnight.

Friday Get Johnnie's room ready. Your parcel arrives but I DON'T look inside. More shopping and get the booze from the off license. Put up the holly.

Saturday Last minute shopping all day long and it pours with rain all afternoon, but is very warm, not Christmassy at all. Buy some pink plastic curtain stuff with red spots for

Johnnie's black and white bathroom and spend most of the evening making THEM. Wrap up presents.

New Years Day Up 6.15a.m. and catch the train to Birmingham for the day to see the new flat. All goes well until I am on the train and then two large lobsters fastened all their pincers violently in the fleshy part of my tum! After about ten minutes I retired down the corridor. I wasn't sick, but I spent the rest of the journey trotting down the corridor every fifteen minutes. SO helpful on buses and trains. However, I 'm glad I went as I simply cannot buy and plan for it without seeing it, and it is a little jewel of a flat and just what he needs and deserves. I had about two and a half hours there, quite long enough for me to rearrange all the furniture the way I wanted it -! -and to say what was still wanted. I caught the 5.10 home and was mighty glad to get home and go to bed. Rupert was very content to come to bed early. It at least ensured I was not going out again that evening! Pooler and I have decided to call him Arthur for a change.

Friday Pooler sails out to the sales, but returns mid afternoon with no bargains, and cross because she had not bought some tweed in Knightsbridge, and now she has got home she decides she wants it very badly. I spend all morning and evening on Johnnie's blue velvet curtains, and make everyone bacon sandwiches and coffee for supper. My stomach not strong enough for bacon sandwiches, but everyone else eats with gusto.

Saturday Poo puts on her hat and goes up to Knightsbridge to buy the tweed. Mrs Jeff and I spend the morning trying to clean up an old pewter pot for Johnnie's sitting room. He has no pictures for his walls and no ornaments. Mrs Jeff thoroughly enjoyed attacking the tankard and I got the shopping for Poo, and lunch for the family, and bought some white voile net for his bedroom windows, so that the spinster ladies can't see his charms! (They are Bachelor and Spinster flats.)

Pooler returns and I am all agog to see the stuff, but she says the sales assistant put her off it!

Tuesday Looked out a few more ornaments for the flat and did a bit more to scouring a little pewter rabbit dish that was as black as Newgate's knocker but is now beginning to sparkle a bit. Mrs Jeff is a big help here. She loves cleaning up the impossible – like I do – and she renews the attack when I flag! The pewter mug is now like silver. Johnnie rang up to say he is tickled pink with all his curtains. I must say I am getting a big kick out of seeing to it all, but it would be easier if it was nearer at hand.

Monday January 22nd I finished the ticking cover for Johnnie's fireside chair and get that ready to post next day.

Tuesday I begin to make a blue velvet cushion for the seat of his big fireside chair, piped and blocked to shape, and get quite a kick out of it and feel clever.

Thursday I finish the velvet cushion and go to Tailoring class in the morning. Spend the afternoon plotting a loose cover for the shabby back of the fireside chair, and have just about got enough over from the blue velvet of the curtains. I cut out the cover at the Soft Furnishing Class and do some more to it when I get back home.

Friday   Up at the crack of dawn. I packed up the chair cushion, the shade for the hall, the black and white gingham curtains with yellow lining for the curtain of the hall door, the pewter mug and the copper ashtray and send them off to Johnnie. He'll be so bally smart he'll be able to charge admission for upkeep.

Saturday 28th January   I am planning to go and help Johnnie choose his armchairs this weekend and so, of course, I wake with a cold on the chest. However, I catch the 11.10 from Paddington. Not a bad morning. Cough and sniff incessantly all the way to Birmingham much to the irritation of the other travellers. Johnnie met me and after we had had lunch we trailed around a lot of cheap furniture shops, and I got more and more snappy and at last I said, "We will now go to a DECENT shop and then go home!" I dragged him up to the Minty shop in Corporation Street, and they had a sale on, and there in the front of the shop were two HEAVENLY arm chairs, eighteen guineas each ! I said, "Have those two and bugger the sofa, "and he said, "There isn't a sofa, there IS only two arm chairs." Anyway, I could see he was almost knocked unconscious by the splendour of those two completely aristocratic super arm chairs, so he bought them, and I wish we could have brought them home with us – but they will not deliver them till after I have gone home.

After this we went back to Walsall and I cooked some haddock and prepared a stew for the morrow, and lit the fire and I put the ornaments round the flat, and it begins to look VERY nice. And after supper I generally turned the place upside down, and had an amicable evening, with me having all my own way, and Johnnie making a few feeble protests which soon died down. A very pleasant evening.

Sunday Up late, tea brought in bed. I spent the morning altering all the curtain lengths that could be altered by hand. Very difficult to make curtains 120 miles away from the windows they are to hang at! I cooked the dinner. Spent the afternoon altering curtains and the evening measuring up for the big fireside chair for loose covers, and doing a bit of knitting.

During the morning there was the most almighty knocking and hullabaloo on the balcony outside the backdoor that serves both flats. Hammering and banging. I said, "What the hell is that?" "It's the chap next door," said Johnnie. I said, "What's he doing?" and Johnnie replied, "I expect he is putting some new buttons on his overalls."

Tomorrow, Monday, if all goes well, we are going to buy shelves for the books and shades for lights and then I catch the train home. I listened this afternoon to a fantastic play on the Third Programme called The Milk of Paradise, based on a new translation of Alain Fournier's novel, Le Grand Meulnes. It was very lovely, I thought, so fay, and queer, and dark and cold.

My cold is on the mend now, so no need to worry.

Monday A heavenly day. On the way to the book- shelf shop I remembered an antique shop which was a mistake! However, we went in and bought a ripping old oak corner cupboard, filthy dirty, for £3.10/- And a lovely little marquetry table that made a lovely bedside table for £2.10/-. Quite frankly the table was worth £10 and the cupboard £15. Then I went and ordered some lampshades made and the woman promised them in two hours! This staggered Johnnie. We took the furniture back to the flat in a taxi, and Edith came for a cup of coffee, and I began to clean up the cupboard while they got the dinner. I bought some steel wool and dipped it in olive oil – the only oil there was in the flat – and the dirt simply rolled off. I found that the door was inlaid. It really is a snip, a dear little cupboard. I caught the 5p.m. train home. Johnnie is most anxious that you should come to stay and see his flat and I said I was sure you would love to!

Wednesday A cold, cold day. I went to the Bargain Shop and bought six yards of good stiff natural corduroy for Johnnie's big fireside chair. It cost me 50/- and I know they sell it for 18/11 a yard in Dickens and Jones. I was very cock-a-hoop! I drafted out all the patterns for the cover from my measurements. After supper we all huddle round the fire. Rupert wears two jerseys to play in the garden this weather and Tig is all bushed out and fluffy.

"…the rest of the day was an endless rush,
with the Grand Dress Rehearsal for the
service, and hundreds of banners thrown in."

Mothers Union Affairs

The Mothers Union was founded in 1876 by Mary Sumner, the wife of a country vicar, to help and support the wives and mothers in her parish. Farm labourers wives had a hard and relentless struggle to raise their families, in poor conditions with little education and often ill treatment. The movement spread rapidly, and now operates world wide throughout the Anglican Communion, and is particularly strong with its practical help in African Dioceses.

Margot was a heart whole Mothers Union member. She was the Enrolling Member for the large parish branch in East Ham. Nearly every parish did have a branch in the 1940s, and they constantly held big area services, and they did love carrying banners. St. Bartholomew's, East Ham, was often chosen as the venue for these services as it was the largest church around. So Margot got landed with the organisation. She was on the Diocesan Council, which met regularly, either in Chelmsford, or in Mary Sumner House in Westminster, and she was responsible for organising the parish monthly meetings.

October 5th 1953 Can't write much tonight as I have to plan out the Mothers' Union Banners' moves for the service they are holding in St Bartholomew's tomorrow. We have got about 150 women coming from all over the Deanery and about 10 banners, so must not get them all jammed up.

Tuesday night 10p.m. in bed Oh DEAR, what a blithering day. Everybody in a flap and more stupid than usual. I got round to the Church Hall in the morning and found that Jessie had told Old Man Gilson there would only be ninety coming at most, so he had taken all the chairs upstairs because of a "do" in the evening. So I said very firmly, "Then so be it, we will have the refreshments upstairs." This is VERBOTEN – unless Jessie wants it – when the rules are reversed! So upstairs it all went. Jessie looked daggers too, when she came round later. It was a good job too, for instead of the hundred and fifty I expected, four hundred turned up! And more Banners! I could have screamed. They didn't crash into each other nor get tangled up, but they were a dumb lot and got all out of place and made life difficult for each other. So, what with getting refreshments ready all morning, and dodging Jessie, and tidying up the flowers, and giving that enormous floor a quick buffer, and changing into smarter clothes, I had my work cut out to keep my head and my temper. Canon Knight preached. He is the one who said Mary Lake and I were the only ones in the Diocese who knew how to walk!!

Wednesday November12th It's a terribly foggy night, just a dirty old gray blanket outside the window instead of black night. I went up to Mary Sumner House this morning for the M.U. Central Council. Got into the chapel by 10.30a.m. The day started with prayers, two hymns, and an address by the Chaplain -!- a man young enough to know better, I should have thought – fortyish – and looked as if he had packed the

266

inside of his gums with cotton wool between his lips and his teeth top and bottom. You do it, and then talk, and it will be just like him! Then we all trooped down to the Assembly Hall. Nearly all morning was spent on discussions on the printing and matter and paper etc. of the Mother's Union Journal. It was very dull and a lot of nonsensical stuff was talked by a lot of very stupid women. I had a lovely view of Mrs Temple though, so I was quite happy. She is a most fascinating woman. About my height but with the strongest face of any woman I know and full of character. I should love to know her. Ask Elizabeth if she knows Mrs William Temple, widow of Archbishop Temple. If so, I can introduce myself next time!

Wednesday November 19th In the morning I sorted out all last year's left over Bazaar stuff and made paper price tags. Then at 2.30 the Mrs Cloake, Porteous, Spivy, Large, Lewis, and Goodman came armed with bags and bags of this year's stuff, and had cups of tea, and priced all afternoon, and left at 5.p.m., and left me to clear up. Which I did by the simple process of dumping the lot in the sitting room and closing the door.

Thursday November 20th I got back from the Tailoring Class about midday, and made the beds, and got up the coal, and had lunch, and them put on my good wool black dress and my black and white coat, and my diamond earrings and fighting cock brooch, and made up my face with considerable care and went off to open the Barking Parish Church Sale. I did it very well though I say it as shouldn't. They gave me a beautiful bouquet, chrysanthemums and carnations, and I went round all the stalls and bought some really pretty things that will be just right for little Christmas gifts, and a sweet Coalport plate that will look lovely on the wall of the attic sitting room, and some very classy Christmas cards of Barking Church. I'll send you one.

Friday night in bed 1a.m. Nonstop day starting at 6a.m. The day before the Bazaar! The stalls are up and duly decorated and all are pleased, except Jessie, who is flouncing around like a maniac. And I've thrown away Gran's hat and she is looking for it everywhere. She says it's the Spirits again. It's that awful thing she turned inside out last winter and I had a presentiment she was going to wear it tomorrow, so I've liquidated it. I heard her say, "I shall simply have to buy another if I can't find it!" I wish she would go and live with Jessie, it would do them both good, and me, too.

Saturday night Midnight in bed Well thank God, that's over for another year. Very successful. £180. Everyone very pleased. Jessie the only fly in the ointment. She only had Mrs Middlebrook and Netta to help her in the morning with the refreshments – no one else would – but quite a lot helped her after lunch to serve the teas, and she behaved a bit better after lunch, but both Muriel and Netta said they would not do it another year. It was quite impossible to work with her. She is getting worse. I think she will go clean off her onions soon.

Tiny Miss Stokes came to open the Bazaar, eighty-four years old and very spruce and game. She said when she lived at the Post Office in the High Street as a girl in the 1880's, she would stand at the shop door and look over the road and right over the fields to Barking Church in the distance with a windmill to the left. And that the trees over hung the road on both sides all the way to the station. There was one butcher's shop and you went down to that through an avenue of trees as you do to the parish church. Next door to the Institute in St John's Road was a big field where they used to have the Sunday School Teas.

Gran arrived about 4p.m. just as we were beginning to think about packing up. She had bought herself a green velvet hat with a green chiffon scarf, not bad at all. Well done the Spirits!

January 11th 1954 I got the dining room ready for the Mothers' Union Committee Meeting at which they decided quite happily to cater for a thousand members for tea at the Deanery Festival on March 25^{th,} Lady Day. They have NO idea what it entails, but that is just as well as they will get though somehow!! And if they realised it they would all stop away! It sounded just like a doctor's surgery in here all afternoon as Mrs Lockyer and Mrs Bush and Mrs Padmore and Mrs Gilson all had bad colds and hacking coughs!

Wednesday A lovely, lovely day, warm and springlike. Got up at 6a.m.and went to 8a.m. Communion. I then put prayer cards on the chairs and got the Lady Chapel sorted out for the Mothers Union Wave of Prayer for the Diocese of George in South Africa which is linked with the Chelmsford Diocese. It began at 10a.m.and ended at 6p.m. Eight hours and eight parishes taking part. We took from 12 noon to 1p.m.

I kept going over to church every hour till 6p.m. It was a very successful day, lots of women came and there was no break at all from ten till six.

Ash Wednesday I got up at 6a.m. and did the chores, and then scuttled off to St Mary's for the Mothers' Union Corporate Communion at 10a.m. There were 26 Members there, GOOD girls! I felt elated.

Sunday March 21st Darling, I m not going to attempt to give you a day-to-day picture of this week. It would be too sordid! All I can say is I must have been very wicked to have deserved this lot! Pooler arrived back from her father's funeral on Thursday night, and retired to bed on Friday teatime, and she looks like being there ALL NEXT WEEK, and NEXT WEEK is DEANERY FESTIVAL WEEK, and I had hoped to have all next week to get ready and plan for it. Well. I am not going to think about it. I shall just plod on and do the best I can. I can't do the impossible. But I wish she had fallen ill in her sister's house and not here!

I battled with the shopping and carting up meals and inhalants to Pooler and then to crown it all I was trying to de-clinker the boiler and slipped and burned my arm on the bars of the blasted boiler. There was no one in except Pooler in bed, so I really let go and yowled and boo-hooed and My-God-ded and dashed for bicarb and bandages and was not at all restrained! I was quick with dealing with it and it is quite safe, but it is a nasty burn and I felt very ill used. But I had to cope with a macaroni cheese for 4.15p.m. so it didn't give me a lot of time to sit and groan. Work is a great healer!

Monday Doctor Bell came to see Pooler by 9a.m. He said she had bad bronchitis and must stay in bed and have constant fluids. Press on! Valiant Mrs Jeffreys came to hold the fort while I dashed about. I cashed a lot of M.U. postal orders, and hired the extra crockery from The Town Hall for the tea on Thursday, and got Pooler's prescriptions and inhalants, and the rest of the day was an endless rush up and down stairs, with the grand Dress Rehearsal in church with hundreds of banners thrown in.

Your Rupert has been sweet to his old Granny during this grim patch. He sticks close and sits near and sits in the hall and waits for me if I go out. Welcomes me with deep bowings and plume wavings. I expect he will break out when it is over, but he is trying so hard to be a dear good dog while it lasts!

On Wednesday I got up at 6a.m and prayed for a clear mind and inexhaustible energy and I must say the dear Lord did co-operate. I don't think I put a foot wrong all day. Pooler was a lot brighter. I cut sandwiches for supper, and made barley soup for Poo's supper, and made four huge "Tea bags" for the urns, (no such things as "tea bags" in the 1950s) and at

6p.m. I armed myself with four old sheets for tablecloths, and presented myself at the Institute and organised the whole show. I lugged chairs and trestle tables upstairs and organised all the women, and coped with Jessie. Finally I fell into bed just past midnight.

Thursday I worked hard round at the Hall from ten until noon. I gave everybody their job to do. We had tea served in the big top hall, big bottom hall and little hall at the back. 220 in the top hall, 250 downstairs, 70 in the little back hall. I had people on the doors counting heads so that we did not get overcrowded in any one area. I even had one person to stir the tea and another to put the sugar in!

The service was very impressive and the church was choc a bloc full. All went like clockwork. The service was not over till 4.10p.m. and by 5.15 the whole bally lot had had tea and gone home, all five hundred plus of them! In fact, most of 'em had gone by 4.45! It really was a triumph. They had a nice tea – two pretty cakes and a piping hot cup of tea for 6d. and there was no waiting and no muddle. I was tired and triumphant.

Tuesday May 11th Perishing cold weather. Pooler went out for the day and I prepared an address for the Mothers' Union at St. Mary's. Mrs Gilson started up her Young Wives group and Mrs Middlebrook helped her look after the babies. She got eleven members the first time so that was very good. And I got thirty at the M.U. so that was good too. Daddy came to the M.U. too, so they all got their monies worth.

June 16th 1954 The Bishop's wife, Mrs Allison, has invited all the Clergy Wives in the Diocese to a Party at Bishops Palace in Chelmsford, and I decided I would go. So I pressed my long grey coat and skirt and tan shantung blouse, donned my diamond earrings and pigskin bag, and I wore new stockings, and had done my hands and my face, and I felt smart and leisurely as I set off. It was overcast and chilly but it didn't rain.

When I arrived at the Palace I was shewn into a vast drawing room crammed with women spilling into a very tatty sort of greenhouse at the end and I found myself a chair here. At the other end of the room were ten women with sheets of music in their hands. They were the Chelmsford Madrigal Singers and they were determined to sing all they knew, and they knew plenty. They sang about six straight off. Then they stopped and we all hoped that was it, but then a weedy young man said he was going to play us Chopin's Third Ballade and did so, twice as slowly as it should have gone, rather like a pianola with no expression stops. It was dreadful. I looked round at the soulful faces of the clergy wives and I thought I was going to have hysterics, so I looked around for something to fix my eyes on to sober up. But alas! The first thing I saw was an enormous and quite hideous garden statue of a nasty adolescent boy, his little arrangements neatly tied up in a jelly bag, (all marble of course) and idly playing a small flute with a battered old Panama hat of the Bishop's larkily placed on his curls. I looked up at the glass roof, but this had been rendered quite opaque by pigeons and house martins. So I gave up and shut my eyes. The Madrigal Singers sang another four, and the young man played some Schumann, which was terrible, and some Arnold Bax, which was worse! It was interminable.

By this time there was a howling gale outside and we watched in dismay as two men came out and put up tables and weighed the tablecloths down against the wind. And maids struggled out with hampers of crocks, and finally at half past four we all trooped out into the inclement weather, and were given small iced cakes and smaller scones, and tepid cups of tea and then a frozen ice cream to follow.

I made my adieux as soon as I decently could. But I came home on the bus with Mary Lake, and we pulled the whole thing to pieces from start to finish, and then we began on the Mothers Union and had a good old pick at that, and thoroughly enjoyed ourselves in an uncharitable way. So it was definitely worth going!

June 26th I got up at the crack of dawn and put on my silk check suit and put a swoosher in that funny little black shaped hat I bought last summer and felt very nice. I arrived at Mary Sumner House in good time for the Council and sat with Mary Lake and Mrs Lord and Mrs Gowing.

After lunch we all trooped down to Westminster Pier and boarded a chartered steamer, and went by river to Putney Bridge where we disembarked and were met and escorted to a Garden Party at Fulham Palace. The Bishop of London and Mrs Wand greeted us. Mrs W. looked very like Rupert when disgruntled and the Bishop not unlike George Robey in his prime only no eyebrows.

But the Palace – oh! The Palace, Lisa, is sheer heaven and hell rolled into one. We approached it from the rear, and were led the short cut from the river into the gardens so that we saw the back of the house first. The back is really ugly, a long flat building with a door at each end, and enormous ground floor windows, from ceiling to floor, with lawns on three sides and trees on the edges of the lawns, and no shade anywhere. The tea tables were set out in front of the house, but still no shade anywhere, and it was scorching hot by now. By the time we had finished the very nice tea it was about a quarter to six, and Mary Lake and I wanted to go home, and we had NO idea how to do it! So we decided to go round to the front of the house and out the other way. We got to the front – and it was absolutely fantastic! There was the most fascinating Tudor Palace, with courtyards and buildings on either side, and an angelic doorway under a porch with a witty little sundial and stone flowers in a glass case on the top of it. In search of a Ladies we set forth inside, and caught a glimpse of vast kitchens and stillrooms, and enormous fireplaces as big as rooms, with spits and gridirons and ovens and coppers and all quite unmanageable!

On the way out after the Ladies we passed through a great hall into a lovely bricked courtyard, and saw into a dining room with a huge round table, and a fireplace with iron dogs as big as me on either side and a replica of the famous painting of Henry VIII, probably painted about the same time as the original. I longed to stop and have a good look round, but no chance, and no time, and I had to be content, and indeed counted myself lucky, to have had even the meagre glimpse. But how anyone could cope with it all in these days I could not think. I felt East Ham Vicarage was like a handkerchief box in comparison – all 23 rooms of it!

July 3rd I trailed over to Chelmsford for the M.U. Executive committee. Deadly. Mary Lake told me Bishop Henry Wilson was back in hospital in Chelmsford, so I decided to visit him before I caught the bus home. I saw the old boy for about quarter of an hour. He was poorly, but pleased to see me – wanted to know my impressions of the "Billy Graham racket". I told him it wasn't my sort of religion. "No!" he said, "NOR mine. I feel like the old hymn, 'I want to go to heaven in the good old fashioned way!'" My sentiments entirely! He said he expected to be in hospital for another week. He was fed up with it and he reckoned he had bought the entire wing already. £14/14/0 a week –   and if he asked them for another cup of tea for a visitor – at tea time – mark you – "I was REFUSED! POINT BLANK!" I could see he was working himself up so I said it was Damnable and that I had better go before we both burst a blood vessel apiece. And he laughed and we parted – but it WAS a bit thick, for it was a nasty little room!

October 1st The Bishop's wife wrote and asked if I could possibly organise a meeting of the local Clergy wives, so I said I could do it for Wednesday week – why did I! – and so on Tuesday I wrote twenty six letters to them all inviting them.

By Saturday I had had twenty-one acceptances. Each acceptance letter brought me out into another sweat. Sunday, Monday and Tuesday I made huge batches of cakes and biscuits. I decided I must get all the guests into one room for the tea. So I pulled the dining room table nearer to the door end of the room, and put all the armchairs the window end and I got fourteen places round the table, and grouped the armchairs round the trolley, so got seven places nicely stowed away there. Then I went to bed.

Tuesday I did all the flowers and arranged the dining room and sitting room as far as possible. Then I got out all the silver for Mrs Jeff to clean. After tea I got out all the china and washed it and dusted it as it required, and laid the table and the trolley and got Gran's supper.

Wednesday dawned fair and bright. I got up at 6.30 and mop-dusted and cleaned the knocker. Then I went to the M.U. Corporate Communion. Then I cut up all the cakes and placed the plates on the table and let Mrs A. make some scones for the party! Great pride on her part! I send her out to lunch with Granny, and I had a bath and changed into the blue stockingette suit and the white nylon blouse and did my nails. Mrs Jeffreys came to help and I borrowed two kettles and a teapot from the Church Hall. The first guest arrived at 2.55p.m. and from then on everything went with a swing .Mrs Allison came and was very nice and friendly with all and twenty women came. Gran came just to show no ill feeling! It went well and I was pleased, but I felt like chewed string afterwards. They had all gone by 5.30, and Daddy and Mrs Jeff and I had another pot of tea and Mrs A. and Mrs Jeff did ALL the washing up and Daddy helped me to put every chair back and all the crocks and silver away and the kettles back to the Hall. And I took a hot water bottle to bed at 9.p.m. and thank God, THAT'S over!

October 31st I had to go to the Church Hall in the afternoon to see the Mothers' Union Overseas Films that had arrived. Ralphie Gilson kindly set them up and ran them through for me. I had two books of commentaries and thought they were not very clear – but I fitted the captions to the pictures nicely. But when I had finished I found I had fitted the captions for the Melanesian film onto the one for St John's Kaffraria, and vice versa. Ralph was very amused – and amusing – over it. However, I said I should just have to hope for the best tomorrow.

Tuesday A very cold morning with thick white frost. All Saints' Day, so I go to church at 8 a.m. and spend the morning round at the Church Hall helping to get the food ready for the fray in the afternoon. We had about ninety women in the downstairs hall and   they thoroughly enjoyed the show. I commentated the films beautifully, but I made half of it up as I was so much more interesting than their script. We had got well started, about 10 minutes into the first film, when in comes old Gran. She gets herself after much groaning onto a

278

hard chair – they were all hard chairs – and then starts to make her way down to the front, completely blocking the line of projection. So I have to commentate AND drag her back out of the line of projection – and she fought me, and struck out at me with her stick! So I gripped like a boa constrictor and hissed, "Yes, you can go to the front, but you will have to go round the side way – HERE IS THE ARCHDEACON OF THE DIOCESE LEADING THE PROCESSION TO THE CENTRE OF THE VILLAGE – No, you CAN'T go that way – NOTICE THE BABIES TIED TO THE BACKS OF THE MOTHERS – if you don't behave yourself you will have to go home – NOTICE THE HANDMADE CROSS ON THE ALTAR – if you give me another slosh with that stick I shall crown you, sit down and stay there! If Mrs Gilson hadn't managed to help me to manhandle her, I should have had to stop the show. She is a MENACE!

11ᵗʰ Jan I woke to snow, lots of snow and lots more coming down. I had planned the Mothers' Union Meeting right down at St. Mary's Hall, and I was pretty damn sure no one would go! However I knew I had got to, and so I made for a 101 bus, when as always, three came along together and they ALL changed drivers and conductors. So I began to walk, and finally walked all the way with a blizzard of snow in my face. When I got there I could hardly speak for lack of wind and coughing and to my astonishment I found thirteen there! I cut it pretty short, but we all had a nice hot cup of tea, and I talked to them for about seven minutes, and then we had a prayer and a nice loud hymn, and came home. I waited for five buses going back, all were full from the Docks, and the snow was really thick then, but I felt I would rather die of cold at the bus stop than die of coughing and exhaustion trudging home! I got home eventually and Mrs Jeff was still there, and made me a hot cup of tea and it was HEAVEN! I made some lovely hot soup for supper which went down very well!

April 8th Annual Mother's Union Party Day and thank God it comes but once a year. But it was a good party and it wouldn't have been without all the work and planning. That's the secret of a good party, they don't just happen on their own, at least, not annually. I got round to the Institute at 10a.m. and the first thing I found was that that bitch Jessie had not left the keys of the crockery cupboard, so I got a screw driver and got the padlocks off THAT! Then I made the custard for fourteen trifles!! And superintended the laying of the tables, white cloths with shocking pink and lime green decorations, EVER so cheerful! Around noon we packed it in, and I went and bought the prizes for the games, and then collared Daddy and Father Witcutt and made them sit on a chair at the cellar head. Mrs Jeff held the cellar light while I pencilled round their shadows on the kitchen door for a game of Silhouettes. This so ruffled them that we all four had to have an alcoholic drink, and thus revived, they became benign again.

After lunch I went back to the fray to "cut-up" (cakes and sandwiches) then home and had a lovely bath and changed. Mary P. came. I warned her what it would be like – but she still wanted to come, and Lou and Charles came as well. The evening was a howling success. There were about seventy there and we gave them masses of food.

We had one relay race where each person had to race with an empty sandwich tin on their head, an orange between their knees, and swinging a cane a la Charlie Chaplin. It so happened that Witcutt, Daddy and Jon Cane were in the same line up and I was nearly sick. I presented Mrs Cloake with a gift Token for £2/0/0 and Ralph Gilson was an excellent M.C.

The Silhouettes gave great amusement. There were twelve and you had to guess who they were. The one of me I thought was very aristocratic, only to have my pride shattered by a woman saying to me, "Would that be Davy Crockett?" We had an acting guessing game – and Daddy had to act a cow in a field watching a passing train, so that we could guess the caption. He went on all fours, put his fingers to his temples and curled them outwards, and said, "Moo! Moo! Chuff Chuff!" I said at once, "A cow being milked by electricity!" Mary P. nearly passed out. Daddy merely said, "ACH! MOO! MOO! CHUFF! CHUFF!"

We rolled home at 10.45p.m. laden with sheets, sausage rolls, a trifle, four glass dishes, a walking stick and an aluminium cake tin!

Bank Holiday Monday Daddy has gone off with Mr and Mrs Gilson and Father Witcutt and a crowd of kids from the Youth Club to Theydon Bois; and Pooler and Johnnie G. and Gran and I have had drinks on the sunp atch, and tried to pretend it was warmer than it was. Johnnie has been putting horse manure on the rhubarb, and I have cut out five Mothers' Union veils, as the Deanery have decided that they will have blue ones, not white ones, for the women who carry the banners. Mary Blue, they call it. Of all the beastly colour blues, I reckon this one takes the cake. Flat, pasty, chalky blue. I feel sure the Blessed Virgin must want to vomit at the sight of it. Still, as long as they don't expect me to wear it, I don't care. I have hemmed four out of the five so far, and feel very virtuous.

"Hello, my mummy!"

The Animals

J.O. and Margot were fond of cats and a succession of cats joined the family over the years. J.O. named the tom cats and Margot named the female cats. The toms all started their lives with esoteric names, various Ancient Middle Eastern kings and emperors, Tiglath Pileser, Hegisippus, but these were invariably shortened to Tig, or Heggie. The girls were Cleopatra, Clotilde, Amelie or suchlike. The only exception to this was one tom, born during the war when Russia was a great ally; He was called Stalin because at birth he looked exactly like him. However, as the Iron Curtain was drawn across Europe, he grew up to be a very handsome peaceful cat bearing no resemblance to that ruthless dictator in either looks or nature. We would have liked to change his name, Joe, for instance, but he would answer to nothing else but Stalin.

Other than cats, our family was not into pets. Lisa won a black and white rabbit called Velvet in a raffle, and this was much loved for five years while we were living in Becontree during the war. The garden was well fenced and so the rabbit ran about in it all day during the summer. On fine days when we had visitors we would have tea in the garden, and the rabbit recognised the sound of the tea trolley as it approached the garden and would steal the sandwiches, jam, lettuce, fishpaste, from the plates on the bottom shelf. It also chased the cat, who was terrified of it and never fought back.

No dogs. J.O. disliked dogs. So diplomacy was needed when Lisa was offered a pedigree Pekinese puppy by a friend at the Central School of Speech and Drama. The puppy was permitted on probation. "As long," threatened J.O., "as I don't hear it yapping, and it NEVER goes in my study."

So Rupert arrived, cheerful and charming, and was confined to the kitchens and the large garden, until one Saturday afternoon, always a busy time for J.O. because of the two or three weddings he always took each week. Lisa and Margot were getting tea and buns ready in the kitchen during a lull in the weddings, when they heard a terrible barking setting up just after J.O. had come in. They peered fearfully round the kitchen door and saw J.O. on his hands and knees in his cassock in the downstairs lavatory, barking at a rapturous, leaping puppy. They crept back out of sight.

From that moment on, Rupert ran the Vicarage with charm and joie de vivre. He lived for nine years, and was never replaced by any other animal.

September 15th 1953 It has been simply baking all day on this sun patch. Rupert has been barking himself sick at Robbers on the Roof. I sat in the sun and wrote letters and Daddy posted them and we had tea out in the sun. Mrs Gilson came round and brought me a lovely bunch of choice chrysanthemums, yellow and white to cheer me up! It WAS sweet of her. Rupert is incorrigible tonight. I think he is protecting me in your absence. He has barked at every sound and chased the cat and eaten a whole leg of rabbit, and had two drinks of tea and some sponge cake, and had a wonderful brushing and ripped Pooler's white pinny, but he sticks pretty close and looks apprehensive if I go out of sight!

September 20th Rupert developed the collywobbles at teatime and looked pathetic, and Gran said he looked like that awful picture of an overblown woman in a full white nightie, clasping a rose or a cross to her floppy bosom. It is called "The Soul's Awakening" and really that is a very good description of him. He had just that soulful liquid brown eye gazing upward in self pity! He recovered about 8.30p.m. and spent a happy half hour chasing the cat all over the kitchen.

October 12th Rupert's appetite has been insatiable today. He has had tea and coffee and shortcake at 11a.m. He had mutton and boiled bacon and a lot of apple and two pieces of apple at lunch. He had tea and sponge cake at tea, a large helping of rabbit and potatoes and greens for his supper and a water biscuit at 10.30p.m. Pooler said to him, "If you go on like this your mother will have to send you food parcels." He is lying on his back in his basket with his fat paws in the air, snoring like claps of thunder.

Monday morning It is a heavenly morning and Roopy is dashing round the garden with his ears streaming out behind him and Spitie is doing entrechats and caricolle dives over his head. I've hung out his basket blankets on the line to give them a nice freshener and he is a very healthy little dog.

November 3rd We have got workmen round the side of the house by Mrs Gilson's door putting tarmac on the path. They are a really rough lot and Rupert has fallen for the biggest bruiser of the lot. I said to him, "You are very honoured – he doesn't take to everybody," and he said, "'E 'ad a go at me feet to begin with, but then 'e smelt me, and that made all the difference!" There's no accounting for taste! This afternoon I walked round the cauldron with Hartley Stokes the builder to pick out the slate slabs and the man shouted out, "Do you want me to cook your dog?" Hartley looked most annoyed, but Rupert gazed adoringly at him and waved his plume in royal greeting, and then stretched forward his neck and pursed up his little mouth, and went fondly "Woo – woo –w-o-o-o" and the man said, "Ah! I shouldn't wonder -!"

Saturday night After lunch I went up to the butchers to get the meat and found I had lost the meat ticket. I'd bought half a shoulder of lamb the day before and told Mr Ayres so, but he said he'd still got a lot of meat booked in his freezer store and would I come back about 4p.m? So I went home cursing and swearing, and then saw Rupert asleep on his cushion with a green meat ticket between his paws! So I woke him up and took him to the butchers to fetch the meat as a treat for finding the ticket!

Tuesday Rupert has been most rambunctious all day and came in out of the garden this evening in a FILTHY condition smothered in soot and mud and with garden dirt CAKED on his little arrangements. "Call yourself a lapdog," I said to him while I rubbed at him with a cloth, to which he replied with vigour, "Ineverperishingwellcalledmyselfalapdogsothere!" and it was so human that both Pooler and I stood aghast! He came in filthy last night too and I had to give him a good washing and wiping and you never heard such swearing. And as Pooler says, "I don't know where he hears it for he doesn't hear it here!"

Saturday November22nd Your dog has got a new trick. If he feels that he is being slighted in some way he GRIZZLES. He makes real "Oh! Mumm-mee! I WANT you to LOVE meee!" noises. Or "Poor, poor Roopy, nobody takes any notice of this POOR little dog, I'm miserable" noises, and he puts on such an injured air with it. It's absolutely killing and quite irresistible.

Friday night I heard a nice tale about a very snooty woman at Crufts dog show with her pampered little darling, saying to another woman, "Yes! He's done very well. He's got First Prize, Second Prize, Third Prize and Highly Commended. What has yours done?" The other woman, who had got no prizes at all, said, "Oh! Mine has had a good Feed, a good Fight, a good F*** and is Highly Delighted!" I feel it's the sort of way Rupert would distinguish himself in like circumstances!

Thursday night Rupert is looking at me all belligerent from his basket – little teeth and one ear cocked – Terrifying! He wants chocolate. I gave him a piece last night and he wants more, and I haven't got any and he doesn't believe me.

Sunday night   Tonight I have been to church to see the Dedication of the new lectern, and to be social with the Misses Davidson who gave it, and they are delighted with it and all is light and joy and peace.

I came home and Rupert went all sentimental. Put his paws round my neck and went all limp and BLAH! He is a funny little dog. Some days he seems he couldn't care less and others he is so loving. He nearly runs his little heart to a standstill when the bell rings three times, and I' m sure he hopes it is going to be you each time. He simply bolts to the door and then stops and looks at the glass panel as if to say – "That's not going to be the right one – she always looked through." I could eat him and do wish I could explain to him WHY you don't come! We don't talk about you too much in front of him as he gets all expectant if anybody says, "Lisa", and begins to look at the door. So I've told them they are not to do it. We don't know what he feels like inside and it isn't fair to tease him.

We are going to keep Rupert's birthday on February 19th as it says it on the Kennel Club certificate. We will give him a pork chop for his dinner and some matzos! And a Bob Martin's the next day!

Tuesday 19th February   It was Rupert's third birthday and when he came downstairs we solemnly opened your birthday card and read it to him and gave him the envelope, and he ADORED the envelope and ran round and round with it in his mouth, and tossed it and pounced on it and ran into the garden with it, and ate a bit of it, and finally went to sleep on it! I wouldn't let him mess the birthday card about though. He had a lovely day. We were all about all day, and he had coffee fudge and a lot of kipper. I didn't get a pork chop as they were very fat, but he had lots of rabbit. And he finished up with two saucers full, one after the other of Pooler's Yerbama Tea. He finished up at midnight. Daddy played with him, and old Gran threw an orange for him. I brushed him and he looked most handsome and knew it.

Saturday This has been a dreadful few days. . As soon as Pooler arrived home from her Father's funeral she retired to bed with a bad bronchitis. And I was hoping to have the next few days free to plan for the huge Deanery Mothers' Union Service which we are hosting at Saint Bartholomew's on Thursday. But no help for it. I just have to cope with all the housework and Gran and every thing and to crown it all I have burnt my arm badly while I was trying to declinker the boiler.

Your Rupert has been sweet to his old Granny during this grim patch. He sticks close and sits near. Sits in the hall and waits for me if I go out. Welcomes me vociferously and with deep bowings and plume wavings when I return, and when I have the potato baskets and can't take him too he just looks resigned, but makes no fuss. I expect he will break out when it is over but he is trying so hard to be a good dog.

I have a feeling That Damn Cat is going to kitten before

the week is out and I feel it is too much to expect me to prepare a maternity bed for her. She is the most unattractive cat – whining and spitting and greedy – and she doesn't improve with age.

When I was at the chemist's this morning waiting for Pooler's prescription there was an old woman before me, and I heard the dispenser say, "You must shew that to your Doctor, I can only give you something to deaden the pain. You MUST shew it to the Doctor." The old girl said, "I don't like 'im." The dispenser said, "Go to another one then." She replied, "I don't like any of 'em." And walked out of the shop. I felt like that – only I would go further than that. I would include all mankind at the moment – but not you, because you are my friend – and Rupert is my friend – but he is not mankind, but dog-kind, and very nice dog-kind too!

Palm Sunday 1954 A lovely, lovely sunny day. Spitie has got two kittens. She had them on Thursday night, one all black and one tabby with lots of white and a ginger spot on its nose. I like the black one best. Thelma is coming tomorrow to sex them! Spitie regards them as more of a duty than a pleasure, I fear. Rupert delights in them. He gets up early and dashes to the cokeshed, where she has them, to see if they are still there, and chases off the other cats and guards them manfully. He is much more concerned about them than Spitie. If the black is a tom we must keep it and forget about Spitie!

Good Friday 1954 It's a funny old Good Friday without

you. I don't like it much. On Monday I streaked round and went up to Grosvenor House for my appointment with Dr. Levin. He has increased my thyroid pills again and I am to go back in another month. My arms have come out in a nest of nettlerash. I put it down to detergents and spring cleaning. But he says I overwork my skin and everything about me and it just revolts. Very undisciplined of it.

I got home at 1.45p.m., just in time, as I thought, for a committee meeting of the Mothers Union. But no! the first thing I noticed was no fire in the sitting room. I was met by Pooler with a face as long as a fiddle saying," The kittens have disappeared – not in their box! Spitie is very distressed, looking for them everywhere. We heard them at lunchtime." I helped search and lit the fire and got cups of tea. No sign of the kittens anywhere. Mrs Lockyer came, and told us a frightful tale of kittens of hers kidnapped and eaten by jealous Tom! I remember seeing Susie, the Gilsons' cat, around looking very sneaky – in fact, I have hurled several buckets of water at Susie when I was sure Mrs Gilson was out, and am sure Susie has had her revenge!

While looking for kittens – me in kitchen drawers, Pooler down cellar grating – we both heard kitten squeakings at the same moment, but they stopped almost at once and both of us are convinced that the Tom has eaten them up and that was their last agonised cries.

Meanwhile avalanches of women arrive at the front door in time for the meeting, so I leave Pooler to search. I hear more gruesome tales in the meeting of frightful fates of kittens from jealous or frustrated toms so that I have little stomach for such matters as food for the Mothers Union Party. MEAT? Sandwiches, Cheese Spread? The meeting is brought to a close about 4.p.m. when Thelma arrives to sex the by now non-existent kittens. She joins in the search, Spitie joining in with piteous yowls and mews all the while.

At 5 o'clock I say, "For the love of God, let's chuck it in and have a cup of tea and SIT DOWN." Daddy came in just as it was made and said, "The poor cat is going upstairs." I said, "I don't care! I am going to SIT DOWN. If you want to go upstairs, YOU go." And upstairs he went, chuntering to the cat all the while. Pooler poured the tea and we sank into chairs with tea to the lips when both heard loud kitty squeakings. Both said, "THERE! Did you hear THAT?" and shot upstairs. We heard a muffled voice from Daddy saying from the Bazaar cupboard, "They are in here somewhere!" And I was petrified as Spitie had turned every box upside down off the shelves onto the floor in her search for a lying- in place last week, and I had not had time to sort it out, and there was Daddy stamping the wine press as it were with his great hooves, and two teeny weeny kittens down there somewhere in the melee! I got him out and began to poke about gingerly among Bazaar streamers and junk and kettle holders and artificial flowers and old curtains – and then all of a sudden one little beastie appeared followed by the other. They were only four days old so not very good on their feet!

That Damn Fool Cat had either forgotten where she had put them or was playing a double deal game. We took them downstairs and put them into their box and she grabbed her star turn and fairly STREAKED off up the stairs again, but my blood was up and I grabbed them both and put them firmly into their box, and shut the door, and nailed up the little window to the landing cupboard in Daddy's dressing room that she must have dropped them in by! I'm not frightfully keen on cats any more.

Rupert was terribly worried but very relieved when they were both safely back in their box.

April 24th Spitie is a terrible mother, but I think there is something very wrong with the black kitten. Its eyes are not opened. It hardly moves. She is in the box very seldom and I am sure she is not feeding either of them sufficiently. Mr Parrish thinks they are a Duff Lot! I fear he may be right.

Later The black kitten died this evening. Spitie couldn't care less.

Wednesday A lovely hot day, but stormy looking. I did washing most of the morning and Parrish came and disposed of the piebald kitten which was a good thing. Spitie was quite openly delighted to see the back of it.

Friday June 18th 1954 When I got back from the hairdresser it was past five o'clock and I had left half a pound of rabbit's liver on the stove – cooked, and with the lid on the pan – for the animals' supper – and when I got back the lid was on the floor and that sod of a Spitie had hiked all the liver out and eaten the LOT! Great greasy patches all over the clean floor too. That did it. I was livid, and desperate too, as all the shops were shut by that time. I managed to scrape the mutton bones and got just enough for Rupert. I had already mixed the curry powder in with the mutton mince, or he could have had some of that. Also Rupert has a painful eye, It is very inflamed and he feels wretched. The vet says it may be an ulcer, but more likely he has got a scratch on it – I am pretty certain it was Spitie – and he has given me some ointment for it.

Saturday I got up early and was well ahead and deciding to get the shopping over, when Mrs Jeffreys turns up with her daughter Marge and produces the most adorable ginger kitten from under her coat! I am quite taken aback and feel I cannot cope with training a kitten as well as Spitie. I begin to explain this, although I had told Mrs Jeff that if she found a ginger kitten I would have it. She said, very wisely, "Well, it is a nice kitten, and I may not chance on another for a long time, and Marge will take the old cat here and now!" So I caught Spitie, and bundled her into the potato bag where she went without any protest. She always did like sitting in bags – and – the liver incident still uppermost in my mind – we parted without a pang. I then gave up all hope of any sewing, and tried to keep up with the kitten.

I need not have worried. He went and mopped up all the milk I gave him. Then I buttered his paws and he obligingly licked them clean. I then put some bread in some rabbit juice and he mopped that up, and then he ran into the garden and dug a little hole and tidied up after himself, and ran back in and ran up the mangle and went to sleep on the shelf at the back. He lives here! He's coffee and ginger stripes with short thick fur and blue eyes and very perky. Daddy has named him Tiglath Pileser, after one of the Emperors of Nineveh. I call him Tiggy, for short. Rupert is very intrigued, but his poor eye makes him feel miserable, and Tiggy likes to pounce on his tail and he doesn't feel up to it, so I have to keep the peace. He likes it when Tig goes mad and prances sideways, but he won't have his tail pounced on. I have been trying to put the ointment on the eye, but Rupert is not having any, and if you want a nice job, YOU come and do it!

Wednesday I got up fairly early but not early enough, and let Tig out into the garden. He generally goes out obediently and then comes straight back and climbs up in my lap while I browse over my cup of tea. But he didn't come in. So I got a little anxious and went to look for him. And I nearly had hysterics for he was jumping up and down all over the grass patch like a jack in the box. He was a-catching of grasshoppers! I longed for you to see; his eyes were bolting out of his head and he was determined to catch them; but there were more than one and it was difficult to change direction in mid air! He's only a LITTLE cat yet and they must have been very wily grasshoppers.

Friday Rupert's eye is better, thank God, and he has

been so imperious lately. Barks for coffee! Barks for biscuits! Barks for sponge cake! Barks for cups of tea! Gets everything he barks for and is more or less satisfied. Finally barks to go to bed!

Tuesday Johnnie G. took Tiggy to the vets to be doctored in the morning. And went to fetch him about six o'clock, and the rest of the evening was spent in tending him. He came home not much the worse for wear, but the anaesthetic hadn't properly worn off and he staggered around and had long sits! We had supper out on the sunpatch, but came in earlier than yesterday. It was not so balmy.

Thursday Johnnie goes off home and after tea I oiled the sewing machine and then began to make the new study curtains, and to line them with the old ones. I worked solidly till midnight and then went to bed.

Friday Daddy has gone off for three days to stay with Ken and Mary Eaves. I got up late. I booked in the funerals when Appleby came, and went shopping. It rained steadily all day so I decided to work at the study curtains. I had hoped Gran would go out, but no, so I got us a scratch lunch, and then on with the curtains, and after getting Gran's tea – that woman turns up for meals with sickening regularity – I finished the curtains and hung them up in the study and they looked grand. So I decided to do Daddy's three big chair cushions before I went to bed.

By this time it is 7.30p.m. and I decide wearily that I

must get Gran something substantial for supper as she only had a boiled egg and some blancmange for lunch. So I made a good batch of ham sandwiches, when it got darker and darker outside, and suddenly, without a word of warning – no sudden spots of rain – the heavens opened and an entire lake descended just like that! It was as bad if not worse than the day in Becontree when poor Velvet Rabbit was out in the garden and Daddy got soaked to the skin trying to get him in. I dashed round the house shutting windows, and then between flashes of blue lightning I continued cutting ham sandwiches. I put the light on in the kitchen and drew the blinds, as Gran is terrified of a storm, but she was busy unravelling a very tangled skein of green boucle wool, and was so absorbed she didn't realise why I was drawing the curtains. In the midst of all this I went into the study to use the phone, to find that even though the windows were shut, the force of the wind and the water had lashed through the sash at the bottom, and there were floods on the floor, and my lovely new curtains were sopping wet from the window sill down. WHAT'S THE USE OF TRYING!!

All through that violent storm, which only lasted twenty minutes, my poor little Tig was out, and I couldn't see him and it was impossible to go out and look for him. When it stopped I donned a mackintosh and went hunting for him, calling and calling under the dripping trees and bushes, and when at last my heart was so full of sorrow I thought it would burst, out crept a little drenched and bedraggled cat covered in black soot from the heavy bushes by the acacia tree. My, poor, poor little Tig. He crept towards me on his belly, his eyes big and black with fear – and when I lifted him up and loved him it was some time before he began to purr. I took him in and dried him, and gave him some warm milk, and all was light and joy and peace once more, but Rupert was very concerned when he saw him so wet and bedraggled – he looked so thin and half drowned! All this while Gran was munching her sandwiches and drinking milky coffee.

Thursday October 22nd Rupert scorched his tail in the electric fire tonight. TERRIBLE smell. Shades of his mother Spitha. I told him I should write and tell you and he said, "YoureadirtyblabbingEuropeanold busybody!" At least it was probably worse than that, but that's what it sounded like.

Boxing Day 1955 Around 3.45a.m. I was awakened by a little whimper, and there was poor Rupert. He tried to jump on the bed, but blow me if he didn't have a fainting turn. He frightened me stiff. I took him to the window and he revived, and I took him to bed with me and got him warm, and then he wanted to go outside. So I took him off downstairs and opened the back door and off he trotted a little unsteadily. I watched him for a bit but he seemed right enough, so I went into the kitchen and made a cup of tea and then suddenly realised he was a long time, so I went to investigate. A dark night, warm and windy. There was not a sign of him. I called softly. No reply. No rustles except windy ones. I searched the whole garden.

I got frantic, and went and woke Johnnie G., as I felt

he could stay in bed in the morning and Daddy could not, and we both searched. We got the long lead and light out of the cellar to help, and went on our hands and knees under the bushes! What in heaven's name anyone who couldn't sleep in Navarre Road would think, I can't imagine. Finally he stumbled into view of the kitchen door and our search was done, but I don't know where he had been, poor lamb. We gave him a drink, and put some whiskey into OUR teas, and went back to bed at 5.30a.m. He was better, but refused to leave me, and lay on my bed, and if I went to sleep he walked on my face! We got up together about 8a.m., and he spent the morning sleeping on the washing pile, and this afternoon he had a nice run in the garden, and tonight he has had a very little chicken, so he is on the mend. I, however, am exhausted!

Monday May 3rd I do wish you had been here this morning to see Rupert meet his Waterloo. He was all busy out in the garden, barking at cats and dogs, and snorting – very cock of the walk – when suddenly – with no warning whatsoever – came the most almighty raucous deep loud bark from the other side of Lockwood's fence. It sounded as though it were a savage wolf hound.   Rupert stood stock still in his tracks by the washing prop, and half turned round, and uttered a teeny weeny bark. A WHISPER of a bark whereupon the barking from the other side of the fence doubled in ferocity, and little Rupert began to trot – tail down – for home. He saw me in the doorway and slowed down to save face, and I said, "I should come in QUICK if I were you! Come in quick!" And he simply streaked in and never stopped until he got into the kitchen by the fire! Pooler and I were in tucks but we daren't show it! Poor little Rupert, but he's a brave boy – it's a brave man who knows when discretion is the better part of valour.

"Daddy has been up to the Passport Office and
Aqua Scutum and bought a new suit and a new
suitcase. Look out, Conneticut, here he comes!"

Holding the Fort

Lisa had decided to return to England in early June 1956 at the end of St Margaret's summer term. However, the plans were altered to mid-July as the Episcopalian church she attended was planning a large outdoor production of G.B.Shaw's Saint Joan and she had been cast as Joan. It was a major undertaking for the church, Saint John's, and for drama groups in Waterbury. The church stood in the central square in Waterbury. A handsome stage was erected in the corner of the square by the church and some traffic was diverted for the evenings the play was on. The Rector of St. John's, John Yungblut, felt it was a pity Lisa's parents could not see her in the play, and invited J.O. to come and preach and speak to several church and civic groups about his life in East Ham. St John's generously put up half the air fare. Margot was invited too; but the problem as always, was old Gran. Who would look after her? So again, as always, Margot and Rupert held the fort back in East Ham.

Monday May 7th 1956   It was a lovely day and very breezy so I fetched the laundry and washed two blankets and my old fox fur! I did! In Daz and it's dried magnificent, all fluffy and gorgeous, and so have the blankets.

Your letter came and we are so excited about the date of your arrival at Southampton in July. O Sapientia! O Radex Jesse! O Attaboy! O golly! And I do wish I could get to see you play Saint Joan. I remember that production that Doris took us to where Bernard Miles was so wonderful as the Inquisitor and Alec Guinness so delicious as the Dauphin. I am sure you will be much better than Celia Johnson. She was all wide-eyes and no guts. I also loved your poem "The Chaperone stood on the stairs." It was superb. You are a silly, clever creature.

Wednesday May 19th 1956 On the sun patch in the sun, a rather elusive sun and plenty of wind, but sun nonetheless.

Up to the present I seem to have done nothing but prepare meals and wash up after meals and by the look of my stomach I seem to have eaten most of what I have cooked! Ghastly! A blackbird is singing a very ribald song and then nearly falls off the chimney pot laughing at it! Quite ridiculous! Rupert evidently understands the language and disapproves, for he is sitting looking up at the bird on the roof and going ORRCH – TCCH – PSHAW – AWRCH – in utter disgust at the abandoned creature.

The laburnum is beginning to flower, the lilacs are full of bloom. The vine is just beginning to leaf and the wisteria is throwing out some feathery flowers first as a promise. The iris are in full bud and should be blooming at Whitsun, but things are very late.

Letter from you arrived about Daddy going to Americky – I opened it first and so was well primed by the time he got down to breakfast, and before he knew it the cable was in the Post Office! He protested every step of the way but he would have been bitterly disappointed if he could not have accepted. I am SO glad for him darling, it will do him a power of good and I don't feel envious, although I should like to see you as Saint Joan, and should be a far better judge of it than he will be! But it is absolutely impossible for me to come and you will be home so soon and that's all that matters. Write him very fully what he is to do, darling, for he really seems in a flat spin over it! - and write it in words of one syllable and in BLOCK CAPITALS!

Well, my best beloved, I guess you are excited at Daddy coming, and I am THRILLED TO BITS about it and you must just remember every bit of it and tell me all about it when you get home. Gran has just come home again from "Up Top" . SUCH a pity that she always comes back!

Tuesday May 25th A lovely, lovely day. Daddy has been up to the Passport Office and to the American Embassy and to AQUASCUTUM AND BOUGHT HIMSELF A NEW SUIT – VERY SMART! Look out Connecticut, here he comes.

I got Gran up and helped to give her a Good Wash, and I gave the garden a Good Watering. The iris are in full bloom on the sun patch and look a picture. Mrs Jeff and Parrish and me had our coffee on the sun patch and he regaled us with a wonderful account of how his son – a devil for speed and long distance driving – took Parrish in his sidecar, "like a bloody little corfin!" down to Leatherhead for an afternoon and evening outing.

This evening I turned up Andrea's frock and made

cake. I do NOTHING but make cake. It goes and goes and it's not me that eats it. Daddy says he never eats cake! But I left half a cake, made in the largest square meat tin we have got , in the pantry on Saturday, and when I came in on Saturday evening it had ALL GONE. It's pitiful the way I have to keep on making cake!

Now I am off to bed. The detergents and general washings have played havoc with my hands again and I have dermatitis and itches fit to send me crazy. I really was not meant for WORK!

Saturday May 29th Up very early and lug the shopping home and then put on my gray costume and have lunch with Elizabeth at the South Audley Street Club and talk talk talk talk talk and came away with a Harvey Nicholls pink wool suit and an Altmans formal grey terylene suit. The latter is lovely material, but fussy, but I can unfuss it when she has gone back to the States. Yippee.

The news has leaked out that the Vicar is going to America. Such a flutter in the dovecote. Daddy pleasantly flattered and trying to be nonchalant.

Now I am going to reiterate about you giving Daddy instructions very clearly and concisely and in good time! He has had letters from both Mr Yungblut at St. Johns and from Miriam and Naum Gabo inviting him to stay with them and in both cases he did not know what to say! I think he told them you were making his arrangements. SO MAKE THEM!! And let him know, so that he can write to those concerned and be grateful. I think he just shelved the question as you had said something about him staying at the school. PLEASE give him some clear instructions.

He says he is going to buy a PROPER thin summer jacket. He will be the proper Tailors' dummy, wait and see.

June 10th Now then darling, thank you for the lovely little dogwood flowers. Lovely little things. Thank you for your letter and the one to Daddy. Now I feel bound to say two things which you will probably say "old sourpuss" but I am going to say them willy nilly! First of all your breath-taking schedule seems to leave one Sunday only for Daddy to preach at St John's Waterbury -! As far as we can make out . You must remember that THE MAIN REASON HE IS COMING IS SIMPLY AND SOLELY BECAUSE ST JOHNS WATERBURY have put up half the fare, and as Mr Yungblut says, "it is a larger honorarium than is usually given in such circumstances." That being so, Daddy must give St. John's the major part of his time. Secondly, he, Daddy, is a very tired man – and is no longer young, and quite frankly he is frightened to have to go careering to Long Island and Lakeville and New York and wherever – so treat him very gently! He fears the heat and has had no holiday for eight years and then only three weeks at Whitstable in acute discomfort with Granny and Grandpa! He wants to see the school and Waterbury and he ought to see New York, but I think unless you are committed I'd go easy on any Long Island jaunts or other visits. He will be afraid of disappointing you to say he doesn't want to do things so YOU MUST JUDGE FOR HIM and remember he is a very tired man and extra strain is not good for very tired men! I don't want to pour cold water, my peachie, he is not on his last legs, but he will last much longer with care!

Sunday June 17th My darlings – Johnnie and Lisa Lou – my globe-trotting pigeons – my venturesome ones. I feel a bit like the rhyme in Lisa's baby church book.

> Angel, pipe thy tune again,
> Long ago I heard it,
> Far away from earthly gloom
> With the choirs I shared it.
> It is a little lonesome here,
> I am so glad to have thee near.

It's a little lonesome here too. I followed Daddy over the Atlantic – now he's fastening his seat belt – now he's unfastening his seat belt - etc, etc, and I wished I could have a teleview of it all. Rupert was desolate for two days after Daddy left, rumble tummy and all, every time the front door went he rushed through and returned with a dejected air, and on Friday night he heard me speak to Petchey's man in the hall and came racing through – and saw it was Petchey's man and gave him a filthy look and went off with his tail on the ground. It nearly broke my heart! However, he is bucking up now and has purloined Daddy's chair at mealtimes and sits in it possessively.

Everything here goes smoothly. Witcutt has been asked

to preach at Westminster Abbey on October 14th at Mattins 10.30a.m. Nothing special in the diary here, so I said to accept. Alice Player rang up to wish you God-speed. I did not let on you had already left. Granny VERY docile, thank God!

On Wednesday I went to St Barnabas M.U. Festival Service and read the Second Lesson and knocked the First Lesson Reader flat! Feel this is not the spirit in which to read the Gospel – but it's the Old Adam coming out!

Johnnie G. rang to wish Daddy God-speed – after he had gone – and also to say that he would come next Saturday for a week, so I shall be well protected!

WANT TO HEAR ALL ABOUT SAINT JOAN.

Monday June 18th Grannie nearly pulverised Pooler at supper last night. After discoursing on the state of the weather and the Government and What Our Men Used to Say, she suddenly said "And I expect Jack will find things in HIS line of business very primitive in America after what HE'S used to over HERE. RIGHT!" Pooler said to me,, "What does she imagine it's like? A rough mission shanty with an earth privy at the back and a crescent moon cut in the door for ventilation?" Get Lisa to take a photograph of St John's Waterbury to bring home to shew her – and me - ! Everyone has been ringing up to know if Daddy has arrived safely. He has no idea what "news" he is this end.

"I love you so dearly, and I DO SO WANT
YOU HOME!!"

The Last Letter

Thursday June 28th 1956 My darling Lisa Lou – This will be the last letter I shall write to you during this stay of yours in Americky and I am going to post it a bit earlier, in case you leave Waterbury before it arrives.

I am so glad you have had such a lovely time together and that Daddy has enjoyed himself so much! His letters arrived with glowing accounts of all the activities – quite breath-taking. And now that he is home he keeps saying, "The food was WONDERFUL," and he never notices food as a rule! I am terrified that now he is back he will spurn his nice grapenuts, and toast and fish paste and demand waffles, and hushpuppies and mint julep and I shall be shamed!

Well, darling, I hope you have a lovely crossing and no seasickness.

I love you so dearly, and I DO
SO
WANT
YOU
HOME!
Your ever-loving mother,
Margot L. Nicholls.